BASKETBALL AND PHILOSOPHY

The Philosophy of Popular Culture

The books published in the Philosophy of Popular Culture series will illuminate and explore philosophical themes and ideas that occur in popular culture. The goal of this series is to demonstrate how philosophical inquiry has been reinvigorated by increased scholarly interest in the intersection of popular culture and philosophy, as well as to explore through philosophical analysis beloved modes of entertainment, such as movies, TV shows, and music. Philosophical concepts will be made accessible to the general reader through examples in popular culture. This series seeks to publish both established and emerging scholars who will engage a major area of popular culture for philosophical interpretation and examine the philosophical underpinnings of its themes. Eschewing ephemeral trends of philosophical and cultural theory, authors will establish and elaborate on connections between traditional philosophical ideas from important thinkers and the ever-expanding world of popular culture.

Series Editor

Mark T. Conard, Marymount Manhattan College, NY

Books in the Series

The Philosophy of Stanley Kubrick, edited by Jerold J. Abrams
The Philosophy of Martin Scorsese, edited by Mark T. Conard
The Philosophy of Neo-Noir, edited by Mark T. Conard
Basketball and Philosophy, edited by Jerry L. Walls and Gregory Bassham

BASKETBALL
(AND)
PHILOSOPHY

THINKING OUTSIDE
THE PAINT

EDITED BY
JERRY L. WALLS AND **GREGORY BASSHAM**

WITH A FOREWORD BY
DICK VITALE

THE UNIVERSITY PRESS OF KENTUCKY

Publication of this volume was made possible in part by
a grant from the National Endowment for the Humanities.

Scholarly publisher for the Commonwealth,
serving Bellarmine University, Berea College, Centre
College of Kentucky, Eastern Kentucky University,
The Filson Historical Society, Georgetown College,
Kentucky Historical Society, Kentucky State University,
Morehead State University, Murray State University,
Northern Kentucky University, Transylvania University,
University of Kentucky, University of Louisville,
and Western Kentucky University.
All rights reserved.

Editorial and Sales Offices: The University Press of Kentucky
663 South Limestone Street, Lexington, Kentucky 40508-4008
www.kentuckypress.com

11 10 09 08 07   5 4 3 2 1

Library of Congress Cataloging-in-Publication Data

Basketball and philosophy : thinking outside the paint / edited by Jerry L.
Walls and Gregory Bassham ; foreword by Dick Vitale.
    p. cm. — (The philosophy of popular culture)
  Includes bibliographical references and index.
  ISBN-13: 978-0-8131-2435-3 (hardcover : alk. paper)
  ISBN-10: 0-8131-2435-2 (hardcover : alk. paper)
  1. Basketball—Philosophy. I. Walls, Jerry L. II. Bassham, Gregory, 1959-
GV885.B343 2007
796.323—dc22

2006039703

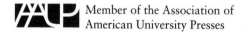

To Brian Marshall and Duke Ruktanonchai, two guys with whom I have had many good hoops arguments, and who have been saved from countless confusions by my insightful observations and analyses.
—JW

To coach Al Padek, who never lost sight of the fundamentals.
—GB

CONTENTS

POWER FOREWORD

Dick Vitale

IF YOU ARE an avid basketball fan, you are certainly aware of my passion for the game that has served me so well. I have been so lucky to have been involved in this game, which was started over a century ago by Mr. Naismith. Interestingly, I bet many of you did not know that Mr. Naismith was a philosopher and a Presbyterian minister as well as a man who was active in many ways in the great game he invented.

My journey has taken me through every level involving the roundball game. I've had the golden opportunity to coach on the scholastic, collegiate, and professional levels. Also, for several decades I have been blessed with the opportunity to share the microphone on ESPN/ABC to discuss this magnificent game. I pinch myself every day thinking how lucky I have been to be able to sit at courtside watching many of our greats, such as Jordan, Magic, Bird, LeBron, Dwyane, Shaq, and many others. I certainly have seen it all in the world of basketball, baby!

But here's something I haven't seen: philosophers sharing their concepts and feelings about the game I respect and revere. Wow—I may not agree with all their theories and arguments, but Mr. Walls and Mr. Bassham have created an exciting concept for hoops fanatics to analyze. They take you on a thrill ride as they and their fellow philosophers express their views of this magical game. Trust me, you will be challenged and amazed by the variety of ways they have found to look at the game. For example, who would ever think to associate basketball with the term "communitarianism"? That's a mouthful, baby! Or who would ever expect to be talking about hoops and Aristotle in the same sentence? Or

Machiavelli and roundball? Believe me, you will find this approach to basketball to be totally different from that in any other book you have ever opened.

Well, my friends, enjoy this fascinating perspective on basketball. Take this philosophical excursion, analyze it, dissect it, and argue with it. I am so proud to know that the game I love has even touched philosophical prime-time players like Walls and Bassham. Who knows? Maybe the next Michelangelo of philosophy will read this book and come to share my passion for Mr. Naismith's marvelous game.

ACKNOWLEDGMENTS

THANKS TO MY children, Angela Rose and Jonathan Levi, for the numerous ways they inspire and amuse me, not always consciously. Jonathan deserves a special word of acknowledgment for still loving basketball despite the workouts. Thanks to various friends with whom I have discussed and debated hoops over the years: Bill Arnold, Tony Casey, Brent Claiborne, Harriet Cook, Joe Dongell, Chris Fowler, Les Fowler, Rusty George, Tony Headley, Derek Keefe, Nick Maples, Brian Marshall, Gabe Pendleton, Duke Ruktanonchai, Reid Walker, and Ben Witherington. Thanks also to Elizabeth Victoria Glass for countless happy hours of watching ESPN together, during which she often shared her estrogen-tinged angle on the game, though I am still not sure how she was lucky enough to pick the national champion the very first time she filled out a tournament bracket.
—JW

THANKS TO BILL Irwin, who read almost the whole book in draft and offered helpful suggestions on every chapter. Thanks too to Jamie McAndrew, Alex Schroeder, J. P. Andrejko, Eric Bronson, Aeon Skoble, and Kelly Clark for providing valuable feedback. Copy editor Cheryl Hoffman and the good people at the University Press of Kentucky were a pleasure to work with at every step. To friends Roger Hurt, Scott Padek, and Mike Kelley: thanks for the great hoops at the CMC. A very special thanks to Dick Vitale for contributing the foreword, and to Tom Morris for putting us in touch with Dickie V. To Al Padek, coach of the Wright Hawks and role model to dozens of kids in South Tulsa, this book is gratefully dedicated. As always, my greatest debt is to my wife, Mia, and my son, Dylan. You make all the difference.
—GB

TIP-OFF

Hoops, Pop Culture, and Philosophy

BASKETBALL HAS PLAYED a long and storied role in American popular culture, and every year it seems to get bigger. Now the most popular team sport in the United States, hoops is high energy, constant motion, spectacular athletic plays, graceful choreography, clutch shots, and dramatic comebacks. Basketball is the big screen and rock and roll rolled into one.

The high-energy, high-drama nature of the game no doubt partly explains why basketball has become so intertwined with popular culture. Past and present NBA stars such as Michael Jordan, Shaquille O'Neal, LeBron James, and Yao Ming are instantly recognizable pop icons the world over. Celebrities such as Jack Nicholson, Woody Allen, Spike Lee, Ashley Judd, Bob Seger, and Kid Rock are regular courtside attractions at NBA and college games. A number of rap and R & B artists, such as Nelly, Jay-Z, and Usher, are part-owners of NBA teams.[1] Popular films such as *Hoosiers, Glory Road, Hoop Dreams, Blue Chips,* and *White Men Can't Jump* offer revealing perspectives on hoops and American culture. And each spring millions of college hoops fans (and office-pool participants) are seized by "March Madness" as colleges from around the country battle their way through a grueling sixty-five-team, single-elimination tournament for the glory of being crowned national champions.

The connections between basketball and philosophy may be less obvious but are nonetheless fascinating and significant. How do you measure true greatness in a basketball player or coach? What can basketball teach us about character and success? Can studying Eastern mystical traditions such as Zen Buddhism and Taoism improve your jump shot? Is intentional fouling unethical, and if so, when? How should you deal with strategic cheaters in pickup basketball? Is women's basketball, with its emphasis on fundamentals and team-centered play, "better" basketball than the more individualistic, physical, and showboating style often favored in the NBA? If a ref makes a bad call and mistakenly disallows a team's winning basket, did that team in fact win the game—or can you win a game only if the refs *say* that you won the game? With constantly changing rosters, what does it mean for a player to play for the "same team"? Is the phenomenon of having a "hot hand" in basketball an illusion, as several prominent scientists and philosophers of sport have argued? What makes basketball such a beautiful game to watch? What can the film *Hoosiers* teach us about the meaning of life? All of these philosophical conundrums, and more, are explored in this volume.

As Dickie V. notes in his foreword, the inventor of basketball, Dr. James Naismith, was himself a philosophy major as an undergraduate and was also actively involved in debate through a campus literary society. Although basketball is sometimes regarded as less cerebral than sports such as baseball and golf, this philosophical pedigree perhaps gives hoops the rightful claim to being "the thinking person's game." Be that as it may, there is no doubt that exploring the philosophical dimensions of the game can make you a more insightful and appreciative fan, a more effective coach, and a better player—not to mention help you win arguments with fellow fans!

In fact, as both professional philosophers and avid hoops fans, we've found that the quality of argumentation among serious basketball fans is often quite high, and that these arguments frequently take on a distinctively philosophical shape. Assumptions are spelled out, terms are clearly defined—both hallmarks of philosophical debate—and theses are clearly defended. A good example is a recent article by *ESPN Magazine* columnist Ric Bucher on the issue of who should be MVP in the NBA in the 2005–2006 season.[2] As Bucher notes, this question is hard to answer with any sort of definitive clarity because "MVP" can be taken in several ways. He mentions several possibilities:

MEP—Most Excellent Player
MVPOAWT—Most Valuable Player on a Winning Team
MSIPOATTWBTE—Most Statistically Impressive Player on a Team That
    Was Better Than Expected

MVPOTBT—Most Valuable Player on the Best Team
MDPDTSOATTFS—Most Dominant Player Down the Stretch on a Team
   That Finishes Strong
MIP—Most Indispensable Player

While Bucher professes to be tiring of this debate, his terminological precision is admirable. His distinctions remind us of the kinds of precise, clarifying definitions we often see in contemporary analytic philosophy. And while they have a slightly humorous edge, they show that the highly contested question of how value is assigned may hinge significantly on implicit assumptions that need to be spelled out.

Though published by an academic press, this is not really an "academic" book. It is written *for* basketball fans *by* basketball fans, most of whom also happen to be professional philosophers. Like the coeditors' two previous books on philosophy and popular culture, it is intended to be a serious but accessible exploration of the often surprising ways that philosophy can illuminate and enrich popular culture and that pop culture can serve as a hook for serious philosophizing.[3] It's a symbiotic relationship of which Dr. Naismith, the philosophical inventor of the game, would surely be proud.

Notes

1. A little-known but intriguing connection between hoops and rock music is that the grunge band Pearl Jam was originally named Mookie Blaylock, after the NBA journeyman point guard, and their first album, *Ten,* was named after Blaylock's number. Luckily, for the good of both rock and hoops, the band members were apparently not big fans of Uwe Blab.

2. "Let's See Your Valuables, Sir," ESPN.com., April 11, 2006. Accessed May 16, 2006. Available at http://sports.espn.go.com/nba/dailydime?page=dailydime-060411.

3. Gregory Bassham and Eric Bronson, eds., *The Lord of the Rings and Philosophy: One Book to Rule Them All* (Chicago: Open Court, 2003); and Gregory Bassham and Jerry Walls, eds., *The Chronicles of Narnia and Philosophy: The Lion, The Witch, and the Worldview* (Chicago: Open Court, 2005).

Baseline Values, Enduring Lessons

Stephen H. Webb

BUILDING COMMUNITIES ONE GYM AT A TIME

Communitarianism and the Decline of Small-Town Basketball

A Question for Rick Mount

WHICH WOULD YOU rather be, a high school basketball star or a professional basketball star? True, most professional players were once high school stars, but not all of them, and it's certainly true that not all high school stars make it to the pros. So pretend you could be only one or the other. Which would it be?

You are probably thinking this is a trick question. What is there to choose? High schools are full of kids walking around with letter jackets, while the pros promise a life of fame and fortune. Why be known only by the people in your hometown when you could be on national TV?

Believe it or not, there are basketball players who have experienced both local and national fame, and they would choose the former over the latter. Rick "the Rocket" Mount was the hottest shooter in Indiana in the 1960s. He played for Lebanon High School and then starred at Purdue, which is right up the road. He went on to a mixed career in the old ABA and retired at age twenty-eight from the game that had brought him so much fame.

Sportswriter Bob Williams asked Mount why he retired early, and he replied: "I still loved the game of basketball, but I didn't enjoy all of the other things about the pro scene. Pro ball is nothing like high school and college—it's a job and too much of a cutthroat proposition."[1] After he retired, Mount moved back to his hometown, where he has lived ever since.

Mount didn't earn a fortune in high school or college, but he had the admiration of the people who knew him best. Hundreds showed up to watch him play when he was just a fifth grader. When he announced that he would be going to Miami for his college career, the people of Lebanon were so vocal in their disappointment that he changed his mind and went to Purdue.

His local fame was so great that the national media caught up with him. He was the first high school–team athlete featured on the cover of *Sports Illustrated*. In that February 14, 1966, issue, Frank Deford wrote that he "may be as good a high school basketball player as there ever was."

Mount's basketball skills were valued by his townsfolk because they epitomized the virtue of hard work. He was not a flashy player, but he had a perfect jump shot, which was the product of countless hours of disciplined practice. When he played for a national audience, those same skills were valued according to the supply and demand of the marketplace. He made more money, but he lost some of the meaning of the game he loved. Clearly, he would choose being a high school star over a professional one.

What Is a Community?

Rick Mount's attitude toward the pros serves as a good example of a philosophical movement called communitarianism. Communitarianism is hard to define because it is known as much for what it rejects as for what it stands for. Communitarians are political philosophers who believe, as you might guess from their name, that the needs of the community outweigh the desires of the individual.

Most modern philosophical theories about what makes for a good society begin with the individual. These theories are often called "liberal," though that shouldn't be confused with the contemporary use of that label. Liberal political theories have shaped the political beliefs of both Democrats and Republicans. These theories argue that the foundation of social order is individual rights and that these rights are universal in scope. Notice that there are two parts to this claim. First, philosophical liberals begin their thinking with individuals. Individuals are the most basic reality, while communities are considered little more than an aggregation of individuals. Second, philosophical liberals insist that *human* rights apply to everyone, regardless of who they are or where they live.

Philosophical liberals thus are more interested in those aspects of human nature that are shared by everyone, not the local customs, rituals, and beliefs that distinguish one group from another.

When philosophical liberals begin with individual rights, they quickly run into the problem of connecting those rights with social obligations. Philosophical liberals understand rights as inherent in human nature. Humans are unique, rational, and of infinite worth. Therefore, all humans should be treated equally and with respect. Rights thus function to protect individuals from each other and from the intrusion of governmental authority. But what about the obligations we have to each other? If rights are the most fundamental expression of our humanity, then what becomes of the social and civic duties that keep individuals connected to each other and to their local and national communities? What is the glue that holds society together?

Philosophical liberals have all sorts of ingenious ways of connecting rights to obligations, but communitarians think that you cannot build a solid community on the shaky foundation of individualism. Philosophers like Alasdair MacIntyre, Michael Sandel, Charles Taylor, and Michael Walzer have set out to dismantle the liberal emphasis on individuals and their rights. Communitarians follow Aristotle in arguing that humans are naturally social creatures. People find value in life through their attachments to various groups, organizations, or teams. The claim that society is composed of individuals with rights doesn't do justice to how people actually lead their lives. In fact, philosophical liberalism is itself the product of many centuries of collaborative thinking on the part of a philosophical community. Philosophical liberalism is a tradition that denies or downplays the importance of tradition, making it impossible for liberals to account for the origin of their own ideas.

Philosophical liberals think they are preserving human dignity when they advocate the enforcement of universal rights. In reality, they are imposing artificial and restrictive norms that don't correspond to how societies actually operate. Communities determine meaning, not individuals. As the familiar example of team bonding in basketball illustrates, people value each other and the places they live because they have shared goals, common beliefs, and public rituals that bring them together. It follows that the best way to preserve the dignity of individuals is to strengthen and enhance the communities to which they belong. The abstract idea of human rights will accomplish nothing if societies don't have the wisdom and the will to enforce those rights.

Philosophical liberals respond to communitarians by arguing that societies can do more harm in the world than individuals. When individuals join together in a group, they have more power than when they act alone, but they also are less inclined to raise questions about the group's beliefs and activities. Groups are so powerful, liberals argue, that individuals tend to conform to the wishes of the whole. Prejudices go unchecked and minorities are often made the victims of collective action. Communitarians answer this criticism by arguing that the law alone cannot protect minorities from majority rule. If a society is to succeed in being both cohesive and diverse, then mutual respect and compassion for outsiders must become part of the daily routine and habits of all its citizens. Individuals learn to put the interests of others ahead of their own by belonging to communities that require them to get along with each other. A just society, communitarians conclude, will consist of many smaller communities where people will learn the values of trusting and respecting each other. Indeed, these are values that can't be learned by individuals in isolation from communal participation.

Communitarians also reject the liberal insistence on the universality of human rights. Communitarians argue that what makes one society good might differ from what makes another society good—just as two equally good basketball teams may have totally contrasting styles. Good societies make demands on their citizens to be involved and to help others, and they can do this only if those citizens have something in common with each other that they don't share with other societies. That is, every community must have a tradition or set of traditions that makes it unique, so that its members feel privileged to be a part of that community. Traditions also help members identify with each other and put the needs of the community above their personal desires.

Communitarians believe that communities need cultivation and protection. Communities are more than a collection of individual persons, just as a basketball team is more than the sum of its parts. Communities, like persons, can grow, change, and die. Each community has its own personality, which it expresses in its own way. Communitarians realize, of course, that communities can become a threat to individual liberty and happiness. Nonetheless, they hold that the needs of communities must often take precedence over the desires of individuals because it is in everyone's interest to live in a society where communities flourish. Without shared moral boundaries and rules, individuals would be set adrift in a sea of moral confusion and social fragmentation. Strong community, not anarchy, is the source of true individualism. It takes courage and communal nurturance to be an individual. As philosopher Thomas Hobbes (1588–1679) argues, in a state of moral anarchy, everyone acts alike.

Because strong communities are necessary for true individualism, America used to be more genuinely diverse than it is today. Before the rise of suburbs and strip malls, the various regions of America looked and sounded different from each other. Each small town had its own character. Small towns were also full of characters—people who were celebrated for their eccentricities. (Think of Goober, Gomer Pyle, and Barney Fife on the old *Andy Griffith Show*.) Local communities had more freedom to exercise authority over their members, which meant that decisions about which groups to join carried more consequences. People expressed themselves through their local affiliations, and their participation in these groups made a difference to their neighborhoods and towns.

The mass media have changed forever the significance of local loyalties and attachments. The world of athletics has contributed to this transformation and has also been a victim of it. Fans used to follow the teams closest to home because they had no way of knowing what the other teams were doing. Now fans root for teams that play hundreds or thousands of miles away. On many of these teams, none of the players are from the city they represent, and several may hail from different countries. Owners move teams to maximize their profits, and players move from team to team for the same reason. Many people still follow their team like true believers, but it's hard to know what they believe in. Perhaps it's inevitable that sports have become part of the entertainment industry, providing distraction rather than edification. It hasn't always been that way, however, as the movie *Hoosiers* attests. Basketball can be a lot more than entertainment by being a lot less than big-time competition.

Gyms and the Making of Small-Town America

Before the advent of television, Bobby Knight, and the Indiana Pacers, Indiana basketball was all about high schools. Indiana basketball exemplified the first rule of communitarian philosophy: the local should have priority over the national. Hoosiers, as people from Indiana are known, identify with their hometowns, and they express that pride by rooting for their high school basketball teams. Towns in Indiana are still known by their best players: "Lebanon: Home of Rick Mount." This was even more true fifty years ago, when Indiana was more rural and there were fewer competing attractions. This lack of diversity no doubt had its downsides, but when people share a common bond and identify with their communities, they take more responsibility for one another and for their own actions.

Liberal political philosophers tend to think that individuals will create good societies if their rights are protected by the government and codified by law. Communitarians think that communities are created and sustained by intentional activity. Communities cannot be left to chance. Communities need public spaces, for example, where people can gather to discuss the issues of the day and just share each other's company. Indeed, one of the most important ways to build a good society is to create buildings that enable people to make connections with each other. For small towns in Indiana throughout the twentieth century, basketball gymnasiums served this precise purpose.

Of the ten high school gyms with the largest seating capacity in the United States, nine are located in Indiana.[2] If you broaden that list, Indiana has twenty-eight of the largest thirty-six gyms in the nation. The largest of them all is the New Castle Fieldhouse, in New Castle, Indiana, which has 9,314 seats.

Hoosiers have been crazy about basketball ever since the Reverend Nicholas C. McKay brought the game to the Crawfordsville, Indiana, YMCA only two years after the game was invented. The first Indiana basketball games were played in attics, Masonic halls, barns, and churches. The first "gyms" were so irregular in size, with protruding walls and low ceilings, that local rules took effect, allowing players to make bounce shots and eliminating out of bounds. When small towns built gyms expressly for basketball games, they designed them to look like the barns that dominate the Hoosier landscape. This common touch had an egalitarian impact on town life. People of all incomes and religious affiliations sat together and rooted for the same cause. Schools were not desegregated for years to come, but Indiana gyms helped begin the process of creating unity amid diversity.

The state tournament, first held in 1911, gave Hoosiers a sense of identity and allowed small towns to express their loyalty and pride. Towns competed to be sectional and regional hosts, so they began building gyms that often held more people than the number of residents who lived there.[3] In many Indiana towns, the gym was the largest building and thus the one place where everyone could gather. The gyms held dances, school plays, and graduation ceremonies, as well as basketball games, but it was the games that gave the gyms their most lasting significance. Even as late as the 1990s, when there were more entertainment options for young people than ever before, nearly a million Hoosiers annually attended the state tournament. To put those numbers in perspective, California, with six times as many residents, was drawing only 250,000 fans to its state tournament.

Few of the gyms built in the 1920s through the 1940s remain in use today. Many were rendered obsolete by school consolidations that began in the late 1940s. In 1950, 766 high schools competed in the state tournament. By 1990, that number was reduced to 386. For many communities, the closing of the gym meant the end of their existence. In 1950 *Life* magazine covered the closing of Onward High School, when state troopers were sent to evict the parents who surrounded the school and the students who stayed inside. The struggle lasted two years, ending only when the state nullified the high school's accreditation. In many cases, old high school gyms became elementary schools or community centers. Some became churches or businesses. Others were preserved only to remain empty, abandoned to the elements, but too full of memories to be torn down.[4]

Anyone driving by these old, decaying gyms today is led to reflect on a radical transformation in American life. Small towns used to be the source of many of America's cultural values and social standards. Residents of small towns did not feel like they were being left behind by the glamour of the big cities. People lived in face-to-face communities where they shopped at stores owned by their neighbors and rooted for the basketball player who lived down the street. Television, as Benjamin Rader has argued, dramatically changed the way athletes are treated.[5] Athletes who are intimately known by their community are expected to uphold the local values. Athletes who are national stars are held to more rigorous competitive standards but, unfortunately, less rigorous moral standards. National stars can get away with outrageous behavior because they are essentially entertainers who have no direct impact on the lives of their fans. Local stars are asked to do their best and to behave in the process. Fifteen years ago, Damon Bailey dominated Indiana high school basketball, and 41,101 fans showed up at the Hoosier Dome to see him play for the state championship in 1990. Yet every discussion of Bailey began or ended with how polite and well mannered he was. Larry Bird was one of the greatest players in state history, but what people respected most was his work ethic and the way he handled adversity. John Wooden, who grew up in Martinsville, Indiana (population 5,200), enshrined these small-town virtues in his famous "Pyramid of Success" by putting industriousness and enthusiasm at the cornerstones.

One way of understanding the impact of television on sports is to draw on the distinction, often made by communitarian philosophers, between virtual and real communities. Virtual communities exist more in the imagination than in concrete reality. They are created by magazines, newspapers, television, and, increasingly, the Internet. They are sustained by advertising and merchandise. Towns used to be united by the team they rooted for. Now you don't know who your fellow citizens cheer for unless they wear the logo of their favorite team. Virtual communities can be exciting and engaging, but something is lost when the local is replaced by the national or international.

When people no longer feel like they belong to local communities, their basic human need for belonging is replaced with nostalgia for the past. Evidence for this claim can be found in the construction of Conseco Fieldhouse in downtown Indianapolis. It was designed to maximize the number of seats, suites, and fan amenities while evoking memories of the state's glorious basketball heritage. With a vintage scoreboard, a roll-out bleacher section, a brick concourse, and ushers dressed in uniforms that look like they were pulled from a Hollywood costume rack marked "Fifties," Conseco looks like an enormous high school gym. The arched roof especially brings back memories of the old barnlike field houses that dotted the cornfields of Indiana. In fact, Conseco Fieldhouse is the first theme stadium, intended, like an amusement park, to conjure up a fantasy world for older fans. A ticket gets you not just a ball game but also a set of memories and a feeling of warmth about the past.

Conseco Fieldhouse has been praised as one of the most attractive stadiums in the nation, but it cannot replace the social functions of the small-town gyms it is meant to imitate. The tickets are expensive, so only the relatively well-to-do can afford to attend games on a regular basis. The gym is in the middle of the state's largest city, so people in small towns are made to feel on the margins of the action, isolated and left behind. Finally, there is undoubtedly a diverse crowd at the games, but the fans come for the glamour of the star athletes and thus have little to talk to one another about except the game itself. Most social interaction takes place in the expensive suites, which businesses rent to entertain their clients. Rather than being active participants in the meaning of the game, fans are passive consumers of a product. The particular and local have been replaced by the general and universal.

The Unmaking of Small-Town Basketball

I could easily be accused of wallowing in the same nostalgia that I have attributed to the designers of Conseco Fieldhouse. After all, high school basketball still dominates the sports pages of the local papers, even though there are more sports to cover and more emphasis is given to professional teams. Even readers who agree with me that small towns have lost much of their significance in modern America might wonder whether the consequences are all that grave. Hoosiers can be proud of an NBA team that is nationally respected, and downtown Indianapolis is thriving. Small towns that took too much pride in themselves and discouraged their children from moving away could be narrow-minded and parochial in their outlook. Perhaps it is good that most of us identify with communities that are national, or even global, in their reach.

A communitarian philosopher would disagree, but arguments about the importance of local community can quickly become colored by passionate rhetoric rather than careful analysis. Ironically, the very state that perfected small-town basketball has threatened its viability, so Indiana can be considered a laboratory of sorts for the plight of small-town sports in a culture obsessed with national fame. In the 1990s, Indiana officials decided to phase out single-class basketball. Single-class basketball tournaments might appear to penalize small schools, whose teams are forced to compete with teams drawn from a much larger student body, and this is precisely the argument made by proponents of dividing the state into classes based on school size. The decision to eliminate the single-class system in Indiana was hard fought and emotional—and for good reasons. Single-class basketball actually was the secret behind Indiana's small-town traditions. When only one team from the state is the champion and a single loss is grounds for elimination from the tournament, every team has a chance. The smallest schools can dream of glory, and the largest schools have to agonize over the possibility of an upset. Players from the smallest schools have an opportunity to prove themselves against the very best.

The iconic legend of Hoosier basketball concerns just this scenario. On March 21, 1954, little Milan (pronounced *Mī'lun*), with an enrollment of 161 students, battled powerful Muncie Central, which was more than ten times bigger, to a 30–30 tie in the waning seconds of the state championship game. When a farm kid named Bobby Plump hit the winning shot with eighteen seconds left to play, Indiana had its own version of the David and Goliath story. The next day, 40,000 people descended upon Milan, a town of 1,500, to celebrate the victory.

The Milan miracle has never been repeated in Indiana, which is one reason why state officials decided to disband the single-class system. It used to be that being from a small town meant dreaming about doing something that was beyond one's reach. Now Americans have apparently decided that every kid should be a Goliath and nobody should be faced with insurmountable obstacles like David.

The whole point of the single-class system was twofold: give everyone a chance, and teach young people to handle adversity. For everyone to want to have a chance, however, there must be something nearly unachievable to strive for. Larry Bird, for example, who called himself the "Hick from French Lick," just wanted a shot at the state title. Oscar Robertson, perhaps the greatest all-around basketball player Indiana has produced, overcame prejudice and discrimination to lead Crispus Attucks to the state championship in 1955 and 1956. In fact, until Robertson stormed through Indiana basketball, small towns were more likely than big-city schools to have integrated teams, because there was just one high school, which everyone attended. In 1930, Dave Degernette was the first black to play for a state championship team, and his school was located in the very small town of Washington, Indiana. Those who wanted to eliminate the single-class system had the noble goal of increasing the number of championship opportunities, but their plan also sent a less positive message to kids from small towns or underprivileged schools: you cannot compete with the big-city schools and the wealthy programs. Small-town basketball is small-time.

Why I Don't Watch the NBA

Communitarian philosophers remind us that bigger is not necessarily better. Players who scramble hard after loose balls can show more excitement for the game than weary millionaires sweating for a mega-paycheck. Small-town basketball is about the virtue of hard work, equal opportunity, and impossible dreams. Professional basketball is fast and furious, with the victory going, more often than not, to the strongest and tallest team, especially when referees hesitate to call fouls and let players perform complex dance steps on the way to the basket. The problem with professional basketball, communitarian philosophers would argue, can't be blamed on any single individual. Instead, the plight of basketball reflects a reversal of priorities that permeates all aspects of our culture. We have let the global and the national take priority over the local. Communitarians argue that what is most important should be what lies closest at hand. Family, friends, the corner store, the neighbor, the local church, mosque, or synagogue, all of these things should be held in higher esteem than people and institutions that we only read about in the papers or see on TV. The local theater, for example, should be where we learn about acting and stagecraft, rather than television and the movies. We should draw our morality from our friends and relatives, not from the stars who are created by the power of the screen.

Communitarians can be accused of nostalgia, but for a time, anyway, basketball really worked the way they want everything to work. In Indiana, high school ball was everything. When the local stars went off to fine professional careers, interest in them just wasn't the same. That way of being a fan seems strange to us today, but that says more about us than about the way things used to be.

Notes

1. Bob Williams, *Hoosier Hysteria: Indiana High School Basketball* (South Bend, IN: Hardwood Press, 1997), 142.

2. Sal Ruibal, "Fieldhouse a Cathedral to High School Hoops," *USA Today Online,* February 27, 2004, http://www.usatoday.com/sports/preps/basketball/2004–02–25-ten-great-hoops-newcastle_x.htm.

3. When UCLA freshman Johnny Moore played his first home game in 1951, a reporter asked him if he was nervous playing in front such a large crowd (2,500). Moore, who hailed from Gary, Indiana, replied: "Well, sir, the UCLA gym is nothing compared to my last high school game in Indiana. They had a crowd of eighteen thousand that night." Dwight Chapin and Jeff Prugh, *The Wizard of Westwood: Coach John Wooden and His UCLA Bruins* (New York: Warner, 1973), 103.

4. For a moving account of the fate of these gyms, see Donald E. Hamilton, *Hoosier Temples: A Pictorial History of Indiana's High School Gyms* (St. Louis: G. Bradley, 1993).

5. Benjamin G. Rader, *In Its Own Image: How Television Has Transformed Sports* (New York: Free Press, 1984).

Thomas D. Kennedy

TO HACK OR NOT TO HACK?

(The Big) Aristotle, Excellence, and
Moral Decision-Making

I'd like to be known as "the Big Aristotle." It was Aristotle who said
excellence is not a singular act, but a habit.

—Shaquille O'Neal

IN THE BEGINNING of basketball, as in almost all beginnings, things
were a lot simpler. Games were thirty minutes long; there was no backboard; and the basket was, well, a basket and the ball had to stay in it in
order to score a goal. There were fouls, of course, and they were pretty
serious business. Rule 5 of Dr. James Naismith's original thirteen rules of
basketball (1891) addressed fouls this way: "5. No shouldering, holding,
pushing, tripping or striking in any way the person of an opponent shall
be allowed; the first infringement of this rule by any player shall come as
a foul, the second shall disqualify him until the next goal is made, or, if
there was evident intent to injure the person, for the whole of the game,
no substitute allowed."[1]

Things have changed in basketball, and mostly for the better. If fouls
were, at first, definite no-no's, that's no longer the case. And if Dr. Naismith had in mind a game in which there would be very little physical
contact between players, that isn't basketball as we know it at any level
today—professional, collegiate, or pickup. Basketball, for good or ill, has
become a contact sport, and even great players commit their share of
fouls. Indeed, in some sense great players seem to be great—or at least,
good—foulers. Consider this: arguably the greatest player in the history
of the game, Kareem Abdul-Jabbar, is also the career leader for personal
fouls (4,657). Granted, he's also the all-time career leader in minutes

played (57,446), and it stands to reason that the more minutes played, the greater the opportunity to foul, as well as the greater the likelihood of fouling, since tired players seem likely to foul more frequently than rested players.

Still, Kareem fouled a lot. As do a lot of great players. If you look at the 1997 NBA selection of the top fifty NBA players of all time, half of those names would also appear on the list of the top one hundred career foulers. It's true that big players foul more frequently than small players in the modern game; only two guards—John Stockton and the amazing Hal Greer of the 1960s Philadelphia 76ers—appear in the top twenty of the NBA career leaders for personal fouls. But big players have no corner on fouling. In addition to Stockton and Greer, recall these other accomplished foulers: Clyde Drexler, John Havlicek, Calvin Murphy, Rick Barry, Isiah Thomas, and Oscar Robertson.

We should find this perplexing. In basketball, as in other sports, a foul is a type of defect, a violation of a fundamental rule of the game. One fundamental of shoemaking would seem to be that the sole of the shoe goes on the bottom, the laces on the top. Can we imagine an excellent shoemaker whose every sixth or seventh pair of shoes had the sole on the top, or on the side, or on the back of the shoe? Would we call someone an excellent driver if she had an accident every ninth or tenth time she got in the car, regardless of her driving accomplishments the other 80-plus percent of the time? Could there be an excellent jazz saxophonist who in his improvisations played notes just because he found them interesting or weird, disregarding what the rest of the combo was playing? In each case, we are inclined to think of excellence in a *regulative* (rule-governed) activity as requiring not only knowledge of the rules but also an adherence to them. So how could an excellent basketball player foul a lot, and thus be a major violator of the fundamentals of the game? Shouldn't that count against basketball greatness? If Kareem wanted to be an excellent player, shouldn't he have fouled less? And, although Phil (from my noontime basketball games) can shoot the three-pointer, isn't his incessant hacking—excuse me for a moment while I change the bandage over my eye from one of Phil's wild swings today—evidence that he is far from a great pickup player? Maybe Kareem isn't the greatest basketball player ever. Maybe, given his fouling record, he wasn't even a great player at all. (Of course, even if that were the case, you and I might still want to play on Kareem's team.)

Or maybe part of what makes a great basketball player great isn't the number of fouls he commits, but how savvy he is about fouling. Maybe great players foul the right person at the right time in the right way with the right aim in view, and feel the right way about the foul, which is a kind of roundball paraphrase of what the philosopher Aristotle (384–322 B.C.) says about having morally excellent qualities. Maybe great players know when fouling is the appropriate thing to do and when it's not. And maybe an excellent player is like a morally excellent person in knowing when to take risks that might lead to a violation of the rules and when to intend not merely the risk but an intentional violation of the rules themselves. That, at least, is what I shall argue.

Intentions, Rules, and Moral Excellence

Almost all of us recognize the existence of moral rules and consider them binding upon us: Don't lie. Don't steal. Keep your promises. Even if we don't understand where these rules came from and why they exist, we believe that they should inform our conduct. That is to say, when we are trying to decide what to do, we think these rules are relevant and should be taken into account. And usually we think we shouldn't only take them into account; we should obey them.

We could put it this way: except, perhaps, in extraordinary circumstances, we should never *intentionally* violate a basic moral rule. Perhaps we can clarify this by thinking a bit more carefully about acts and actions.

In everyday life, we use the terms "acts" and "actions" interchangeably, but part of what philosophers do is to try to bring some precision to everyday language. We can say that both actions and acts are human *doings*, things you and I do. But some things we intend to do and some, like blinking and breathing, we don't. It's a fast break, the other team has the ball, and I'm trying to get down to block the shot when I barrel into Dan, who has set a smart pick just below the foul line. I didn't mean to slam into Dan. I didn't even know he was there. Still, I did it. It was my *action*. Call the foul if you want to. Actions are the broad category that covers everything we *do*.

But within that broad category, we can distinguish some things, namely, *acts,* that we do intentionally. Earlier in the game on a fast break I was just behind John as he broke for the basket. John's about my age, and I'm not trying to dribble the ball as I run, so I think I've got a good chance of getting down the court and stopping him from scoring. But John's team wins if he makes a basket, and if John's team wins, I sit the next game out. So I form the intention to foul John; that is something I aim to do. It won't be a dangerous or a hard foul, but I'll keep the ball from going in. Having formed the intention, I *act*—a gentle, artful swat of his right arm that deflects the ball out of bounds.

So part of the act is simply the *physical movement* I perform with my body, and another is the *intention* that informed the act—what I aimed to do. There are other features as well. All acts have *consequences,* things that result from, that follow from, the act—John's team has to work for the next point, my ego is inflated and John's is deflated by my effective foul, Phil gets another shot at hammering someone, and so forth. (And, of course, there may be consequences of these consequences; the world of human acts is very complex and messy.) Finally, there's the *motivation* for the act I performed, the why of the act, what value I was trying to realize or what desire I was trying to satisfy in acting. In this case, I desired to show that even at my age I've still got game, I wanted to win, and I wanted to get back at John for smoking me on that reverse layup in the last game.

The relevance of the act/action distinction is that it helps us see that many fouls are actions, not acts, and typically we consider people blame-worthy only for their acts, for things they intended to do, and not for their actions.[2] Many fouls (although almost none of Phil the Hacker's fouls) are unintentional actions that we couldn't help because our bodies were out of control or we followed the fake. We don't know how many of Kareem's fouls were acts, or intentional fouls; how many of his fouls were actions in which he intended to block a shot, or steal a ball, or blockout for a rebound, but was called for a foul; and how many of his fouls were cases in which his intention was to perform a risky act that might or might not be called a foul.

The interesting questions for us have to do with acts and how inten-tional violations of rules fit with excellence in the activity governed by the rules. If we think of morality, would the morally excellent person intentionally violate those rules we normally recognize as binding? If we think of the practices of investing money or creating a musical work, would the excellent person violate the rules that govern those practices? In basketball, how frequently, if at all, might an excellent player intend either to foul or to make a risky play that might well be called a foul? We can't cover everything here, so let's start by trying to think more carefully just about intentional fouls. Would an excellent player ever intentionally foul another player? Or is the intentional violation of the rules always a defect?

Two Modern Traditions of Moral Thought

There are two major modern schools of thought about the moral life—about how we should live, what we should intend to do, and what we should intend not to do, as well as what we should not intend to do.[3] The first tradition is *deontological ethics,* a school of moral thought that maintains that certain actions are wrong because they are violations of duties we owe to others or violations of the rights that others have. For example, some deontological ethicists maintain that there is a dignity and worth that attaches to human beings because they are human or, perhaps, because they are rational creatures. We ought never do anything that violates the respect that is owed to another person as a result of his nature as a human being.

Perhaps the best-known proponent of deontological ethics is the eighteenth-century German philosopher Immanuel Kant (1724–1804). It's hard to imagine the periwigged and barely five-foot-tall Kant playing basketball, although in Monty Python's brilliant "International Philosophy" sketch he does appear as a member of the "back four" (along with Hegel, Schopenhauer, and Schelling) of the German soccer team playing against the Greek philosophers (Plato, Socrates, Aristotle, and others) in a match refereed by Confucius, St. Augustine, and St. Thomas Aquinas. But though it's hard to visualize Kant as a basketball player, it's easy to think of him as a great ref or an NCAA Men's Basketball Rules Committee member, for he is one of the greatest rules-men of all philosophical history.

Kant thought that you and I and most everyone else are pretty much on the money in our recognition of the rules that are morally binding upon us. "Don't steal," "Keep your promises," and "Don't lie" are sound moral rules, and we should obey them. Part of what is distinctive about Kant's philosophy is his account of *why* these moral rules are binding upon us. Kant's explanation is that there is one fundamental principle of morality, one superrule—the *categorical imperative*—that is binding on all people. Every moral rule that we ought to obey is an application of the categorical imperative.

Kant offers several different formulations of the categorical imperative, the most famous of which are *Act only according to that principle which you could will to be a universal law* and *Act always in such a way that you respect humanity, whether it's your own humanity or that of another person.* Why is it wrong to lie? Because when we lie to a person, we deny him or her access to information that is needed to make a rational decision, and in doing so we fail to respect him or her as a rational person. Rational people have a legitimate claim to all available information relevant to their making an informed decision. Why is "Don't lie" a good moral rule? Because no rational person would want to live in a world in which her word had no value because everyone lied whenever it suited them.

A second school of moral thought agrees with Kant that there is one fundamental principle of morality that justifies valid moral rules, but concurs with Kant and deontological ethics on little else. The basic principle of *utilitarianism*—the *greatest-happiness principle*—maintains that human acts are "right in proportion as they tend to promote happiness, wrong as they tend to produce the reverse of happiness." Utilitarianism is a *consequentialist* theory, since it claims that it is the consequences of one's act that determine what one ought to do. This is in contrast to deontological ethics, which emphasizes the character of what one is intending to do and whether the intended act comports with respect for persons. Consequentialist theories maintain that results are what matters; your act should bring about the best set of consequences. If Phil is trying to determine whether or not to hack me as I pivot toward the basket with my crafty hook shot, he should compare what is likely to result from his hacking me (I'll miss the shot, and I'll get really mad at him) with what is likely to result from his not hacking me (I'll make the shot, but I won't get mad at him) and determine which consequences are more desirable. But any consequentialist theory will have to answer two questions: (1) Whom should we consider in calculating which consequences are best? Just myself? Just my team? Everyone affected by actions? And (2) what type of consequences should one seek to maximize? Consequences in terms of what?

Classical utilitarianism's chief spokesperson is the philosopher John Stuart Mill (1806–1873), who argues that since pleasure is the only thing we desire for its own sake, we should try to maximize pleasure. More pleasurable for whom? For everyone affected in any significant way by the action. Mill (like Kant) insists upon *impartiality*—the person considering which act to perform counts as one, but no more than one, in her calculations about which act will bring the most happiness. *The greatest good* (in terms of pleasure) *for the greatest number of those affected* (each one equally counting as one) is the guiding principle of classical utilitarianism.

What do utilitarians make of moral rules? Typically, they will view moral precepts like "Keep your promises" and "Don't steal" as good rules of thumb based on the experience of the ages. We've learned that, ordinarily, breaking promises does not maximize the pleasure of the individuals involved and that only in the rarest of cases does stealing bring about the best consequences. So, typically it's best to obey these rules as a means to bringing about the most desirable state of affairs. But when you have good reason to think that obedience to a commonly accepted rule won't maximize pleasure, you should aim at pleasure, not at obedience to the rule.

What happens if we apply these two ethical theories to fouls in basketball? Consider *strategic* (or *tactical*) fouls. One type of strategic foul occurs near the end of the game, with the losing team using every opportunity to send the winning opponents to the charity stripe, hoping that they (the defense) may rebound a missed foul shot and thus get back into the game. Or think about coach Don Nelson's Hack-a-Shaq strategy—what Shaq himself described as "clown basketball." Assuming that you can't stop the other team's big man—a notoriously poor free-throw shooter—rather than risk his scoring, you hack the big man as soon as he touches the ball, sending him to shoot a free throw, which he is as likely as not to miss. How should a great player, an excellent player, feel about committing such strategic fouls?

Typically, something like the following consequentialist argument will be offered:

1. In competitive games such as basketball, the best consequences usually result when each team tries its hardest to win.
2. We don't stand a chance of winning unless we commit these strategic fouls.
3. Therefore, we ought to hack.[4]

The first premise is, of course, disputable. Basketball isn't rollerball, and if "playing one's hardest" means "doing whatever it takes to win," few people would be inclined to accept the premise. Still, it seems that a consequentialist might reasonably support strategic fouling unless the consequences of such fouls would make the game of basketball significantly less enjoyable to play or watch than otherwise.

What about a deontologist? It isn't clear how deliberately fouling a player is a violation of what one owes another—whether, that is, there is a *right* never to be fouled in a game. So one is hard-pressed to agree with Shaq that there is something *deeply* problematic about strategic fouls, at least on consequentialist or deontological grounds. Thus, tactical fouling, even the Hack-a-Shaq strategy, seems not to violate any easily recognizable principles of either deontological or utilitarian ethics.

Despite this, isn't there something to Shaq's objection? Even if we can't find any compelling consequentialist or deontological objections to the Hack-a-Shaq strategy, doesn't it nevertheless seem in some sense to be "clownish"? Tactical fouling, even when one is willing to accept the consequences of one's actions, ought to be a source of embarrassment, shouldn't it? It may not be goon basketball, but it is clown basketball. It isn't basketball the way an excellent player would play it.

Goon Basketball and Clown Basketball

Imagine that you're a reserve on the team of one of college basketball's winningest coaches. You haven't seen a lot of playing time, but you are big—6'8" and 250 pounds—and your coach is frustrated by what he thinks are uncalled illegal screens set by your opponent. He decides to send you in to do some damage, to send a message. You are to foul your opponents and to foul them hard. That's what "Coach" wants you to do. And pleasing Coach might win you more playing time in the future.[5]

Both consequentialist and deontological ethicists have an easy time making a compelling case *against* obeying your coach when he orders you to intentionally harm another player. Consider the consequences of your hard fouls. Can you know that your foul won't end another player's career? Is sending your coach's message worth that? What would be the consequences for your team if the opposing coaches gave orders like your coach? What would be the consequences for basketball if all players went into the game with the intention of taking out an opponent or two if the calls weren't going their way? Who would enjoy playing that game? Who would enjoy watching it? This is vigilante justice, something that isn't really just, something that not only harms the alleged wrongdoers but also ultimately fails to protect the innocent.

Deontological ethicists would also find your coach's order to be morally repugnant. Respect for others requires respecting their rational agency, and the rules against hard and dangerous fouls, rules present from basketball's origin, are in place to protect players. No rational person would want to play a game in which he or she might become the permissible object of a vicious attack whenever an opposing coach was frustrated. That would be goon basketball.

So it seems that consequentialist ethics and deontological ethics can help us determine which rules we ought to obey, and why. But these theories won't go very far in helping us explain why we're uneasy with "clown basketball." Perhaps we (and Shaq) are mistaken in thinking that these infractions are clown basketball. Or perhaps we're correct, and we need a different type of moral theory to explain why we shouldn't play either goon basketball or clown basketball.

Aristotle and the Big Aristotle

One response to the suggestion that we need a different type of theory would be: "Indeed we do. We can't expect moral theories to address nonmoral situations." The assumption behind this response is that we can neatly distinguish the moral from the nonmoral, that moral theories appropriately address only actions in the moral domain, and that goon basketball is clearly in the moral domain but clown basketball is not.

What should we make of this response? Shaq seemed to believe that he was being wronged by the Hack-a Shaq strategy and that the institution of basketball was being wronged as well. But as we've seen, there don't seem to be any moral rules that prohibit strategic fouling. Here, I suggest, Aristotle can help us out. Aristotle persuasively argues that there are some things we shouldn't do even if there are no moral rules against doing them. Perhaps strategic hacking—maybe all hacking—falls into this category.

Let's go back to Phil, the incorrigible hacker from my noontime basketball games. No one refuses to play on Phil's team. He won't help out much on defense, but perhaps the opposing team has an older player (like David) who won't fast break on Phil. Even though Phil can't dribble or rebound, he may help out significantly on offense because if you set the screen for him and give him enough time, he can nail the three. But although no one refuses to play on Phil's team, not many people on Phil's team (and even fewer on the opposing team) are enthusiastic about playing with Phil. Why? Because Phil is a hacker, and, well, there's just something base and unsportsmanlike about being a hacker.[6]

Why is hacking so unsporting and "clownish"? It isn't altogether easy to say. In part, there's the harm that may come to others from hacking. But in more than ten years of playing basketball with Phil (and more than a couple of trips to the hospital as a result of basketball play), I've never seen anyone seriously injured by one of Phil's hacks. Mostly, people get ugly bruises and scratches that heal within a couple of weeks. Physical harm is done, but it's minor harm.

There are also *aesthetic* considerations that come into play, considerations about the ugliness and inelegance of hacking. There's no such thing as a beautiful hack. You can't hack someone with style and grace. And hacking prevents a good many beautiful moves and graceful shots from coming to fruition.

Perhaps there are considerations of etiquette or what we might call social pleasantry as well. Even if no one is likely to be harmed by the hacking, games in which people are routinely hacked are rarely as sociable or as much fun as games in which the fouls are "good" fouls, honest attempts to stop one's opponents from scoring through good defense. And there are considerations external to the game as well: What will it be like for Kennedy and his philosophy students if he has to teach a class with an unsightly cut on his nose from my hack? If I routinely hack John, will that have a negative impact on our friendship? And so on.

In short, it appears that we'll get a truer grasp of the clownishness of hacking, not by trying to identify some moral rule that prohibits it, but by reflecting on what basketball is and why we value it. Most of us don't want our kids to play basketball for a coach who will send in the goons. Most of us don't want a coach who advocates clown basketball. Instead, we want our kids to play for someone who understands basketball and the fundamental values of the game. That's the kind of person who sees what's wrong with hacking. That's the kind of person who sees that there's something cheap and base about clown basketball. That's the kind of coach who can help players develop the knack of risking a foul, of playing at certain times (but only at certain times) in a way that makes you more likely to be called for a foul. Whether or not great players learn it from their coaches, that is something that great players have learned.

What I'm suggesting here about fouling is similar to what Aristotle suggested for living well. Great players are like excellent people. And the excellence of excellent people is more a matter of correctly seeing and reading the complexity of the world than it is a matter of learning how to make judgments based on an appropriate set of moral rules. With respect to both actions and feelings, the excellent person can see what is fitting and can distinguish between what is too much and too little for any situation. The excellent person has somehow developed a character such that she has "the right feelings at the right times, about the right things, toward the right people for the right end, and in the right way," as Aristotle says.

We might put it this way: In basketball, as in life, excellence is not a matter of making the right decisions; it's a matter of having a good character, of being the right sort of person. The right sort of person is one who is able to see things well and, having correctly seen the way things are, understands and desires what is fitting for the situation. Her decisions are good ones because they are made the right way by the right sort of person. It's because she sees the game rightly that she sees the inappropriateness of hacking, as well as the appropriateness of sometimes risking a foul call. And, as the Big Aristotle reminds us, excellence isn't about single acts; it's about living in the world in such a way that you always see things rightly and well. Seeing well and acting and feeling in a manner appropriate to what one sees are habits for the right sort of person. Hacking can become a habit, but so can not hacking. And the same is true of the many other qualities that make for excellence in life as well as in basketball.

How does one become the right sort of person? That's no easy question, but I suspect that the secret to becoming an excellent person is much the same as that to becoming an excellent basketball player. It helps to be born into the right sort of family and to have some genuinely good coaching, especially at an early age. But ultimately, as Aristotle said, it is a matter of forming good habits and always striving to be one's best.

If you are inclined to think that it is too late for you to become either a good person or a good player, let me remind you that Michael Jordan was cut from his high school basketball team his sophomore year. Find a good coach, and be like Mike.

Notes

1. Naismith's notion of fouls was actually a bit more expansive than this. Essentially, a foul was any violation of the rules of basketball; for example, striking the ball with a fist (rule 6), running with the ball (rule 3), and holding the ball with some body parts other than one's hands (rule 4) were also fouls.

2. Not surprisingly, things are a little more complicated than this. Consider what we should say about a drunken fan who throws ice on the court. In some sense, he may not have been in control of what he did. "That wasn't me who did that," he may genuinely say in a sober moment. Most of us at the very least would say that he was culpable for knowing that were he to get drunk, he might very well throw ice on the court. He was culpable for getting drunk, and one consequence of that act that he should have foreseen was that his drunkenness might lead him to act like a buffoon.

3. You (and Phil!) should think about the difference between not intending to slash my chest when you are guarding me and intending not to do me harm when I shoot. Phil never intends to hurt people, I am convinced—he's a nice guy. The problem is that, apparently, Phil too rarely intends *not* to hurt people.

4. Former North Carolina State coach Jim Valvano offers a similar rationale for ordering his team to foul in the last ten minutes of the 1983 national championship game against Houston, which NC State won 54–52. See Jim Valvano and Curry Kirkpatrick, *Valvano* (New York: Pocket Books, 1991), 165.

5. This imaginary case, and the description of this type of basketball as "goon basketball," owes more than a little to coach John Chaney of Temple University.

6. What is it to *be a hacker,* in contrast with just occasionally hacking? Think of a hacking foul as a foul aimed at stopping the play by physically impairing the opponent. A hacker is someone who makes a habit of hacking rather than genuinely challenging the opponent by trying to block a shot or box out.

R. *Scott Kretchmar*

BASKETBALL PURISTS
Blind Sentimentalists or Insightful Critics?

BASKETBALL PURISTS HAVE had something to crow about recently, and they haven't been quiet. When the U.S. basketball team embarrassed itself at the Greek Olympic Games in 2004, purists jumped at the opportunity to point out our lack of good passing, shooting, and teamwork. And when Detroit and San Antonio ended up in the 2005 NBA finals, sports columnists noted that this would be a series for basketball purists. With the likes of Tim Duncan and Richard Hamilton leading their respective squads, fundamentals would be featured over raw athleticism, good shooting over brute force, hitting the open player over taking forced shots or going one-on-one, strong defense over a run-and-gun offense, and perhaps most important, selfless teamwork over chest-thumping individuality.

The recent defeat of the talent-laden U.S. men's basketball team in the 2006 FIBA semifinals at the hands of the Greeks has only added fuel to the purist-stoked fire. Purists would agree with one AP report noting that the U.S. had dazzling skills, but the Greeks had a dazzling team.

Basketball purists, however, also have their critics. Some regard the patient team-oriented, passing, and back-door-cutting kind of offense, often associated with the Pete Carril–coached Princeton teams, as utterly boring. This view would seem to be supported by influential sports entertainment programs such as *SportsCenter*. They are far more likely to feature thunder dunks and in-your-face showmanship than they are a well-set screen, movement away from the ball, or sound defensive footwork. In addition, *Streetball, City Slam,* and other basketball-related ventures that feature spectacular individual capabilities coupled with "attitude" are now multimillion-dollar businesses that have attracted the attention of such mainstream sports media as ESPN. All this would tend to suggest that the basketball purist is something of a sports dinosaur. Unable to accept the fact that the game has changed, the purist stubbornly and mindlessly holds on to some overly sentimental version of basketball's "good old days."

Who's right? Which brand of basketball is better? Is this the kind of debate on which philosophers should weigh in? Can their insights shed any light on this issue? Or are the skeptics and relativists right when they say that this is simply a matter of opinion, much like the battle between those who prefer vanilla ice cream over Ben and Jerry's coffee-coffee-buzz-buzz-buzz?

My sense is that there is something here into which philosophers can sink their teeth. The "purist debate," after all, is not all that different from traditional philosophic arguments over the nature of the good life. Some have argued, for example, that the good life is built on a foundation of enlightened self-interest. Others suggest that prudential living doesn't go far enough and that alternate principles like humility, love, justice, and altruism provide keys to a better existence. While most contemporary philosophers don't believe that any "slam-dunk" arguments can be given for either view, most are convinced that persuasive arguments can be offered even if they are not absolutely conclusive.

I agree with this contemporary view and believe that persuasive philosophical arguments can be marshaled in the purist-modernist debate in basketball. In what follows, I try to build a case for what I call a "modified purist account." I call it a modified position because I fully agree with the modernists that basketball is an evolving phenomenon. Like all cultural activities, basketball changes, and many of these changes have improved the game. It would be foolish to go back to the "good old days" of basketball when equipment, skills, strategy, courts, and training techniques were, at least by contemporary standards, primitive. Nevertheless, I shall argue, purists are correct in thinking that many modernist changes in basketball have been unfortunate and should be resisted.

A False Test: Which Version Works Better?

Some might argue that the debate over different versions of basketball can be resolved by examining which style works best—on the court, in face-to-face competition. If teams that play modern versions of basketball typically beat comparably skilled squads that use a purist style of play, then the former brand of basketball wins. Case settled! Likewise, if the purists who criticized our less-than-stellar Olympic effort or our loss in the FIBA semifinals can trace these poor performances to a lack of fundamentals, poor teamwork, too little patience, and other bedrock principles of purist basketball, then they will be proven right. Purist versions of basketball, in other words, work best on the court.

It should become quickly obvious, however, that this cannot be the final court of appeal for this debate. Arguments between purists and modernists are primarily about different visions of what basketball *should be,* not about which techniques work better. Few purists, for instance, would argue that a flashy one-on-one move is not tremendously useful and effective on certain occasions, given certain matchups. And few modernists would argue that teamwork and good passing have little to do with effective play. But purists and modernists disagree significantly on how we should design, teach, officiate, and value the game. One side finds excitement and beauty in one set of abilities, skills, and attitudes. The other side finds excitement and beauty in an overlapping but partly different set of abilities, skills, and attitudes. So even if one side were able to show that its version of the game typically worked better, the case wouldn't be settled. Those with the less-effective style of play could simply ask why anyone would want to ruin the game by playing it the other way.

Their question is very much to the point. How we want to shape our games is a separate issue from how best to play them once they have been shaped, and maximal effectiveness can be a liability rather than an asset. The rule makers who form games, in fact, have outlawed new equipment that, in their judgment (or the judgment of the broader sporting community), was actually *too* effective. Consider the banning of square-grooved golf clubs, automatic hunting rifles, corked baseball bats, and various technologies related to everything from steroids to new composites for tennis rackets.

These prohibitions show that athletes and fans alike want to preserve core tests that are part and parcel of our various games. Because these central challenges can be ruined by certain rule changes and equipment innovations that lock in maximal effectiveness, efficiency can never be a trump card in any debate over what form the game of basketball should take. This underlines the fact that the purist-modernist controversy is at least partly over how we *want* basketball to be played—which skills we want to honor, how we hope to teach youngsters to play, and what values have attracted us, and countless others around the world, to this marvelous sport.

How Purist and Modernist Basketball Differ

When I reflect on the differences between purist and modernist styles of basketball, I come up with a cluster of characteristic tendencies rather than a hard-and-fast set of necessary and sufficient conditions. Nevertheless, a list of such tendencies will suffice for my argument. I will be pushing for the tendencies that go with the purist style of play, even though they will appear in any number of combinations and in a variety of strengths.

Comparisons between the two styles of play at issue in this chapter are listed below:

Purist	Modernist
Centered on team capability	Centered on individual capability
Based on honing of skills, fundamentals	Based on exceptional athleticism
Emphasizes team-related skills and group achievement	Emphasizes individual skills and one-on-one matchups
Requires good team spacing/ passing	Requires clearing out, beating a single opponent
Based on patience; more half-court play	Based on pressure; more full-court play
Grounded in help-defense	Grounded in man-to-man defense

Emphasizes quickness, deception, sound footwork, good positioning	Emphasizes raw speed, strength, brute force
Based on excellent shooting skills, often outside shots that come from half-court plays	Less emphasis on shooting skills; shots often come from transition play and feature inside opportunities, dunks, and put-backs
Emphasizes defense	Features offense over defense

This is certainly not a complete list of differences, and the comparisons provided may look like caricatures of basketball play. Most teams blend elements of the two styles, and most good coaches shift one way or the other depending on the talent they have on their current squads. Nevertheless, these contrasts show us what is at stake in this debate and lay out unmistakable differences in how we play and value the game. Furthermore, when I read or hear about this debate in the media, these are the factors that are typically mentioned. Thus, while the list is surely incomplete and debatable, it should still serve us reasonably well by clarifying the general tendencies of purist and modernist basketball.

Why the Purist Game Is Generally Better

I believe that purist basketball, generally speaking, is better than modernist basketball, and I offer three arguments for this view: the functionalist argument, the variety argument, and the communitarian argument. The functionalist argument, which focuses on how games are constructed and evaluated, is the most fundamental. I am indebted to John Searle, a well-known American philosopher, for the gist of this argument.

The Functionalist Argument

Searle was more interested in languages than he was in games, but his argument can be used for either. He notes that languages are conventions—that is, artificial constructs that are the product of what he calls constitutive rules. Conventions are built to serve a purpose. With languages the purpose is to facilitate good communication. In other words, the rules that determine how language works—rules of vocabulary, syntax, and grammar, for example—should build a language system that performs various communication functions well. For instance, these rules allow us to record information accurately and efficiently. They help us to understand one another clearly. They give us the means to ask questions, make statements, raise doubts, and perform other communicative tasks well.

A similar line of reasoning can be used for games, including basketball. Games, too, are conventions composed of constitutive rules and created to perform a function. This function, according to Bernard Suits and other leading commentators on games, is to provide an artificial test. Good games, in short, provide good tests. These tests can be used for any number of purposes—among them, to while away the time when we are bored, to make money if we are professional athletes, or to teach children useful lessons and values. But regardless of the uses to which games are put, the fundamental principle of gamewrighting remains the same. It is to create a good test.

This Searlean line of reasoning puts us within reach of some objective criteria that could be used to evaluate the rules of language—or the rules of games. If some rules of syntax, for example, make it *more* difficult to understand what someone is saying, we would have a reason to change the rules. And we would have good reason for concluding that any language system using such rules would be inferior to another one that avoided them. Likewise, if some rules of basketball make it a lesser test, we would have reason to change those rules or simply avoid that brand of basketball.

Purists rightly claim that a game that involves ten individuals in tightly interactive relationships both offensively and defensively is more complex than a game that emphasizes only two individuals in these relationships. More complexity exists in a ten-person test because more variables are involved in making things go right (or wrong). Players, I would argue, appreciate this complexity because there are more possibilities to be exploited. Informed fans who watch basketball enjoy ten-person complexity because there is more to see and understand.

Complexity is valuable in games for another reason, namely, durability. Complex games like basketball and chess continue to attract us, even after years of play, training, or observation as a fan. Excessively simple games like tic-tac-toe, on the other hand, lose their charm quickly. Some of us, for instance, have tried our hand at solving interlocking-ring puzzles. Even though some of them are tremendously difficult, they lack complexity. Once we solve them, or in my case, once someone shows me how to solve them, we put them aside. Once solved, always solved. They lack complexity and no longer attract.

Basketball, in this respect, is more like chess than it is like tic-tac-toe. Any "solution" in basketball always stands in relationship to additional problems and future improvement. And importantly for the argument here, the complex, ten-person basketball game favored by purists offers the richer and more durable test. Searle would undoubtedly agree that games function better when their constitutive rules promote appropriate levels of complexity.

The Variety Argument

A second argument for the purist style of basketball focuses on the importance of multiple opportunities and their role in promoting social equity. I will call this the "variety argument." Once again, I am indebted to others for this defense of the purist tradition.

Ethicist Robert Simon has argued that social justice requires the acknowledgment of differences between people for the distribution of some goods.[1] This fair distribution can be promoted in at least two different ways. Society can guarantee access to goods by setting aside opportunities for special groups. This is roughly the separate-but-equal strategy promoted by *Plessy vs. Ferguson* (1896) and is present in the current Title IX legislation that supports women's college athletics. Alternately, society can provide and value such a variety of opportunities that individuals with different skills and interests would all flourish. Fewer set-asides or safety nets would be required under this scenario because most people could find their own niche and would be honored for their unique strengths.

This second route to social justice is based on an idealistic vision of diversity and equality. Unfortunately, it is doubtful that any contemporary societies exemplify anything close to what Simon has in mind. Nevertheless, in our current collection of far-less-than-perfect societies, such thinking places a value on variety as we work toward ever more complete forms of social justice. Variety in sporting opportunities better serves communities that have diverse sets of skills and interests for playing and watching sports. From this it follows that we have a moral responsibility to promote diversity, not uniformity, in our collection of sports—assuming, of course, that we have an interest in promoting social justice via this method.

Of course, a huge variety of sports and other kinds of games can be found across the globe and within the boundaries of any one country. It would seem that almost everyone, regardless of body shape, muscular strength, gender, age, wealth, or ethnicity, could find something suitable either to play or watch. Variety, in other words, would seem to be a foregone conclusion. But as the philosopher John Stuart Mill argues in his classic *On Liberty* (1859), variety is always under fire from vested interests like business, ruling powers, custom, tradition, and other homogenizing influences.

Philosopher William Morgan has shown, for example, that capitalism and gamewrighting can run at cross-purposes.[2] In capitalist societies if a game will "sell" better, even though its improved marketability requires that it be pushed in the direction of other sports that already sell well, so be it. If basketball becomes a bit more like football, for instance, no entrepreneurial hackles are raised so long as football-like skills and activities are profitable. When the external logic of business takes precedence over the "gratuitous logic" of gamewrighting, variety may be sacrificed as a result.

One conclusion that might be drawn from these considerations is that both purist and modernist versions of the game should be preserved because this adds variety to basketball. Those who culturally or physically prefer the team-oriented purist game can play or watch it. And those who are drawn to the modernist game can follow their druthers as well.

This is not a bad conclusion in principle. We want a reasonable degree of flexibility in our games so that they better fit diverse cultures, genders, age groups, and other subpopulations. Furthermore, virtually all of our current games—from golf to poker—take on slightly different shapes for diverse groups of people who play them and for the diverse purposes to which they might be put. Basketball games promoted by religious organizations to attract converts, for instance, are organized and conducted differently than basketball activities in a gym class that are designed to promote health and physical fitness.

That level of diversity, however, is not what is at issue here. Cultural pressures work across all these diverse populations and purposes to reduce the differences between basketball and other popular games. Women, men, children, religious devotees, physical education teachers, and others who play and watch basketball are all influenced by celebrity players, *SportsCenter* coverage of the game, the style of play they typically see on television, and the like. If cultural pressures exerted by these phenomena push in the direction of less difference between basketball and other popular games, the results will infiltrate virtually all domains and forms of basketball.

This is where the rub lies. Basketball, arguably, has become more like football under influences of the modernist game. Play in the post area has grown tremendously physical. One very large person leans against another very large person in an attempt to dislodge that individual from a desired spot on the court. One center uses vigorous "swimming motions" to hook the opponent and again forcibly move him or her out of the way. A power forward or a very strong shooting guard will post up and then literally butt their way backward toward the hoop and an easy basket or foul-shot opportunity. Some of these power moves near the basket result in a slam dunk, a kind of basketball shot that is predicated on power, not on touch or accuracy. In addition, pure foot speed becomes a premium in fast-break or transition forms of play. Modernist basketball has moved in the direction of a contest to see who can beat the other team down the court.

Many of these basketball actions are similar to those we see in college or NFL football. The skillful use of brute strength and force wins the day. Dislodging individuals from positions by using tremendous body mass, momentum, and muscular strength plays a major role in football. Speed, in contrast to quickness, is important when running the ball, going deep for a pass, or defending against the ground game or an aerial attack. Such vigorous play and blinding speed lie very much at the heart of what both players and fans love about the game of football. The core of its game test, in other words, has a great deal to do with hitting and outrunning.

Basketball should be different. Purists better than modernists, I would argue, resist the evolution of basketball toward the excessively muscular, outrun-the-opponent, football-like game. Basketball, while still a very physical activity that includes a good amount of body contact, retains its distinctive charms if it emphasizes such qualities as quickness, touch, positioning, footwork, accuracy, and deception over brute force and blinding speed.[3]

These distinctive qualities of basketball were present from the start. The inventor of the game, James Naismith, was given the assignment of developing an activity that could be played indoors during the winter months. Because of constrained space and safety considerations, he felt that he needed to develop rules that would honor accuracy over speed, and deception and quickness over brute force. He mulled over two kinds of goals or targets that might be used in this new game: a vertical one, like those used in soccer or football, and a horizontal one, like those used in golf and horseshoes. The problem with vertical goals, he reasoned, is that they put a premium on fast, forceful shots and excessively physical play. Thus, he selected a horizontal goal or basket and placed it well above the player's reach so that scoring would require accuracy combined with a "soft touch." In short, many of the distinctive charms of basketball were enabled, quite intentionally, by basketball's horizontal, elevated goal.

Of course, neither history nor Naismith's intentions provide strong philosophic arguments for one brand of basketball over another. But a knowledge of history helps us understand the distinctiveness of this game—how and why it is different, for example, from games that use vertical goals. An understanding of the game's roots also allows us more clearly to make choices about preserving a rich diversity of gaming opportunities. The promotion of social justice through variety requires nothing less.

The Communitarian Argument

My third argument for the purist style of basketball, the communitarian argument, focuses on the relationship between individuals and their communities. Contemporary philosopher Alasdair MacIntyre emphasizes the importance of human interactions in promoting the good life, in general, and virtuous living, in particular. His reconstruction of ethics starts with something he calls a "practice." He chooses this entry point because the excellences of various practices require virtues like justice, courage, and honesty. Cheating and taking other shortcuts prevent one from meeting "the best standards [of a practice] realized so far."[4] They also prevent one from experiencing what MacIntyre calls the "internal goods" of such challenges—the joys, excitement, and meaning that go with excellent performances whether they be in raising a family well, teaching a philosophy class with style, or playing basketball beautifully.

Because any erosion of practices in a culture would harm both the development of virtues and the availability of internal goods, it is important to understand what counts as a practice for MacIntyre. He writes:

> By a "practice" I am going to mean any coherent and complex form of socially established cooperative human activity through which goods internal to that form of activity are realized in the course of trying to achieve those standards of excellence which are appropriate to, and partially definitive of, that form of activity, with the result that human powers to achieve excellence, and human conceptions of the ends and goods involved, are systematically extended. Tic-tac-toe is not an example of a practice in this sense, nor is throwing a football with skill; but the game of football is, and so is chess. Bricklaying is not a practice; architecture is. Planting turnips is not a practice; farming is.[5]

On this account, both the purist and modernist forms of basketball are practices. As MacIntyre argues, practices are evolving phenomena with ever-new standards of excellence as they are found, acknowledged, and endorsed by their respective practice communities. This would seem to leave room for modernists' version of the game and their complaint that purists refuse to accept new (and possibly superior) versions of basketball excellence.

Be that as it may, a flexible purist position that acknowledges change within important community-grounded constraints best honors MacIntyre's commitment to practices. The modernist game tends to emphasize technical skills displayed in serial fashion and places less weight on "a coherent and complex form of socially established cooperative human activity." Many one-on-one moves in the modern game, and many of the actions that require tremendous athleticism, are analogous to MacIntyre's "throwing of the football with skill." That is, the modernist game relies more on isolated technical skills than on complex, interactive, multifaceted capabilities. The modernist values of "doing your own thing" and "expressing your individuality" once again detract from the consensus goods of a practice community. This is seen in modernist players on ESPN's *Streetball* who earn their individual monikers through signature styles of plays—Half Man Half Amazing, Syc Wit It, Spinmaster, and the Pharmacist (so named because his moves are "morphine-based").

Indeed, many of the modernist moves that are the steady fare of *Streetball* and occasionally find their way into the NBA are remarkable athletic feats. They are also tremendously entertaining. But they emphasize the individual over the community, the isolated feat over the game. Basketball as a practice wanes under such individualism and its attendant entertainment pressures.

This is important for MacIntyre, and also for us, because practices provide richer challenges than do isolated skills. The good life is grounded in meeting complex challenges with integrity and excellence, in building coherent stories around our repeated encounters with practices—as parents, basketball players, or professors. Isolated feats, or skills, or displays, as remarkable and breathtaking as they sometimes are, function far less effectively in doing this job.

Has This Chapter Produced "Slam Dunk" Conclusions?

It has not, but I have already argued that slam dunks are overrated. This chapter has attempted to persuade more than prove, to work a little team offense rather than go one-on-one "in your face."

Accordingly, we have noted that all games change, and we need to honor that progress. Nevertheless, purists have a sense of the limits of change, limits that preserve what is good about our games while allowing new forms of play to emerge. I offer three arguments for this view: the functionalist argument, which focuses on the importance of complexity and durability in building good games; the variety argument, which emphasizes the importance of variety in promoting social justice, and the related significance of keeping basketball distinct from such games as football; and the communitarian argument, which shows purist-tending basketball to be a better practice, and thus a better foundation for the delightful excellences we experience in the game of basketball.

A number of changes in the world of contemporary basketball would suggest that the pendulum is swinging back in the direction of the purist-tending game. First, basketball rule books and officiating seminars have consistently included "points of emphasis" that discourage rough, football-like activity, particularly in the post. Double fouls and charging calls for overly muscular offensive moves are now the norm. Second, NBA rules against zone defenses were recently changed, in part to discourage tediously repetitive one-on-one play. Offenses now need to be more team oriented, and defensive schemes are now far more cooperative and collaborative in nature. Both, arguably, have made the game more complex and interesting. Third, the point guard has again emerged as perhaps *the* key player on a team. The point guard is the player who stimulates team play and creates scoring opportunities for his or her four teammates. The election of Steve Nash as the 2004–2005 NBA MVP in a very close vote over dominant big man Shaquille O'Neal exemplifies this subtle shift in priorities.

A new style of superstar may be emerging, one who, while flashy and entertaining, brings a diverse set of team-oriented skills. I am thinking of someone like the Argentinian Manu Ginobili, from the San Antonio Spurs. He dribbles well, goes to the hoop, shoots nicely from the outside, plays good team defense, and plays as if the whole is always greater than the sum of its parts.

Rigid purists might not like him because his remarkable passing and dribbling may seem a little excessive, a bit like showboating. Furthermore, his game doesn't look anything like the one played in the 1960s and before. But moderate purists like me see in his style of play solid fundamentals and a good measure of what is wonderfully unique about the game of basketball. Besides, he led his Argentine team to the gold medal in Greece. I like the fact that purist basketball works pretty well too.

Notes

1. Robert L. Simon, *Fair Play: The Ethics of Sport* (Boulder, CO: Westview, 2004), 132–36.

2. William J. Morgan, *Leftist Theories of Sport: A Critique and Reconstruction* (Urbana: University of Illinois Press, 1994), 128–75.

3. Former UCLA coach John Wooden makes a similar point about the importance of preserving the distinctiveness of the game of basketball. When asked if he enjoys watching the NBA, Wooden replied: "I watch the pros, but if I want to see wrestling, I'll go to a wrestling match. If I want to watch traveling, I'll go to a track meet. And if I want to see showmanship, I'll go see the Globetrotters." Quoted in Steve Bisheff, *John Wooden: An American Treasure* (Nashville: Cumberland House, 2004), 201.

4. Alasdair MacIntyre, *After Virtue,* 2nd ed. (Notre Dame, IN: University of Notre Dame Press, 1984), 190.

5. MacIntyre, *After Virtue,* 187.

Gregory Bassham and Mark Hamilton

HARDWOOD *DOJOS*

What Basketball Can Teach Us about Character and Success

A coach should be a philosopher of hoops.
—Digger Phelps

LIKE MOST OTHER sports, basketball as such doesn't teach anything about values or character. If your daughter learns to play soccer from the win-at-all-costs coach played by Will Ferrell in the 2005 film *Kicking and Screaming,* she'll learn that the rule is "play dirty, but don't get caught." Likewise, if your son learns basketball from watching ESPN's *Streetball,* he's not going to learn a great deal about discipline, respect, fair play, or teamwork.

Clearly, basketball can teach rotten values if a player has bad coaches and role models. But is the reverse also true? Can basketball teach good values if a player has good coaches and good role models? In the language of Eastern philosophy, can a basketball court be a *dojo,* a "place of enlightenment" in which disciplined athletes train their hearts and minds through the pursuit of physical excellence?

To help us think about this question we looked at the coaching philosophies of four highly successful college basketball coaches: Dean Smith, Rick Pitino, Pat Summitt, and Mike Krzyzewski. All of these coaches are widely respected for their high ethical and professional standards, and all have written books explaining their values-based coaching philosophy. Studying these coaches' philosophies, we came to see that basketball *can* teach fundamental lessons about character and success, both on the court and in the greater game of life. What's more, these are precisely the same lessons that great philosophers have been teaching for thousands of years.

Four Famous Coaches, Six Key Principles

The four coaches we've selected will need no introduction to most readers of this book. Dean Smith coached the North Carolina Tar Heels for thirty-six years, winning 77.6 percent of his games and two national championships, and graduating more than 96 percent of his players. His 879 career victories are the most by any coach in college basketball history. He is the coauthor (with Gerald D. Bell and John Kilgo) of *The Carolina Way: Leadership Lessons from a Life in Coaching* (Penguin Press, 2004).

Mike Krzyzewski has coached the Duke Blue Devils for more than a quarter century. A five-time ACC Coach of the Year, he has won three national championships. He is the author (with Donald T. Phillips) of *Leading with the Heart: Coach K's Successful Strategies for Basketball, Business, and Life* (Warner Business Books, rev. ed., 2004).

Pat Summitt is the legendary coach of the University of Tennessee Lady Vols. In her thirty-three years at Tennessee, she has won six national championships, led her teams to fifteen Final Four appearances, and graduated 100 percent of her players. Her 1998 book *Reach for the Summit: The Definite Dozen System for Succeeding at Whatever You Do* (cowritten with Sally Jenkins) was a New York Times Business Bestseller.

Rick Pitino has coached the New York Knicks, the Boston Celtics, and four college teams, including the 1996 national champion Kentucky Wildcats. Now head basketball coach at the University of Louisville, he is the author (with Bill Reynolds) of *Success Is a Choice: Ten Steps to Overachieving in Business and Life* (Broadway Books, 1997).

Though differing greatly in their personalities and coaching styles, these four coaches have remarkably similar philosophies of success. Each sees basketball as a microcosm of life, a Bally's gym of the heart in which the fundamentals of success on the court are also the cornerstones of success in life. Although there are minor differences of emphasis, six key principles stand out in these coaches' philosophies of success:

Set demanding goals.

Make hard work your passion.

Establish good habits.

Be persistent.

Learn from adversity.

Put the team before yourself.

Let's examine these six principles to see why these famous coaches—as well as some of history's greatest thinkers—view them as critical to success in sports, business, leadership, or virtually any other worthwhile endeavor.

Set Demanding Goals

"The quest for success," says philosopher Tom Morris, "always begins with a target. We need something to aim at, something to shoot for."[1] To achieve success in basketball, or any challenging task, Morris says, "we need a clear conception of what we want, a vivid vision, a goal or set of goals powerfully imagined."[2]

Aristotle (384–322 B.C.) would strongly agree. In his *Nicomachean Ethics,* his classic work on excellence and achievement, he argues that all conscious human activity is done with some goal or end in mind. Some goals are obviously more important than others. What should be our ultimate goal, our highest good, the thing we should work hardest and most persistently to achieve? For Aristotle, it is making the most of our potential, striving for excellence in all that we do, but particularly in those capacities of heart, mind, and spirit that make us distinctively human. Being all that we can be, living at the top of our powers—this, for Aristotle, is what each of us should strive for, however humble or exalted our station in life may be.

To achieve one's potential in something as difficult as basketball requires years of hard work, dedication, and practice. We need goals in this process both to *motivate* us and to *guide* us.

In basketball, as in life, the road to mediocrity is paved with good intentions. It's easy to lose focus, to become lazy or distracted. Goals can motivate us to stay the course. As Coach Pitino reminds us, goals "give us a vision of a better future. They nourish our spirit; they represent possibility even when we are dragged down by reality. They keep us going."[3]

Pitino tells the story of Billy Donovan, a little-heralded 5'11", 170-pound point guard who played for Providence College in the mid-1980s. Donovan was a classic underachiever his first two seasons at Providence, playing only part-time and averaging fewer than three points a game. When Pitino took over as the Providence coach prior to Donovan's junior year, he met with Donovan and asked him about his goals. It quickly became apparent that Donovan had no real goals except maybe getting a little more playing time and scoring a few more points per game. Pitino challenged him not to settle for such modest goals but to work hard and aspire to excellence. That summer Donovan worked his tail off and dramatically improved his conditioning and his skills. By his senior year he averaged 20.6 points per game, led his team to the Final Four, and was drafted in the third round of the NBA draft by the Utah Jazz. Today he is the highly successful head coach of the 2005–2006 NCAA champion Florida Gators.

Goals not only motivate us to aim high, but they also keep us on track and guide our progress along the way. As Pitino remarks, "goals provide our daily routine. They show us where to start and they establish our priorities. They make us organized and create the discipline in our lives."[4]

The key to sustained excellence, Pat Summitt says, is to "think big, focus small."[5] Dream big, shoot for lofty general goals, but also have clear, specific, short-term goals for daily and weekly improvement. Like UCLA's legendary John Wooden, Dean Smith was famous for his detailed, minute-by-minute practice schedules, which stressed daily improvement achieved through intense conditioning and repetitive drills.[6] Smith also made it his practice at the end of each season to give each returning player two or three specific areas of improvement to work on over the summer.[7] By setting ambitious yet realistic long- and short-term goals and working hard to achieve them, we can often do more than we imagined we could.

Make Hard Work Your Passion

For former U.S. senator and New York Knicks great Bill Bradley, basketball "was a clear example of virtue rewarded."[8] Why? Because in basketball Bradley found an unambiguous demonstration of one of life's most important lessons: that there is no greater secret to success than hard work.

The value of hard work is something that all great coaches teach. As Rick Pitino observes, "If you look closely at all great organizations, all great teams, all great people, the one common denominator that runs through them is a second-to-none work ethic. The intense effort to achieve is always there. This is the one given if you want to be successful."[9]

Pat Summitt also puts hard work at the core of her coaching philosophy. She writes:

> How am I going to beat you?
>
> I'm going to outwork you.
>
> That's it. That's all there is to it.
>
> You've just learned my most valuable secret. . . . [T]here is no great intangible quality to success. It's not a gift people are born with . . . or a knack. It's a simple matter of putting your back into it.[10]

Throughout history, great philosophers have stressed the importance of effort and hard work. Aristotle taught that happiness is an activity, an exemplification of excellence, rather than any kind of feeling or state of mind.[11] Marcus Aurelius (A.D. 121–180), the famous Roman philosopher-emperor, believed that humans naturally find fulfillment in "action and exertion" rather than in idle pleasure or creature comforts.[12] John Locke (1632–1704), the great seventeenth-century British philosopher, maintained that one of the first duties of a teacher is to teach his or her pupils "vigor, activity, and industry."[13] And American philosopher William James (1842–1910) argued that effort is the true measure of a person, because "effort is the one strictly underived and original contribution we make to this world."[14]

In emphasizing the importance of hard work, our four coaches often sound much like the ancient Stoic philosophers. Stoics like Seneca (4 B.C.–A.D. 65) and Epictetus (around A.D. 50–130) believed that we can control our thoughts and attitudes but we cannot control "externals" like wealth, reputation, or health. Happiness, they believed, lies in learning to accept hard knocks with equanimity and to concentrate our energies instead on developing healthy, positive thoughts and a good character. In a similar spirit, Summitt writes: "There is not much you can control in this life. Freak accidents, good or bad luck, these things are out of our hands. But how hard you work *is* within your control. Rather than complain about bad breaks . . . make a few breaks of your own."[15] Likewise, Dean Smith used to tell his players: "Never let anyone play harder than you. That is part of the game you can control."[16]

Few basketball players ever worked harder to improve their skills than New York Knicks forward Bill Bradley. In high school, Bradley practiced three to four hours a day on Monday through Friday, and five hours a day on Saturday and Sunday. He put weights in his shoes to improve his vertical leap, wore a blindfold to prevent him from looking at the ball when he dribbled, and stacked chairs to practice shooting hook shots over an imaginary seven-footer. To improve his shooting, he shot set shots and jump shots from five different places on the floor. Only when he hit twenty-five set shots and twenty-five jump shots in a row did he move to the next spot. If he missed number twenty-three, he started over.[17]

Teams built on a strong work ethic tend to draw closer because of all the shared suffering, hard work, and sacrifice.[18] There's also a motivational factor eloquently expressed by Michael Jordan in a note to U.S. Olympic basketball coach Bob Knight just prior to the gold-medal game against Spain in 1984. Jordan wrote: "Don't worry. We've put up with too much shit to lose now."[19] Teams with a passion for hard work tend to play harder in clutch games. Why? Because they feel like they've worked too hard and suffered too much to accept anything short of victory.

Establish Good Habits

Philosophers have long recognized the powerful role that habit plays in human life. For Aristotle, forming good habits of character and intellect is crucial to leading a happy, fulfilled life.[20] The greatest thinker of the Middle Ages, Thomas Aquinas (around 1225–1274), thought habits were so important that he devoted a whole treatise to the subject in his magisterial *Summa Theologica*. And American philosopher William James believed that "all our life, so far as it has definite form, is but a mass of habits . . . systematically organized for our weal or woe."[21]

A habit is a stable and not easily altered disposition to act in a certain way, usually acquired by repetition of such acts. Good habits, like punctuality, politeness, and diligence, help us do good things easily, readily, and without much thinking. Bad habits, like eating a bag of chips every night while watching ESPN, can be a curse.

Since so much of what we do is based on habit, and habits are so hard to break, it is important to form good habits. As Rick Pitino writes: "Good habits prevent laziness. They prevent floundering. . . . Good habits create organization and discipline in our lives. It's virtually impossible to achieve success without having good habits. . . . And in times of stress, times when you are being severely tested, good habits become even more important. They become the rock, the standard of behavior that we must stick with so that we don't get off track."[22] Good habits are especially important in basketball, because so much of the game is repetition. By forming good habits when we shoot, dribble, or defend, we make muscle memory our ally and avoid the dangers of overthinking.

Great coaches and players understand the power of habit. John Wooden, who coached the UCLA Bruins to ten national championships in twelve years, said, "I believe in learning by repetition to the point that everything becomes automatic."[23] And Dean Smith writes that in his years at Carolina, "we worked hard on fundamentals in practice. . . . We repeated things until they became habits. I believed that once we introduced something new, we should cover it in practice for several days to make sure the players got it. We hammered it home: repeat, repeat, repeat until we got it right."[24]

Few NBA players worked harder on developing good habits than Boston Celtics star Larry Bird. Each summer Bird would go home to French Lick, Indiana, and work tirelessly to improve some aspect of his offensive game. One year it was shooting with his left hand. Another year it was the up-and-under shot coming off a fake. During the first week of the Celtics' preseason camp, the other players liked seeing what new dimension Bird had added to his game.[25]

When Phil Jackson became coach of the Los Angeles Lakers in 1999, he gave his superstar center, Shaquille O'Neal, a copy of Aristotle's *Nicomachean Ethics*. Aristotle, as we have seen, taught that the key to a happy, successful life is sustained excellence through the formation of good habits. After reading the book, Shaq said that he'd like to be known as "the Big Aristotle," because "it was Aristotle who said excellence is not a singular act but a habit."[26]

Be Persistent

Great thinkers have long emphasized the value of persistence. To achieve long-term success and fulfillment, the Roman philosopher Seneca said, we must "work hard with all the courage we can muster, ignoring any distractions, and struggle with a single purpose."[27] Samuel Johnson noted that "great works are performed not by strength but by perseverance." And contemporary philosopher and corporate adviser Tom Morris reports that in his experience "the biggest difference between people who succeed at any difficult endeavor and those who do not is not usually talent. It is persistence."[28]

Socrates (470–399 B.C.) was a model of persistence, as he was of many other virtues. Early one morning when he was on a military campaign, Socrates stopped to ponder some philosophical perplexity he wished to think through. Around noon, word began to spread around camp that Socrates was lost in one of his (in)famous fits of abstraction. When evening fell, some of Socrates' fellow soldiers spread their bedding around him to see if he stood there all night. He did, and when dawn came, he offered up a prayer to the sun and went on his way.[29]

Persistence seems to be something of a lost virtue today. Our newest university graduates expect to find top-level jobs immediately out of college, and athletes expect to achieve success without struggle. But every successful person must learn the lesson of persistence, a personal quality underscored by each of our four coaches. Persistence is holding steadfast to a purpose despite obstacles and setbacks. It is perseverance and tenacity in the face of hardships and disappointments. It is sticking with something even when you don't feel like it or see the final goal. As Pitino says, "It's persistence that makes you great. It's persistence that allows you to reach your dreams. It's persistence that enables you to perform at your fullest potential."[30]

Dean Smith tells the story of an unnamed Carolina basketball player who was better at football than he was at basketball. He was a player Smith loved having on the team, but after two years it was clear he didn't figure into the team's future plans. Before summer break, Smith told this player that he wasn't going to get much playing time in the future and encouraged him to think about whether he wanted to return. To Smith's surprise and delight, a week later the player called and said he was returning. The player "spent hours and hours each day over the summer working on his shot, his ball handling, all his basketball skills," Smith writes. "I couldn't believe my eyes when practice opened on October 15. He was vastly improved. He won a starting position for us and made All-ACC first team before he graduated."[31]

Learn from Adversity

Persistence is easy when things are going smoothly, but the true test of character comes when one encounters adversity. As many philosophers have noted, a world without challenges and disappointments would be a world without growth. Coaches have shortened this to "no pain, no gain." Winners don't give up in the face of failure; they become more determined to succeed the next time. Adversity teaches self-knowledge, revealing our true strengths and weaknesses. As Seneca remarked, "If a man is to know himself, he must be tested. No one finds out what he can do except by trying. . . . Disaster is virtue's opportunity."[32]

Learning to turn negative events into positive ones is essential to success. Summitt points out that failures often cause people to reevaluate their lives and recommit themselves to excellence.[33] Krzyzewski notes that adversity can sometimes work in one's favor. "Instead of feeling sorry for yourself and using it as an excuse," he recommends, "accept the situation and try to make the most of it. That's how a team develops resilience and character."[34]

Sport teaches us the inevitability of failure. No one makes every shot or wins every game. As Pitino reminds us: "The best hitters in baseball fail to hit seven out of every ten times they come to the plate. Many of the best home run hitters strike out a lot. The best salespeople have days when they don't sell anything. Artists have days when nothing creative happens. We all fail sometimes. The question is what do you do with that failure?"[35] Again the Stoic approach to life is relevant in knowing what one can control in life. As Summitt remarks, echoing a constant Stoic theme, "You can't always control what happens, but you can control how you handle it."[36]

Krzyzewski recalls: "One year I received a note from a former player

I had coached back in the early 1970s. It seemed that he had recently received a double-lung transplant and was told by his doctors that the main reason he survived was due to his will and determination. Then he credited me for instilling that quality in him at a young age."[37] The player had learned as a young man to persevere through adversity without falling into despair. As St. Paul—a man well acquainted with adversity—stated, "Suffering produces endurance, and endurance produces character" (Romans 5:3).

Put the Team before Yourself

Thomas Hobbes, a seventeenth-century British philosopher, believed that humans are naturally nasty, violent, brutish, and selfish. Hobbes's view may be extreme, but basketball coaches know firsthand that teamwork must be drilled into athletes because it is against their natural inclinations. Summitt writes: "Teamwork does not come naturally. . . . We are born with certain inclinations, but sharing isn't one of them. . . . When two or more children get together in one room, what do they fight about? Sharing, that's what. They hate to share. . . . I've seen whole teams act that way. . . . My point is, teamwork is taught. . . . As a coach, I have to be at my most inventive and articulate when I talk about teamwork. But basketball happens to be a wonderful tool with which to teach it."[38] As LA Lakers coach Phil Jackson points out, creating a successful team "requires the individuals involved to surrender their self-interest for the greater good so that the whole adds up to more than the sum of its parts."[39] But this is a tough message to communicate in our increasingly individualistic and celebrity-crazed culture.

Self-interest shouldn't be confused with selfishness. Self-interest can operate in ways that are not selfish. Was Michael Jordan a selfish player because he took more shots than anyone else or because he wanted to take the climactic final shot of a game? Not at all. If Jordan had refused to take last-second shots to avoid appearing selfish, this wouldn't have put the team before himself; it would have made him *appear* to be a team player while actually hurting the team.[40] Similarly, Dean Smith has been criticized for overemphasizing team play, thereby delaying the development of individual skills. But as Jordan aptly remarks in Smith's defense:

"The one thing I was taught at North Carolina, and one thing I believe to the fullest, is that if you think and achieve as a team, the individual accolades will take care of themselves."[41]

Summitt offers a great example of individual/team synergy. Her 1996 team was filled with high-profile players like seniors Michelle Marciniak and Latina Davis, but it also had a dynamic freshman, Chamique Holdsclaw. Summitt called in Marciniak and Davis and told them they probably wouldn't be All-Americans but that Holdsclaw would. She then challenged them by asking whether they would rather be All-Americans or win a national championship. Both said that they'd prefer to be national champs. Summitt writes: "Michelle and Latina swallowed whatever feelings they had. What happened next is a credit to both of them. Latina became the Most Valuable Player in the NCAA East Regional. Michelle was the MVP in the Final Four. Chamique was named Kodak All-American. And Tennessee was national champion."[42]

To help her players appreciate the value of teamwork, Summitt often uses a simple analogy. "Let's say I hand out pencils to our twelve players. I tell them, 'Now I want each of you to break your pencils in half.' They will do it, no problem. You'll hear the snapping of pencils all over the gym. But what if I take twelve pencils, and I bind them together with a rubber band? Now try to break them. You can't. That is the basic principle of teamwork."[43]

Basketball's Enduring Lessons

During the 2005 NCAA basketball tournament, CBS ran an American Express commercial featuring coach Mike Krzyzewski. In the commercial Coach K says:

> I don't look at myself as a basketball coach. I look at myself as a leader who happens to coach basketball.
>
> When [my players] get into the workplace, they're armed with more than just a jump shot or a dribble, but I want you armed for life. I want you to develop as a player. I want you to develop as a student. And I want you to develop as a human being.

Some fans objected to the commercial, claiming that it gave Duke an unfair recruiting advantage over other schools. Maybe so, but the commercial was nevertheless an effective and much-needed reminder that basketball is ultimately a game, and that "success" is about something much larger than simply "winning." Basketball, when well coached and well played, can prepare us to succeed in the greater game of life. At the end of the commercial, as Krzyzewski walks across the court in Duke's venerable Cameron Indoor Stadium, we are reminded that a basketball court can be a "place of enlightenment"—a place where vital life lessons are taught, and spiritual warriors aim not simply at baskets but ultimately at themselves.

Notes

1. Tom Morris, *True Success: A New Philosophy of Excellence* (New York: Berkeley Books, 1994), 35.

2. Morris, *True Success,* 35.

3. Rick Pitino, *Success Is a Choice: Ten Steps to Overachieving in Business and Life* (New York: Broadway Books, 1997), 45.

4. Pitino, *Success Is a Choice,* 47.

5. Pat Summitt, *Reach for the Summit: The Definite Dozen System for Succeeding in Whatever You Do* (New York: Broadway Books, 1998), 125.

6. For an example, see Dean Smith, *A Coach's Life: My Forty Years in College Basketball,* rev. ed. (New York: Random House, 2002), 128.

7. Dean Smith and Gerald D. Bell, with John Kilgo, *The Carolina Way: Leadership Lessons from a Life in Coaching* (New York: Penguin Press, 2004), 230.

8. Bill Bradley, *The Values of the Game* (New York: Artisan, 1998), 14.

9. Pitino, *Success Is a Choice,* 2.

10. Summitt, *Reach for the Summit,* 117.

11. Aristotle, *Nicomachean Ethics,* 1099a.

12. Marcus Aurelius, *Meditations,* book 5.

13. John Locke, *Some Thoughts Concerning Education,* in *John Locke on Politics and Education* (Roslyn, NY: Walter J. Black, 1947), 281.

14. William James, *The Principles of Psychology* (New York: Dover, 1950), 2:579.

15. Summitt, *Reach for the Summit,* 132.

16. Smith, *Carolina Way,* 30.

17. Bradley, *Values of the Game,* 29–30.

18. Lisa E. Wolf-Wendel, J. Douglas Toma, and Christopher C. Morphew, "There's No 'I' in 'Team': Lessons from Athletics on Community Building," *Review of Higher Education* 24, no. 4 (2001): 378–79.

19. David Halberstam, *Playing for Keeps: Michael Jordan and the World He Made* (New York: Random House, 1999), 150.

20. Aristotle, *Nicomachean Ethics,* 1103b.

21. William James, *Talks to Teachers on Psychology and to Students on Some of Life's Ideals* (1899), reprinted in *William James: Writings 1878–1899,* ed. Gerald E. Myers (New York: Library of America, 1992), 750.

22. Pitino, *Success Is a Choice*, 98.

23. John Wooden, with Jack Tobin, *They Call Me Coach*, 3rd rev. ed., (New York: McGraw-Hill, 2004), 106.

24. Smith, *Carolina Way*, 77.

25. Halberstam, *Playing for Keeps*, 166.

26. Quoted in Dennis McCafferty, "Now They Can't Call Me a Bum," *USA Weekend Magazine*, October 29, 2000.

27. Quoted in Tom Morris, *The Stoic Art of Living: Inner Resilience and Outer Results* (Chicago: Open Court, 2004), 44.

28. Morris, *True Success*, 175.

29. Plato, *Symposium*, 220c–d.

30. Pitino, *Success Is a Choice*, 192.

31. Smith, *Carolina Way*, 19.

32. Quoted in Morris, *The Stoic Art of Living*, 29.

33. Summitt, *Reach for the Summit*, 237.

34. Mike Krzyzewski, *Leading with the Heart: Coach K's Successful Strategies for Basketball, Business, and Life* (New York: Warner Business Books, rev. ed., 2004), 111.

35. Pitino, *Success Is a Choice*, 220–21.

36. Summitt, *Reach for the Summit*, 266.

37. Krzyzewski, *Leading with the Heart*, 271.

38. Summitt, *Reach for the Summit*, 159–60.

39. Phil Jackson and Hugh Delehanty, *Sacred Hoops: Spiritual Lessons of a Hardwood Warrior* (New York: Hyperion, 1995), 5.

40. Once when Chicago assistant coach Tex Winter reminded Jordan that "there's no *I* in the word *team*," Jordan responded, "There is in the word *win*." Halberstam, *Playing for Keeps*, 259.

41. Michael Jordan, *I Can't Accept Not Trying* (New York: Penguin Books, 2004), 24.

42. Summitt, *Reach for the Summit*, 165.

43. Summitt, *Reach for the Summit*, 163.

Regan Lance Reitsma

WHAT WOULD MACHIAVELLI DO?

Confronting the Strategic Cheater in Pickup Basketball

I'M A LITTLE embarrassed to admit that I vividly recall several "strategic ticky-tackers" my college friends and I encountered in pickup basketball games—eleven years ago. A strategic ticky-tacker is a species of cheat. A "ticky-tacker" is a person who routinely calls nonexistent fouls; a "strategic" ticky-tacker is someone who does this intentionally, to gain a competitive advantage. It's not my habit to keep a moral ledger of past transgressions against me. But the thing is, cheats are infuriating. With little effort I can resurrect the personal contempt, righteous indignation, and helpless frustration I felt when confronted with such unscrupulous scheming.

I'm going to bring up a few old stories about cheats, but it's not that I plan to hunt down old perpetrators to exact vengeance. (Surely the statute of limitations for punishing moral violations in pickup basketball expires within a decade.) My intentions are more forward looking and philosophical. For future confrontations, is there a good strategy to beat the cheat? No strategy will be foolproof, of course. However clever we are, the cheat's shots might be falling, and ours not. But perhaps a little hard thinking will point the way to methods that neutralize, or at least minimize, the benefits the cheater gains from his machinations.

Since pickup basketball, like international relations, is an arena that lacks neutral and authoritative rule-enforcers—no third-party referees or (moralistic) league commissioners—why not seek out practical advice from that master of realpolitik, Niccoló Machiavelli? Machiavelli (1469–1527) is well known for his frank and unvarnished advice to would-be princes seeking political power. Maybe Machiavelli also has something to say to would-be kings of the basketball court. If a cheater stands in your way, how best to defeat him? What would Machiavelli say, and is he right?

Two Types of Ticky-Tacker in Pickup Basketball

Ticky-tacky (or *ticky-tack*) refers to "a cheap facsimile," something "of inferior quality, made to appear as of greater quality." The term is a put-down, and it comes from the home-construction business. Say Chuff wants desperately to own a grand, beautiful house but can't afford it. If Chuff simply won't do without, he might build a cheaper facsimile of the house he covets by skimping on both construction materials and labor costs. Such a house is constructed by "ticking" (hitting lightly) "tacks" (a poor man's nails). Chuff is trying to pass off a flimsy reproduction as the real thing. When snobby Margaret—unfooled, her aesthetic sense offended—calls Chuff's house "ticky-tacky," she means to say not only that it's not the real thing but also that it's done in poor taste.

As in home construction, so in pickup basketball. In pickup, players call their own fouls, and to accuse a player of "ticky-tacking" is to say he is attempting to pass off a cheap facsimile of a foul as the real thing. The accusation is also a put-down; to call someone a ticky-tacker is to say he habitually, and annoyingly, makes these lousy calls. As I see it, in pickup basketball, there are two types of ticky-tacker: honest and strategic. Neither type is admirable, but only the strategic ticky-tacker is a contemptible cheat. In college intramurals, we regularly played a team that had both sorts.

One player, Arjen, was a muscular, hairy-chested seminarian from the Netherlands. If Arjen had the ball in the lane, our players invariably bodied him up, and he invariably called a foul. Arjen took seriously the claim that basketball is not a contact sport. This idea doesn't make much sense. Try to teach blocking out or setting a pick without saying anything about making contact with a player from the other team. Anyway, Arjen's foul-calling was ridiculously ticky-tacky, and, given how frequently players come into contact during the flow of a game, his foul-calling rate was ridiculously prodigious.

We strongly disagreed with Arjen's calls. (And we noted—sometimes publicly—the discrepancy between Arjen's burly physique and his acute sensitivity to the slightest bump.) But we tended to think Arjen came by his ticky-tacking honestly. He didn't grow up watching or playing basketball, so we weren't sure he knew any better. We considered his calls misguided, but not a clear case of cheating.

Arjen's teammate, "Brian," was a different story. Brian had the mug of a car salesman in a movie chock-full of nauseating stereotypes, and his foul-calling was as calculated as his grin. Most anytime his shot was contested, Brian predictably called a foul, whether or not any physical contact was made. As an American who had long played both pickup and organized basketball, Brian didn't have any of Arjen's excuses. Naturally, Brian came in for the strongest reactions: the personal contempt and righteous indignation. He was a "strategic" ticky-tacker; he deliberately called phantom fouls to help his team win.

The Logic of Strategic Ticky-Tacking

To maximize our odds against the Brians of the world, we must understand what they are thinking and anticipate how they will act. "Know thine enemy." So what chain of reasoning leads a Brian to strategic ticky-tacking?

The motive is generally the desire to win. At least at first glance, strategic ticky-tacking increases a player's chance of winning. The idea is simple. The team with the most points wins. To score points, a team must take shots. To take shots, a team has to possess the ball. And calling fouls permits a team to get or to keep possession. For example, if you call a foul in the act of shooting, your team keeps the ball even if you miss the shot. In this way, a foul call benefits a team in much the way an offensive rebound does, and without the effort.

Several background conditions make strategic ticky-tacking both possible and enticing. The first is the absence of a neutral referee and a formal system of governance with a penalty for cheating. One vivid way to get at this background condition is to compare pickup basketball to a common idea in political philosophy, the state of nature. The state of nature is the condition of human life in the absence of political institutions. Commonly, the state of nature is portrayed as a place in which human beings are living in the time before a political state—a government with laws and a police force—has come into being. What is life in the state of nature like? Most conspicuously, human beings enjoy great liberty; there is no state to lay down laws, and no state-sanctioned police force to enforce them. You have the freedom to do whatever you are able to get away with, without threat of formal prosecution or punishment. There are, by definition, no laws or police to protect *others* from *you*. But it is also a place of considerable insecurity, for everyone else enjoys the same liberty as you, and there are no laws or police to protect *you* from *others*.

English philosopher Thomas Hobbes (1588–1685) famously stated that life in the state of nature would be "nasty, brutish, and short." But that depends not only on what the state of nature is like but also on what kind of people live in it. Hobbes thinks of people as selfish, violence-prone egoists, deeply alienated from each other. This disaffection, along with the desire to acquire maximal power and pleasure, leads them into a "war of all against all."

Another important political thinker, John Locke (1632–1704), had a different view of humanity. He considered human beings to be naturally social creatures. So he imagines the state of nature as a place in which at least many people have some measure of fellow feeling and a sense of duty to others, but they are joined together only in loose, informal arrangements. A person is a mixed bag, motivated by self-interest, no doubt, but also by some level of concern for others. And so, in Locke's view, at least many of the people in the state of nature are willing to constrain their own behavior not merely for self-interested reasons but also, to varying degrees, out of conscience or a sense of friendship.

As I see it, pickup basketball resembles a Lockean state of nature. Without neutral third-party referees, there is no "government" to act as judge, jury, or police officer. But it isn't a Hobbesian war of all against all. First, at least many players come into the game with a measure of conscience and with loose and informal connections to other players, as my college friends and I did. (I'm still grateful to teammates who were willing to set picks and play defense for the sake of the team.) Second, basketball is by its very nature a team game, which encourages cooperation—passing and setting picks, for instance. Third, since basketball is an artifact, a game that has been created, it has rules. Even in pickup basketball, most players bring with them a rough set of rules they're generally willing to follow. Traveling isn't called tightly in pickup, but no one grabs the ball and runs the length of the court without dribbling. All that said, the cheater enjoys, as people in the state of nature do, freedom from official prosecution and punishment, and this makes cheating easier to get away with. There isn't a night watchman assigned to watch out for the cheat.

What makes a strategy of ticky-tacking especially tempting is that human motives are hidden behind a veil of ignorance. Strategic ticky-tacking is a matter of intentions. But it isn't possible for us to tell for sure what a person's motives are. Since we can't crack open a player's head to see, how can we know whether a given ticky-tacker is an Arjen or a Brian? Brian's smile and too-friendly manner signaled insincerity. But clever cheaters will better disguise their motives. The prudent strategic ticky-tacker is able to hide behind this veil of ignorance.

Moreover, in pickup basketball, as in international relations, there are many disputes and no clearly established way to settle them. In pickup games, disputes frequently concern not only whether a particular call is true, but also what rules ought to be enforced: Is it permissible to call offensive fouls in pickup? How tightly do we regulate traveling? Players disagree. From my experience, when disputes of either variety arise, basketball etiquette is to defer to the call maker: "Respect the call." This principle has the virtue of resolving disputes quickly. But such deference to the foul-caller also benefits the strategic ticky-tacker; his calls will tend to be respected—though, perhaps, only in one sense of the word "respected."

Why Strategic Ticky-Tacking Is Wrong and Contemptible

My friends and I felt in our guts—in our gut of guts—that strategic ticky-tacking is morally wrong and contemptible. Contempt and indignation seem a bit much, I know. Pickup basketball is not of world-historical significance. There are greater social ills to combat than a bit of cheating in an informal playground game. (Political corruption and white-collar crime come to mind.) Even though the case could be made that our emotions were outsized, I think they were the right "shape": cheating is wrong and contemptible.

As I see it, strategic ticky-tacking is wrong for at least three general reasons: it breaks moral rules, it reflects poor moral character, and it has morally bad consequences.

First, strategic ticky-tacking is a form of cheating, and cheating is morally wrong. By definition, strategic ticky-tacking is lying with the aim of gaining a competitive advantage. To ticky-tack strategically is to claim, knowingly and intentionally, that a foul has happened when it hasn't. As a form of cheating, ticky-tacking is unfair. The strategic ticky-tacker is attempting to take advantage of the willingness of other players to play by the rules. As the German philosopher Immanuel Kant (1724–1804) would say, the ticky-tacker "makes an exception of himself": he aims to violate the rules of good sportsmanship that he wants his opponents to follow. In this way, he is a parasite—a "free rider"—upon a healthy institution: his flourishing depends upon the general conscientiousness of others.

Second, strategic ticky-tacking reveals a lack of moral virtue. To take up a *strategy* of ticky-tacking reveals a lack of love for the truth and a poor sporting attitude, as well as a strikingly calculating character. If our desire to win is strong, most of us will be tempted in the heat of the moment to make a ticky-tack call to gain an advantage, and most of us—being human, all too human—will succumb to the temptation from time to time. But strategic ticky-tacking is not a brief episode of weakness of the will, in which a player is momentarily overcome by a strong or even irresistible urge. It is a sustained strategy, a game plan. And sustained wrongdoing is more culpable than momentary weakness. Whatever moral scruples a particular cheat happens to have, his calculating self is even stronger. It is at the helm.

Finally, strategic ticky-tacking often and predictably causes frustration, anger, and ugly basketball. Commonly enough, a ticky-tacker will provoke—sooner or later—suspicion and then anger from opposing players. Bickering and disputes ensue. An aggrieved party might easily begin to give tit-for-tat: "If he calls every little thing, so will I!" Play often becomes more aggressive: "If I'm going to get called for a foul, I might as well make it count!" A game that at its best is a festival of graceful and flowing athleticism degrades into a slow, tedious string of calculated fouls and cycles of angry revenge.

This threefold moral case against strategic ticky-tacking is exceedingly strong. It establishes the conclusion that "first-strike" strategic ticky-tacking is morally impermissible. A first-strike strategic ticky-tacker is someone who cheats unprovoked. Brian cheated simply because he wanted to win, not in response to the cheating of others against him. In the last section, I will consider whether "retaliatory" ticky-tacking, as a strategy to combat the cheat, is morally justified.

Honor and Excellence

As I've said, strategic ticky-tacking is contemptible. It fails not only by moral standards but also by an ideal of excellence in competition. By this standard, mere winning—being first to a point total—isn't everything. There is a right and proper way to win. Victory has to be earned by skill and effort, not deceit and treachery. But the reason for this is not so much a matter of fairness as it is of athletic excellence.

In Homer's epic works, a good warrior is not willing to do just anything for victory, or even for personal survival. He must follow a standard of excellence in warrior craft. In the *Iliad,* for instance, Achilles prefers death to the staining of his personal honor. Likewise, in pickup basketball, a desire for athletic success and personal honor demands fair play.

Think of the platitude "Cheaters never prosper." This might seem to be mere wishful thinking: in all likelihood, some cheats will benefit from their tactics. Brian's strategy probably won him a few intramural games. But, at a second glance, there is an interpretation according to which the platitude is true. To prosper is to flourish, to do exceedingly well. A cheater's strategy might help him win in a technical sense. But since he hasn't earned it, the cheat is not nearly in the exalted position of the person who has earned victory through skill and effort. Really, the cheater's very act of cheating cuts him off from the possibility of true success. Great basketball players don't *need* to cheat in order to win. Cheating, therefore, is a confession: "I'm not good enough to win fair and square." The cheat is insecure in his ability and so falls short of the combination of courage, self-confidence, and sporting ability that makes for a great athlete.

Contempt is the standard feeling toward those who are base and dishonorable—in this case, the person who lacks the dignity to compete in the right way. Despite moral reservations about the heroic ethic, I admire the Homeric tradition's willingness to honor the great warrior who goes down to glorious but admirable defeat, and its disdain for cheating.

These reflections provide *some* consolation to the cheater's victim. Without lifting a finger, the victim is assured that the cheater is condemned by a standard of athletic excellence. This matters for our discussion, I think. I suspect that many players who do not care much about moral considerations do value athletic accomplishment and would strongly prefer winning without having to cheat. These cheats fail to satisfy their own preferences.

Unfortunately, if a cheat, undetected, wins in the technical sense, his personal shortcomings, however real, might well be hidden from public view. His public reputation might be better than he deserves. Is there a way to beat him in the technical sense, so that his cheating doesn't gain him status points? Let's see what practical advice Machiavelli has.

Machiavelli and Would-Be Kings of the Court

Machiavelli is sometimes regarded as a cynical amoralist who rejects all conventional moral values and believes that, in politics, might makes right and ruthlessness is a virtue. His name has been a byword for immorality and cruelty. Among contemporaries, his name was often shortened to "Old Nick," a popular nickname for Satan; and "Murderous Machiavel" is a favorite reference in Elizabethan plays, including Shakespeare's. The reputation comes from Machiavelli's remarks about "political necessity." A wise prince, he claims, guides himself above all by the dictates not of morality but of necessity: if he "wishes to maintain his power" he must always "be prepared to act immorally when this becomes necessary" (*The Prince,* chap. 15). Machiavelli encourages more than a little political spin-doctoring; he suggests that the prince "act treacherously, ruthlessly, or inhumanly" if this is necessary to maximize his power (*The Prince,* chap. 18).

It is a mistake, however, to regard Machiavelli as a thoroughly cynical amoralist or a diabolical immoralist. Though not an advocate of Christian virtues such as meekness, humility, and universal love, Machiavelli does recognize the values of honesty, temperance, fair dealing, and hard work, and, like Nietzsche, he frequently praises the "heroic virtues" of courage, strength, boldness, resourcefulness, and resiliency. There are only two conditions in which he endorses "immoral" actions: when "glory" demands it, and when immoral means are necessary to achieve a great and overriding public good.

Machiavelli greatly admires the classic Roman virtue of *glory,* that is, exalted and well-deserved fame. If glory requires it, Machiavelli argues, treacherous cruelties are justified. Thus Machiavelli condemns the Italian tyrant Giovanpaolo Baglioni for failing to secure his own "eternal fame." Pope Julius II, attempting to remove Baglioni from power, impetuously entered Baglioni's stronghold without adequate protection. In Machiavelli's eyes, greatness called for Baglioni to murder Julius, his known enemy, but Baglioni squandered the opportunity (*Discourses,* bk. 1, chap. 27). However, Machiavelli makes clear that glory can *forbid* resort to immoral means. Thus Machiavelli condemns the savage cruelties of Agathocles the Sicilian: "Yet it cannot be called virtue to kill one's fellow citizens, betray one's friends, be without faith, without pity; power might be gained in this way, but not glory" (*The Prince,* chap. 8). In all such instances, the highest standard of right conduct isn't conventional morality but lasting and resplendent renown.

The second type of case in which Machiavelli endorses immoral behavior is when "the end justifies the means," or more precisely, when urgent "reasons of state" override ordinary moral considerations. Like Hobbes, Machiavelli believed that most humans are weak, selfish, and violent (*The Prince,* chap. 17; *Discourses,* bk. 1, chap. 3). This is especially evident in politics, which is dominated by corrupt and unscrupulous power seekers. Politics, Machiavelli writes, is no game for saints or idealists,

> for how we live is so far removed from how we ought to live, that he who abandons what is done for what ought to be done, will rather learn to bring about his own ruin than his preservation. A man who wishes to make a profession of goodness in everything must necessarily come to grief among so many who are not good. Therefore it is necessary for a prince, who wishes to maintain himself, to learn how not to be good and to use this knowledge and not use it, according to the necessity of the case. (*The Prince,* chap. 15)

Machiavelli is here offering what philosophers today call a "dirty hands" argument. According to such arguments, there are times when dirty pool must be met with dirty pool. If countries A and B are at war, and A is carpet bombing B's cities, it may be necessary for country B to resort to similar measures, though ordinarily, of course, such tactics would be seriously wrong. Similarly, if you are in a street fight and your assailant is fighting dirty, you are justified in returning ill for ill if this is necessary to save your life or avoid serious injury. Machiavelli believed that "dirty pool" is ubiquitous and unavoidable in politics. As a result, to be guided by a desire for moral purity ("Never has a lie passed these lips") is folly. A high-minded ruler with a taste for moral purity will not provide the strong, iron-fisted leadership needed to protect himself and his subjects from subjugation and violence.

So what would Machiavelli say about strategic ticky-tacking? Can it be justified by an appeal to either glory or the necessity of dirty hands?

Machiavelli would surely condemn first-strike tactics. As we've seen, this practice is contemptible, not glorious. And dirty-hands justifications don't apply; first-strike strategic ticky-tackers, by definition, are not answering wrongs suffered; they are simply aiming for an advantage.

Would Machiavelli endorse retaliatory tactics? Glory probably isn't going to do the trick. As we've seen, Machiavelli thinks of glory in the classical Roman sense as enduring and deserved renown. In this classical sense, there isn't much glory to be won in pickup basketball games, no matter how brilliantly you or your team may play. (A little, I submit, but not much.) Also, to the degree that considerations of glory do apply, if you defeat the cheater without adopting his tactics, that is far more magnificent.

Still, the question of dirty hands is legitimate. Suppose the game is close and your opponents are calling blatant, and blatantly dishonest, ticky-tack fouls. May dirty pool be met with dirty pool?

How to Fight the Strategic Ticky-Tacker, and Win

There are a few strategies I won't treat as practical options, at least not for me. The first option is serious violence. Confronted with a strategic ticky-tacker, one source of frustration is the absence of any formal process to use against cheating—no ethics committees or ten-game suspensions. Absent the long arm of the law, you might think to extend your own arm—in the direction of the cheater's face. An elbow to the teeth is one way to make a cheater suffer for his sins. But it's not how I would go about it. That's not to say that I won't take seriously lesser forms of aggression, a bit of hand-checking or blocking out harder than normal, for instance. But as Locke persuasively argues, in a state of nature we may only pay back an offender "so far as calm reason and conscience dictate, proportionate to his transgression, which is so much as may serve for reparation or restraint."[1] Causing injury, even a bloodied mouth, seems disproportionate to the offense, and the bloodying of teeth might lead to a protracted, bloody fight. The cheat makes me mad, but I'm not looking to beat him up or start a brawl.

The second strategy I won't take seriously is walking off the court. My wife asks, "If the cheater makes you so mad, why don't you just quit?" But quitting won't do. From my experience, walking off doesn't usually frustrate the cheater so much as it gains for the person who refuses to play the reputation of being a quitter. More importantly, quitting is terribly unsatisfying. Perhaps leaving the court makes sense for the more casual player, but (as I've already admitted) I'm a bit more intense. When I'm confronted with a cheat, I want to stay and compete. The cheat wants the personal glory that comes with victory, but without earning it. Defeating him puts him in his rightful place. That's satisfying.

So I choose to stay on the court and play. If you join me, how could we maximize our chances of succeeding at this public service? I suggest a threefold strategy.[2]

Step 1: Step Up Your Game

The strategic ticky-tacker has a strong incentive not to be detected. A suspected cheat confronts an angry opponent, who generally fights harder. My college friends and I were already passionate. We set picks, double-teamed weak ball handlers, and played help defense. And we got on any teammate who didn't. But we gave absolutely no quarter to cheats. Against the cheat, we blocked out even more aggressively and went after every loose ball. We also revoked our general commitment to sporting etiquette; we hand-checked (more), and we never gave up a layup. We'd rather hack the cheat going in for an easy shot and send him back to the top of the key.

Step 1 is to turn the cheat's cheating into your greater motivation to compete: overcome the benefits the cheat receives from his schemes by winning every loose ball and by securing all the benefits of hustle and mildly objectionable tactics.

Step 2: Shame and Accuse

The strategic ticky-tacker also has a strong incentive not to be detected for fear of retaliation. The cheater is likely to believe that if he is detected, there will be consequences: his reputation will suffer, for instance. And he might fear physical retaliation. (Presumably, you haven't *told* him that you don't intend to elbow him in the mouth.) If you accuse him of cheating, you give him a strong reason to attempt to "disprove" your accusation, and how is he to do that except by subsequently making a few "fair" calls? If you have the cheater making true calls—even if from a calculated instead of a moral motive—then he is not benefiting (as much) from his scheming. He isn't snatching up (as many) extra possessions for his team. The benefits of his strategy are at least minimized.[3]

Step 2 is to make clear—verbally or nonverbally—that cheaters will pay. Don't stew in your indignation; speak up and accuse. Perhaps you can shame or frighten the cheat into greater conformity with the rules.[4]

Step 3: Give Tick-for-Tack

Suppose you've intensified your game and made your accusations, but the cheaters are still benefiting, maybe even winning. And, however skillful, your sheer ability and effort might not be enough to defeat the cheat. Now, finally, you've reached the moment when, according to Machiavelli—and probably Locke, too—tit-for-tat is morally justified. For every possession the cheat steals by an unfair call, make an unfair call to balance the scales.

I suspect that the most common objection to retaliatory tit-for-tat-ism would be this: In meeting dirty pool with dirty pool, haven't we committed the dreaded fallacy of "two wrongs make a right"? Haven't we sunk to the level of Machiavelli's cynical power politicians? Aren't we, if we're making intentional ticky-tack calls, also wrong and contemptible?

There is a compelling reason to think the answer is no. A strong moral case can be made for retaliatory dishonesty against the strategic ticky-tacker. If there is no neutral third party—no properly appointed agent of justice—to punish the cheater's wrongdoing, then any justice that is going to be achieved must be brought about by the victims of the cheater. There is simply no one else to bring it about. As Locke argues, in a state of nature, such as a pickup basketball game, "everyone has a right to punish the . . . transgressor . . . to such a degree as may hinder its violation."[5] Since there are no courts, police officers, or referees in a state of nature, there is no other way in which justice can be served and "criminal" conduct deterred. Are we to stand by and let the oppressors benefit from their oppression? Does morality demand passivity in the face of wrongdoing? I don't think it does. I don't think, in any case, that morality *demands* that we be categorically unwilling to ticky-tack back. The retaliatory ticky-tacker can be seen as an agent of justice, a balancer of scales.[6]

Of course, the willingness to retaliate must be accompanied by discernment. Retaliation is permissible only under the right conditions. As Locke notes, one of the "inconveniences" of the state of nature is that "self-love" naturally makes humans "partial to themselves and their friends,"[7] making it hard for them to judge fairly in their own cases. (As evidence, think how quickly fans jump to the conclusion that a referee is biased against their favorite team.) In returning a lie for a lie, therefore, we must be careful that our response is unbiased and proportionate. Nevertheless, as both Locke and "murderous Machiavel" would probably agree, there are times when retaliatory ticky-tacking is morally justified.

It bears mentioning, too, that the strongest reason not to meet carpet bombing with carpet bombing is that huge numbers of innocent people are inevitably killed. But when it comes to retaliatory ticky-tacking, no one gets injured. Retaliatory ticky-tacking is not a violent strategy.

My own moral outlook is not, generally speaking, Machiavellian. Both my anthropological and my moral views are closer to Locke's than to "Murderous Machiavel's." But as I see it, Machiavelli gets it right, at least this time.

Notes

1. John Locke, *Second Treatise of Government* (1690), sec. 8, in *Two Treatises of Government and a Letter Concerning Toleration,* ed. Ian Shapiro (New Haven: Yale University Press, 2003).

2. Another option is to change the rules. What if pickup basketball were to adopt the strategy of "defense calls" instead of the more common "offense calls"? Doing so would prevent the strategic ticky-tacker from making phantom calls. Unfortunately, this strategy is not immune from cheating either; it might encourage "hacky-slapping": aggressive play by defenders with too few calls made.

3. Perhaps, of course, this chain of reasoning will lead a clever strategic ticky-tacker to "endgame" ticky-tacking: waiting until crucial possessions near the end of the game to cheat.

4. A shaming strategy will work more effectively, presumably, if there is a good chance that you will play this cheater again in the future. I suspect the rate of cheating increases when players believe that they will not meet their victims again.

5. Locke, *Second Treatise of Government*, sec. 7.

6. Locke, *Second Treatise of Government*, sec. 13.

7. Is it better yet to take the moral high road? Someone might wonder, "Why give up our moral integrity to do something as trivial as beat the cheat?" If my argument is sound, retaliatory ticky-tacking is not morally wrong, and so it doesn't cost you any moral integrity. In my view, a categorical unwillingness to lie about foul calls is morally admirable but not morally required.

Luke Witte

BASKETBALL, VIOLENCE, FORGIVENESS, AND HEALING

ANYONE WHO IS even a casual basketball fan will readily recall the ugly brawl that disrupted the game between the Detroit Pistons and the Indiana Pacers in November 2004 and resulted in suspensions for several players. The incident was a major story in the media and was replayed over and over. Like almost everyone else who saw it, I was sickened by the continuous stream of video showing the violence erupting on the court and even into the stands. For me, however, the incident touched a deeply personal nerve because it brought back memories of a similar event I was involved in more than three decades ago.

Sports Illustrated called it "the most vicious attack in college basketball lore." ESPN ranks it as one of the ten worst fights or brawls in twentieth-century sports. Today, most basketball fans wouldn't recognize my name. Many, however, have seen clips of the infamous brawl in which I participated on January 25, 1972, in a game between the Ohio State Buckeyes and the Minnesota Golden Gophers. In this chapter I tell my story, and as you'll see, it's a tale in which both faith and philosophy play an important role.

The encounter was a media heyday. Ohio State and Minnesota were two nationally ranked teams with the winner likely to be the Big Ten representative to the NCAA tournament. Ideologically and philosophically, the two programs seemed to be at opposite ends of the spectrum. Ohio State was a predominantly white team with a rich basketball history that emphasized hard work, discipline, fair play, and integrity. Minnesota was an emerging Big Ten power with nothing traditional about it. Under young new coach Bill Musselman, the predominantly African

American Gophers featured slick Globetrotter-type warm-ups, glitzy marketing, junior college recruits, a fast break / no-set offense, and a win-at-all-cost attitude that culminated a few years later in a major recruiting scandal and Musselman's resignation.

The game was tense and emotion packed from the beginning. Our Buckeye team was booed when we came out on the floor, and the loud music and slick Gopher warm-ups seemed to whip the large crowd into a frenzy. The first half was relatively cleanly played, but at halftime, as the two teams were going to their dressing rooms, Gopher Bob Nix passed in front of me with his left arm raised in a clenched-fist salute. I tried to shove his arm out of my face and accidentally clipped him lightly on the jaw. Later, Musselman claimed that it was this incident that incited the brawl.

Things turned ugly in the second half. After Ohio State went ahead 40–32 with less than ten minutes to play, the crowd began to boo and throw debris on the floor. With less than a minute to play and the Buckeyes up 50–44, the Gophers had to press, which left me open near midcourt. I received the pass and headed down court for an easy layup. As I went up for the shot, I saw Clyde Turner coming in from my right side. I expected the block attempt, shifted the ball to my left hand, and used my right arm and the basket to ward off any attempt to block the shot. Turner had other thoughts. Instead of going for the block, he came across with a right hook that hit me in the face. I crashed to the floor dazed and disoriented. The crowd cheered when I went down, then booed when Turner was called for a flagrant foul and ejected from the game.

My head spinning, I managed to get to my knees. As I sat on my haunches, Minnesota player Corky Taylor extended a hand of assistance, and I took it. Instead of helping me, however, Taylor jerked me forward and kneed me in the groin. I fell back to the floor and lay on my side holding both hands to my groin.

Chaos ensued as both benches unloaded, followed by fans from the stands and even student-athletes from other sports. Dave Merchant, a starting guard for Ohio State, pushed Taylor away from me and also from Minnesota's Jim Brewer, who had come to see what was going on. As Merchant tried to fend off the much bigger and stronger Golden Gophers, he realized that this wasn't going to work and ran, pursued by their players. That left me alone on the floor still reeling from the two blows.

Ron Behagen, a starter for Minnesota, was on the bench, having fouled out of the game earlier, and had a clear line of sight on me. He ran onto the court and kicked me three times in the head, landing the last blow with Ohio State coach Fred Taylor holding him from the rear in a bear hug, trying to pull him off me. Taylor said that Behagen was screaming, "Let me go, man, let me go."

Skirmishes were everywhere on the court. Among the Minnesota players who participated in the brawl was future baseball Hall of Famer Dave Winfield. According to sportswriter William F. Reed, Winfield, who had recently joined the Gopher varsity, "joined the fray too, dodging to mid-court where some Minnesota reserves and civilians were trying to wrestle Ohio State substitute Mark Wagar to the floor. Winfield leaped on top of Wagar when he was down and hit him five times with his right fist on the face and head. When the stunned Wagar managed to slip away, a fan pushed him to the floor and another caught him on the chin with a hard punch from the side."[1] After reviewing the videotapes, I think "bedlam" is the only word that properly describes the scene. The police had left the arena early to assist in emptying the parking lots and now ran back in to help restore order. The Ohio State team had huddled around me as I lay on the floor, some looking in to see how I was doing and others with their backs to us in a circle, an island in the middle of infested waters, not knowing what was going to happen next.

The officials called the game and announced Ohio State as the winner. I was lifted up by my teammates and carried off as we left the court en masse. Then the most startling event of the night happened. The fans and players uproariously booed us as we walked toward the locker room. Interestingly enough, I didn't know this had happened until years later when I watched a videotape of the incident.

As our team sat in the dark, dingy locker room, plans to get us out of there were made. Mark Wagar and I would be taken by ambulance to the University of Minnesota Medical Center, and the rest of the team would follow in a team bus. At this point I emerged from a near-comatose state and jumped up, wanting to finish the game. I have no memory of anything that occurred from halftime to the next morning (from what I understand this is called retro-amnesia), with the exception of a few lucid moments, just memory bites of being restrained in the locker room, an extremely cold ride in the ambulance, and my teammates standing around my bed in the hospital.

My first conscious memory came the following morning when the phone rang next to my bed. One contact lens was still in, and the phone was way too loud for the splitting headache I had. I saw Wagar in the bed next to mine, and I knew we were in a hospital. I wasn't quite sure why, but I ached everywhere. I fumbled around for the phone; it was my brother Verlynn calling. I don't remember the conversation, but I must have said I was fine.

Later that day, the team boarded a commercial plane to return to Ohio. I had a patch over one eye, a large bandage on my chin, a huge scrape down the right side of my face, and an oversized, discolored ear. My cornea had been damaged from an impact that forced the hard contact lens that I was wearing to slice across my eye. I sustained a concussion and had numerous cuts on my face that required twenty-seven stitches. The knee to the groin didn't help matters. A flight attendant asked me if I had had an accident. I could only reply, "You could say that."

Physical scars heal, but the heart takes a little longer. Many people pressed me to sue the players involved, Minnesota coach Bill Musselman, the university, the state and campus police, and anybody who had even a remote connection to the incident. My father, a professor of systematic theology and a Presbyterian pastor, even pushed me to retaliate with a lawsuit. But I just couldn't.

Something was going on within me that was much deeper than a scar, a game, or even money. Even though Ohio State's basketball program stressed fair play and doing your best, I was still very competitive and wanted very much to win at everything I did. But I felt my desire to compete fading away; I kept thinking that a game is never really worth physical aggression or fan violence. The game of basketball should be a thing of beauty, not a blood sport of anger and hostility.

What happens to the human psyche when a person suffers traumatic harm? What does a person do with the deluge of emotions that infiltrates his mind and changes from minute to minute? One minute I felt that everything would be fine, that healing was happening, that I was surrounded by loving and supportive family, teammates, and friends. The next minute all I could think about was hatred and retribution. The kaleidoscope of changing emotions made normal daily functioning almost impossible.

In the weeks that followed, I had a class in a large lecture hall that began at 9:00 A.M. I arrived and sat through the lecture. Sometime later one of my teammates came up to me and asked what was going on. I had been sitting at that desk for two lecture periods and was about to start a third. I couldn't remember a thing about the lecture or the following class, which wasn't on my schedule. I don't want to suggest that I was a stellar student who excelled in every subject, but I did well when I put my mind to it. This memory lapse could be blamed on the concussion I sustained, but the truth is, I couldn't escape from the constant mental gymnastics going on in my mind.

Emotionally and philosophically, I was in a crisis. Ron Behagan, Clyde Turner, Corky Taylor, and Coach Bill Musselman had become objects of what philosophers Jeffrie G. Murphy and Jean Hampton call "moral hatred." Hampton defines moral hatred as "an aversion to someone who has identified himself with an immoral cause or practice, prompted by moral indignation and accompanied by the wish to triumph over him and his cause or practice in the name of some fundamental moral principle or objective, most notably justice."[2] In my case, moral hatred meant an intense revulsion to flagrant acts of violence, accompanied by an overwhelming desire to have justice served and the love that I had for the game of basketball restored.

Here is where the rubber met the road for me. I wanted to feel again the excitement of getting ready for a game and the emotional drama of playing, but I simply couldn't get over my intense feelings of hatred and resentment. Moreover, I took this personally as I looked in the mirror and saw my face scarred and distorted. I felt violated and demoralized, and my hatred was like a cancer that drained me of my energy and sapped my will to compete.

Prior to the Minnesota game, there was nothing complicated about my feelings for basketball. Although my family moved around a great deal when I was younger, I spent my adolescent and high school years in Marlboro, Ohio, a rural community of about 350 people. My high school had never had a winning record until our team, which had played together for years as kids and was made up of hardworking, disciplined farm boys, began to play. Every year we lost in the state tournament to powerful Canton McKinley, led by future University of Illinois and NBA player Nick Witherspoon. Nick and I went head-to-head, and those games are still talked about as some of the greatest games fans had ever seen. I remember those games with great fondness, for they were what competitive sports are all about: the banging bodies, the use of talent and strategy, a healthy respect for the opposition, and even the *Hoosiers*-type matchups pitting the speedy, flashy urban kids against the hayseeds from the country. Witherspoon's team won all those games, but I had little victories by outscoring Nick 13–12 our sophomore year, 27–26 as a junior, and 37–36 as a senior. Nick and I loved the game, and we genuinely cared for each other, but when we walked onto the court it was all business. Up until the Minnesota game, this is how I viewed the game. I may have been an "Opie from Mayberry," but for me basketball represented everything that was good about sports and about America.

As a first-team High School All-American, I was recruited by just about everybody, but I was attracted to the coaches who had obvious integrity. Among them were Frank Truit of Kent State University (just thirty minutes from home), Jim Snyder of Ohio University (where my oldest brother played), Bucky Waters of West Virginia and later Davidson College, Ray Mears of the University of Tennessee, Dean Smith of North Carolina, and Fred Taylor of Ohio State. Not all these schools were among my final choices, but these coaches all had my respect. My final five were Duke, Maryland, North Carolina, Tennessee, and Ohio State.

Each of these teams' coaches offered me only two things: an education and a chance to play basketball. On my official visit to the University of North Carolina, I was in Dean Smith's office, and there was a stack of UNC golf shirts on his desk. He noticed that they had caught my eye. As I was taking my seat, he picked them up and moved them to his credenza, saying that he would love for me to have one but it would be a violation of NCAA rules.

I was especially impressed, however, by Ohio State coach Fred Taylor. Taylor once offered a scholarship to a young man who, before he had a chance to sign the papers, suffered a serious injury that blinded him in one eye. As soon as Taylor heard about it, he drove to the recruit's house with the letters of intent and told him that he still wanted him, even if he never put on a Buckeye uniform. Fred was a man of transparent goodness and authenticity. I heard Coach Taylor say a number of times that he would never recruit men whom he wouldn't invite to sit at his dinner table with his family—quite a statement for a man who had four very attractive daughters! At Fred's funeral, of the 107 men who had played for him at Ohio State, more than 70 of us were there to pay our last respects.

On the other hand, there were plenty of schools in those days that were out to tempt recruits with all kinds of goodies, ranging from preferential treatment in housing to promises of "vehicles for the choosing for a recruit like you." Other coaches appealed to players' desires for personal glory. One small-college coach asked me why I would want to be a big fish in a big pond when I could come to his school and "be the biggest fish in our tiny pond." That may have been true, but it wasn't very exciting or challenging.

At the end of my senior season, the recruiters were everywhere. During that time my brothers and I had recognized that this might be the only opportunity for us to play together on the same team, so we entered a number of tournaments. We had a ball, but college coaches were always around, and all we wanted to do was have some fun together. I think University of Maryland coach Lefty Driesell was at every game and practice.

At one tournament we were resting in the locker room between games when a coach came in whom I had never met before. He introduced himself as the coach of a small school not far from where I lived. I told him that I was interested in schools with more of a national presence, but he continued to press. My oldest brother, who never let an opportunity to mix it up go by, said, "Didn't you hear him? He said no thanks." The coach then said he was representing one of the schools I was interested in, the University of Tennessee. I found this strange, as did most of the people in the room, and he was asked to leave again, but he refused. Finally, he was literally escorted from the locker room. I had never in my life been around a man who was as relentless and tenacious as that man, Bill Musselman.

Forgiveness and Healing

After college, I played for a few years with the Cleveland Cavaliers in the NBA, but I never played with the same intensity or enjoyment that I had before the Minnesota game. When my basketball career ended, I ran my own business for a while and then spent several years in banking. I have been a Christian most of my life, although not a very good one, but as I approached age forty, I felt a different calling, attended seminary, and became an ordained pastor. For seven years I served as a chaplain for the Charlotte Hornets and today serve as a pastor in a large church in Charlotte, North Carolina.

As the years passed, something told me that I had to let the whole incident go, that I couldn't possibly hold on to the anger and bitterness and desire to retaliate. Eventually, I realized that the only logical response was forgiveness. But here many questions filled my mind: What is true forgiveness? How does one forgive? How do I restore my soul?

Over the years, through philosophical and theological reflection, I've been able to put a vocabulary to the process I underwent to experience healing. "Restoration" implies a recovery to normal or at least to a previous condition. Medically, to restore, say, a broken arm, three things must happen: First, the bone needs to be set right. Next, a cast must be put around the limb to protect it. Finally, time is required for the bone to heal. Forgiveness is the first step in this healing/restoration process. Forgiveness is the act of *setting it right*.

Here philosophers, with their conceptual tools, can help. Canadian philosopher Anne Minas points out four senses of "forgive":

- to condone an offense by overlooking it or treating it as nonexistent
- to remit punishment for an offense
- to reverse or retract a previous condemnatory judgment
- to give up or cease to harbor resentment, rancor, or wrath[3]

There was never any question of my condoning the actions of my attackers, and it was never my place to impose or remit any punishment. Nor was it ever a question of reversing my judgment of the serious wrongness of what my attackers did. For me the key issue was Minas's fourth sense of forgive. How could I bring myself to give up my intense "resentment, rancor, or wrath" and heal the breach not only between myself and my attackers but also the breach I felt within myself?

There is something just shy of a miracle when two people reconcile and friendship is restored, especially when forgiveness is unconditional and has nothing to do with the other person. If the offender chooses to say that he or she is sorry and expresses remorse for the offense, then true reconciliation becomes possible. In a marriage, in a family, in business, in churches, and in other settings where harmony is essential, reconciliation is mandatory. In my case, I had no significant prior relationship with the

University of Minnesota, the players, or their coach, so harmony wasn't an issue, and I didn't see a need for them to say they were sorry. My objective was simply the cleansing of my heart, and for that I needed to forgive, or rather to "set my heart right."

As a pastor, I often encounter individuals and families demanding an apology from an offender, but frequently such demands are meaningless. Saying you're sorry outside a committed relationship often means very little. For the offender, the path to healing lies through admitting guilt, feeling remorse, repenting of sin, and making restitution if possible. The offender, however, may not be interested in repenting and making restitution. If he's not, the injured party mustn't become preoccupied with the offender's responsibility in the matter. For ultimately, as Robert Jeffress says, "repentance is the offender's responsibility; forgiveness is our responsibility."[4] So the one who is offended against must stay focused on his own responsibility to forgive for his own healing.

The second step in emotional healing is to create and maintain a supportive cast around the wounded. When a person has been seriously hurt or offended, they experience myriad emotions. Elizabeth Kübler-Ross, in her classic book, *On Death and Dying,* claims that people go through five stages of grieving: denial and isolation, anger, bargaining, depression, and acceptance. Unfortunately, a clear path to healing really doesn't proceed in that way. It's much more like firing a shotgun in a bank vault: the ricochets—or emotions, in this case—come at you from every direction, and there is no telling which one will be next. You, as a victim, are attempting to negotiate a steep slope to recovery, laboriously climbing to acceptance and health only to slide back, often without warning, to depression, anger, bargaining, isolation, and denial.

The supportive cast of characters should be both encouragers and challengers to get you out of the bank vault and to the top of the slope. These people shouldn't necessarily be friends or relatives but wise, objective counselors who can not only listen but also think dispassionately about your decisions and actions. They need to meet with you regularly and ask the tough questions about how you are dealing with your anger, coping with depression, and keeping truth at the forefront of your mind. Yes-men or yes-women are undesirable because purity in your walk is the sole objective.

Last comes time. It has been said that the healer of all wounds is time.

That is true if you really don't care if you are scarred and don't mind carrying a huge scab that could be easily pulled off, even years later. In other words, healing does take time, but time alone does not heal. If not properly treated, wounds can be reopened over time, inviting infectious organisms to infiltrate the body and potentially starting a destructive cycle all over again. The proper treatment of those damaged emotions over time can allow an individual fully to heal even from the most grievous hurts we sometimes inflict on one another.

Forgiveness requires us to extend grace to fellow sinners, grace that steps over the offense and says the deed and debt are canceled. It is an intentional choice of an offended person to extend goodwill to someone who doesn't deserve it. Should Ron Behagen, Corky Taylor, Clyde Turner, Dave Winfield, or Bill Musselman take responsibility for their actions and make some sort of restitution? As I say, that's not my call. Only time will tell.

Reaching Out

In the winter of 1982, my wife and I celebrated the birth of our second child, and the ten-year anniversary of the Minnesota incident went by with little fanfare, except for a few calls from reporters and a surprising letter I received from Corky Taylor. I agonized over my reply for days and started many times to pen a response. My wife finally said, "Just call him." And I did. The conversation was stilted, but we talked about our wives, children, and jobs. He talked about his two young basketball players and wanting them to understand integrity and good sportsmanship and to respect the truth. Most of it would have seemed like small talk to an uninformed listener, but to us huge chasms were being backfilled with understanding and trust. Even the silence was filled with receptivity toward one another.

For many years, Corky and I wrote infrequently to one another, until the age of e-mail, when we began writing more often. With each Send button pushed we divulged more of our emotions and hurt, connected by a moment in history that put our names always in the same breath. We even talked about coauthoring a book. We exchanged ideas, and we started to become extremely aware that a spiritual bond had formed between us. Our thoughts about forgiveness and grace were very similar, and we became intentional about our openness to the psychological effects of violence and race and about the blessings we had encountered because of our openness. In a letter, Corky wrote:

> I know that the events of that January 25th game many years ago has taken a mental toll over the years. I don't think anyone else can totally understand those feelings. I do think you are as close to those feelings as anyone. First of all your spiritual (as opposed to worldly) reaction to the event lets me know that God has helped you heal. It has helped me a great deal in seeing things clearly. In some ways it was necessary for God to get my attention. He makes all things right in time.

He then added:

> If it had not been for the incident, would I have continued to use the blessings from God to attract sins of the world, or might you not be in the ministry right now? Would I feel this spiritual connection and understand you? I know it took courage to stand up publicly and talk about the incident. Courage to tell people that you have chosen to react to it in a spiritual and not a worldly manner. The courage you have shown helps prepare me to tell the truth. As distasteful as the situation was, it can be used by God to help people.

In April 2000, I boarded a plane to Minneapolis. The airport was almost deserted when I arrived, and as I walked to the baggage claim area, I saw a lone figure pacing near the exit. We stared at each other for a long second, and then Corky and I hugged each other as two brothers would after a long absence. The two of us talked over dinner that night, and the next day I met his family. Our conversations were about people, basketball, character, and the freedom that forgiveness has brought to our lives.

On Corky's deck that afternoon, he said he had a surprise for me. As Clyde Turner stepped out, I told him I would recognize him anywhere—a little heavier perhaps, but Clyde all the same. Later, in Corky's den, we watched the tapes of the incident, Clyde and I sitting on the couch, and Corky pacing back and forth. At first we watched in silence, conscious of the strangeness of the scene. We felt like characters in a play watching a replay of an event that we somehow hoped would turn out differently than we remembered. Questions bubbled out of the rush of emotions: Who was that guy? Where is he today? What were your thoughts? How did that happen? When did we realize the enormity of what just happened? It was surreal.

Later, we took Corky's son to play soccer, and the three of us sat on a bench. A guy from Columbus, Ohio, recognized us and seemed totally freaked out. "What are you doing here?" he asked me. "Just checking in with some old friends," I replied. We felt like battle-scarred wartime adversaries who through the years had reconciled without words, sharing a bond that was deeper than we could express.

Before we left the soccer field, I stood up and looked down at my two aging friends and told them that I had opportunities to speak and write and asked if I could use their stories. "Only if you give them the gospel," Clyde responded. The gospel is "love one another," for there is no game worth the loss of a relationship or even the potential loss of a relationship. There is no place for violence but always a place for grace.

Notes

1. William F. Reed, "An Ugly Affair in Minnesota," *Sports Illustrated*, February 7, 1972, 21.

2. Jeffrie G. Murphy and Jean Hampton, *Forgiveness and Mercy* (Cambridge: Cambridge University Press, 1988), 61.

3. Ann C. Minas, "God and Forgiveness," *Philosophical Quarterly* 25 (1975): 138–50. Reprinted in *Philosophy and Faith: A Philosophy of Religion Reader*, ed. David Shatz (New York: McGraw-Hill, 2002), 26–31.

4. Robert Jeffress, *When Forgiveness Doesn't Make Sense* (New York: Waterbrook Press, 2000), 80.

Scott A. Davison

THE BREAKS OF THE GAME
Luck and Fairness in Basketball

Luck and Skill

IN BASKETBALL, AS in everyday life, luck plays a role in the outcome of things. In fact, sometimes luck appears to play such a pivotal role in a game that we are tempted to think that the outcome wasn't fair. Should we ever draw that conclusion? How are luck and fairness related?

First, let's consider the connection between luck and skill. Daniel Dennett, a contemporary American philosopher, describes it this way. Over time, luck tends to average out in sports, because it is randomly distributed. As gamblers routinely discover, there's no reliable way to be lucky. There are no true lucky charms or habits, for example, although believing in them may have positive psychological effects. By contrast, skill leads to predictable results. As Dennett says, "The better you are, the less luck you need, and the less your successes count as merely lucky. Why? Because the better you are, the more control you have over your performance."[1]

Since control is always a matter of degree, so too is luckiness. Consider someone who makes a half-court shot, for example. If this person is a randomly chosen fan who makes the shot during a halftime contest and wins a million dollars, then we would say that it was a very lucky shot indeed. If the shot is made by an NBA player at the end of a quarter, then we would say that the shot was a little bit lucky, but not as lucky as the fan's shot, since the NBA player has more control over his shot than the fan does. As Dennett says, for star athletes, "the threshold for what counts as luck is considerably higher."[2] Finally, if the half-court shot happens to be a hook shot made by Meadowlark Lemon, the former Harlem Globetrotters great, then we wouldn't say it was a lucky shot at all, since he made that shot all the time. (His contemporary heir apparent is Matt "Showbiz" Jackson, who regularly makes an unbelievable behind-the-back half-court shot.)

So the more skill a person has, the less luck is involved. Since skills are relative to persons, as we can see from the examples just discussed, it follows that luck is relative to persons and their abilities. What counts as lucky for one person might not count as lucky for another. Many of Michael Jordan's improvised layup shots (after being fouled in the lane) seemed to be lucky, but he made so many of them that it seems unlikely that they always were. The very same shots, if made by Kurt Rambis, would certainly have been lucky. (Sorry, Kurt.)

Luck is also relative to times, since what is lucky for someone at one time might not be lucky at another time. For example, the first half-court hook shot that Meadowlark Lemon made was certainly a very lucky shot, but the five-hundredth one certainly wasn't so lucky.

So luck is a matter of degree, it is relative to persons and their abilities, and it is relative to times. The more skilled a person is, the more reliably and predictably he or she can accomplish something, and the less luck is involved. Luck is not a special kind of force in the world that can be reliably exploited, like gravity or solar radiation; instead, we use the word "luck" as a convenient way to refer to those good and bad things that happen in people's lives that are beyond their intentional control.

Luck and Fairness

Now that we've explored the connection between luck and skill, we should consider the relationship between luck and fairness. There are two conceptions of fairness that are worth considering here: one is the conception of fairness in terms of equality, and the other is the concept of fairness in terms of desert. Let's consider each of these in turn.

One common conception of fairness is the idea of equality: a game is fair to the extent that all things are equal. Fans sometimes object to what they perceive as bad officiating by saying, "Call it both ways, ref!" This indicates a desire for things to be equal, so that each team faces the same challenges and opportunities, without any favoritism on the part of the referees.

But if we think carefully about the idea of fairness as equality, we will realize that it is an ideal that is practically unattainable. There is no way to guarantee that everything will be the same for each team. In fact, since the players never occupy exactly the same places at exactly the same times, things are never literally the same for any two people on the court (or anywhere else, for that matter). There will always be differences, no matter how small, that make a difference, and many of these will involve luck. So fairness in the sense of equality is impossible to achieve.

If an all-powerful and all-knowing God exists, though, perhaps God can judge things in an absolutely fair way. Some philosophers have wondered, in this connection, whether or not there could be luck with respect to God's judgments concerning the eternal salvation of human beings.[3] There does seem to be a degree of luck with respect to morality in general, as a number of authors have pointed out.[4] But by analogy with athletic contests, we might expect God to serve as the ultimate referee in such matters and to make sure that luck does not play a significant role in the outcome.[5]

To return to basketball, it is important to note that the game does have some built-in mechanisms for eliminating certain kinds of lucky inequality. To see this, consider the scope of luck in basketball as compared to other sports. In football, for example, there is an added dimension of luck that comes from the shape of the ball. When a football falls to the ground, it is very hard to predict where it will bounce. (Have you ever tried to dribble a football like it was a basketball? I have. It's not pretty.) One of the luckiest plays in football history, Franco Harris's so-called Immaculate Reception in the 1972 Steelers-Raiders AFC semifinal game, depended upon the luck introduced by the shape of the football. Physicists today still debate whether or not this deflected pass was legal according to 1972 NFL rules, which depends upon whether or not the ball hit the Oakland Raiders' Jack Tatum before being caught by Harris, who then scored the winning touchdown for the Steelers with only five seconds remaining in the game.

Of course, in the early days of basketball, there was a tiny bit of luck introduced by the fact that the ball had laces in one seam (between the last two panels of leather to be sewn together). Thanks to improvements in technology, though, this bit of luck has been eliminated. Today all basketballs are spherical and hence symmetrical, so it is highly predictable where the ball will bounce when it hits the floor (unless it's spinning wildly). In this respect, basketball depends less on luck than football does.

In addition, football relies upon a coin flip to determine the first offensive possession of the game and the first possession of each overtime period. Not even this method is completely foolproof, as we saw on Thanksgiving Day 1998, when the Pittsburgh Steelers' Jerome Bettis appeared to call "heads" and the referee heard him call "tails," leading to a Detroit Lions victory after the first possession in overtime. (Maybe the Steelers had it coming, since they benefited from the good luck involved in the Immaculate Reception.) Since then, the NFL has introduced new rules about how to call a flipped coin in order to avoid this kind of confusion.

By contrast, basketball relies upon the jump ball. Like the coin toss, in a well-executed jump ball, each side has an equal opportunity to reach the tossed ball. But unlike the coin toss, which is a matter of pure luck, in a jump ball the player with the best timing and highest vertical leap will have the best chance to tip the ball to a teammate. So here again, basketball leaves less room for luck than football does.

Of course, the first possession of the game or overtime period is not nearly as important in basketball as it is in football, so this isn't a big difference. This is because basketball includes the opportunity for many possessions by each team and many opportunities to score points, even in overtime periods. (This is one reason why the shot clock is so important, by the way: it tends to create changes of possession on a regular basis.) If a basketball game (or an overtime period) lasted only two minutes, we might well regard the outcome as unfair or too dependent on luck. (Basketball games are never decided by "sudden death" for the same reasons.) As it is, though, we think that the game is long enough to cancel out differences in time of possession due to luck.

It's also interesting to note that the referees in basketball are responsible for eliminating certain kinds of lucky inequality from the game. For instance, they are charged with preventing fans of the home team from inappropriately disrupting the play of the opposing team. They call fouls, which are defined in terms of gaining an unfair advantage over an opponent by means of bodily contact. They are expected to stop play if the court is visibly wet or strewn with debris. They must also ensure that the ball is round and symmetrical, that the hoops are tight and stand at regulation height, that a shot clock is equally visible from both ends of the court, and so forth. (In one sense, then, the referees are supposed to play the role of God in terms of ensuring that a contest is as fair as possible and practical.) And just to make sure that any differences between courts and hoops do not favor one team over the other for the whole game, at halftime the teams exchange goals and sides of the court.

When these sources of luck are eliminated, we tend to think that a game situation is fair (in one sense of that word), even if the teams aren't evenly matched. We don't generally think that what philosopher Bernard Williams calls "constitutive luck"—the lucky breaks that allow one team or individual to be more talented than another—necessarily makes a contest unfair.[6] Dennett puts the matter this way: "In sports we accept luck, and are content to plan and strive while making due allowance for luck— which is, after all, the same for everyone; no one actually has more luck than anyone else, even though some have been lucky enough to start off with more talent. But that is fair too, we think. We don't suppose that the only fair contest is between perfectly matched opponents; the strength of one may defeat the finesse of the other, or vice versa."[7] So fairness doesn't require literal equality, which is impossible to achieve anyway, but requires instead that certain sources of luck are eliminated from the game. In this way, we think that the outcome of the game will depend upon skill, strategy, and hard work, and this will be fair.

But things don't always work out that way. Even though basketball is designed to eliminate luck in certain ways, as noted above, there are still lucky shots, lucky bounces, bad calls, lucky tournament draws, fortunate draft choices, and lots of other sources of luck in the game. These things are often called "the breaks of the game." To turn now to the second conception of fairness, in terms of desert, we might wonder whether the breaks of the game can result in an unfair outcome, in the sense that the winning team doesn't deserve to win (or the losing team doesn't deserve to lose, or both). If the breaks of the game can result in unfairness, then do they always do so? If not, what's the difference? Let's consider some famous cases of luck in basketball in order to answer this question.

Three years before winning game 5 of the 2005 NBA finals on a last-second three-point shot as a San Antonio Spur, Robert Horry did something very similar as a Los Angeles Laker in game 4 of the 2002 Western Conference finals, beating the Sacramento Kings at the buzzer. (Had Sacramento won this pivotal game, they would have led the series three games to one, and probably would have won the series; as it happened, though, they lost the series in seven games.) There was some luck involved in Horry's game-winning shot against the Kings.

On this final play of the game, leading by two points, the Kings had already successfully defended a shot in the lane from Kobe Bryant and a follow-up attempt by Shaquille O'Neal. Hoping to put the game away for good, Sacramento's Vlade Divac batted the ball away from the basket as time began to expire. Much to Divac's dismay, the ball went right to Horry, who was standing behind the three-point line. "Big Shot Bob" (as his current San Antonio teammates call him) promptly drained the three-pointer to win the game for Los Angeles at the buzzer.

In postgame commentary, the players involved tried to isolate the lucky element in this play. Sacramento's Hedo Turkoglu said, "It's the luckiest thing I've ever seen in my life." Divac agreed. "It was just a lucky shot, that's all," he said. "You don't need to have skill in that kind of situation. You just throw it. If it goes in, it goes in." By contrast, Sacramento's Chris Webber was more cautious: "I'm not saying the Lakers lucked up and won the game. I said it was a lucky play and that was a lucky play. Coach didn't draw that up. That wasn't a second or third option. That was a lucky play, a fumble out of the inside to the outside. Now Horry shooting it wasn't lucky. That's a big shot. I have to give him credit. That's a big-time player but that was a lucky player."[8]

So Webber distinguishes between a lucky play, which this was, and a lucky shot, which this wasn't. In response to Divac's suggestion that Horry's shot was lucky, Horry himself said: "If you go back and look at the shot, a luck shot is one of those guys who has no form. If you look at the shot, it was straight form. He shouldn't have tipped it out there. It wasn't a luck shot. I have been doing that for all my career. He should know." In other words, Horry claims that his shot manifests skill, not luck. And this seems clearly right. But Webber also seems clearly right in saying that it was a lucky play, because the way that the ball ended up in Horry's hands was completely unforeseen and unintended.

That the Lakers won the game on a lucky play does not by itself imply that the game was unfair, or that Los Angeles didn't deserve to win. Sacramento had its chances, as people say, leading the game 50 to 26 at one point in the first half (and still leading by five points with only 1:17 left in the game). So even though luck was involved in the outcome of this game, we shouldn't say that the result was unfair.

Something similar happened in college hoops several years earlier. On April 4, 1983, sixth-seeded North Carolina State beat a heavily favored, top-ranked University of Houston Cougar team to become the first team in history to win the NCAA tournament after suffering ten or more losses during the regular season. NC State benefited from a bit of good luck in beating Houston (otherwise known as "Phi Slamma Jamma" because of its fast-paced, high-flying style, which featured future NBA Hall of Famers Clyde Drexler and Hakeem Olajuwan). With the score tied, NC State spent the final forty-four seconds of the game trying to set up a high-percentage shot (there was no shot clock then) but couldn't do so. As time finally expired, Dereck Whittenburg launched an off-balance, desperation shot from thirty feet away, missing the hoop entirely. But his teammate Lorenzo Charles caught the ball in the air and dunked it home as time expired, giving the Wolfpack the improbable victory.

Where exactly does luck enter into the NC State win? Whittenburg's shot missed badly, but it could have missed in lots of other ways. For example, his shot might have missed on the far side of the hoop rather than on the near side, or it might have bounced off the back of the rim and into the air, or it might have glanced off the rim and bounced on the floor. Had any one of these things happened, Charles would have had no play on the ball before time expired. Of course, it wasn't luck that Charles was in a position to make a play on the ball: he was playing the game properly, waiting for a rebound. But it was lucky that the air ball came right to him as time expired.

Since there was luck involved in the NC State victory, should we say that it was unfair, that NC State didn't deserve to win? I don't think so. First of all, the game was tied at this point, so we can't say that Houston would have won if the lucky play hadn't occurred. (We can't say that NC State would have won, either; I think we just don't know what would have happened in overtime.) Also, NC State had played a masterful game under coach Jim Valvano in order to be in a position to win. In fact, they fought their way back from a 42–35 deficit late in the second half. So even though there was luck involved in the outcome of this game, once again we are not inclined to say that NC State didn't deserve to win.

Consider a third case that is slightly more problematic. Roughly a year after Michael Jordan's (first) retirement, the Chicago Bulls faced the New York Knicks in the Eastern Conference finals. In game 5, with only a few seconds on the clock and the Bulls leading the Knicks by two points in Madison Square Garden, New York's Hubert Davis attempted a three-point shot to win the game. Scottie Pippen challenged Davis's shot and was called for a foul, although replays showed that Pippen's defense produced no unfair advantage over Davis. Davis made all three free throw attempts, and the Knicks went on to win the series in seven games.

In this case, the Bulls seemed to suffer from a case of bad luck in the form of a bad call. Had the foul not been called on Pippen, it seems clear that the Bulls would have won the game. Should we say that the outcome of the game was unfair because it was determined by an unlucky break? Did the Bulls deserve to win this game? Were they robbed?

Things are not as clear here as they were in the previous examples. Even if the Bulls would have won had no foul been called on Pippen, can we really say that this one unlucky call determined the outcome of the game? We have to remember that there are always lots of other lucky breaks that occur throughout a game, each of which contributes to the outcome. This final piece of luck was only one of many events that shaped the final outcome.

We also need to remember that although referees introduce an element of luck (in the form of bad calls), they are an essential part of the game. First of all, they are necessary to see that the rules are followed, to ensure fairness in the sense of equal opportunity, as discussed above. For example, as we've seen, the concept of a foul is defined in terms of bodily contact that results in gaining an unfair advantage over one's opponent. But not every instance of bodily contact results in gaining an unfair advantage, so calling fouls correctly requires having a clear sense of how the game works and what is fair contact. It also requires a lot of judgment, because as former Knicks great Bill Bradley notes, basketball is "a game of subtle felonies," and calling literally every foul that is committed would make the game take forever.[9] For these reasons, it would be impossible for a computer to take the place of a human referee.

But if human referees are necessary, they are also fallible, which introduces an element of luck to the game. Humans make mistakes. Sometimes they "see" what isn't there (maybe like the so-called phantom foul called on Scottie Pippen mentioned above). There are ways of minimizing the impact of human error, such as having more than one official to corroborate calls and consulting instant replays in certain situations, but there is no way to eliminate completely the element of luck introduced by human referees. There can be only a few referees, for instance, because their observations need to be coordinated into a quick decision to keep the game moving. Consulting instant replays throughout the game would bog things down considerably, since replays require additional human judgments. This was illustrated recently by the controversial call involving a dramatic last-second, rolling-around-the-rim three-point shot by Kentucky's Patrick Sparks that sent the game against Michigan State into overtime on March 27, 2005.[10] Michigan State eventually won the game in two overtimes, advancing to the Final Four, but it took the officials six minutes and twenty-five seconds to decide whether the replay showed that Sparks's foot was on or behind the three-point line. If instant replays were always consulted whenever an important call was made, basketball games would lose their flow and take too long to complete.

Since human referees are necessary, and they can only be judged on the basis of what information they have available to them at the moment a call is made, it's usually unfair to criticize referees. Observers of the game never see exactly what the referees see, since they are in different places (and so are the television cameras that provide instant replays). So it's generally unreasonable to criticize referees for making bad calls when we can't see exactly what they saw, even though fans routinely do this on the basis of instant replays. (The NFL's television feature "You Make the Call," in which fans are encouraged to second-guess officials on the basis of instant replays alone, surely encourages this unfortunate practice.) Luckily, professional referees are very good and rarely make mistakes given the information they possess.

Of course, there are cases where referees are biased or deliberately alter the course of a game in a direction that is unfair. The dispute over the extra time added onto the clock in the 1972 Olympic gold medal game between the United States and the USSR may be a case of this sort. When cheating occurs and determines the outcome of a game, then of course the result is unfair, whether the cheating is perpetrated by players, coaches, fans, or referees. But the lucky breaks of the game do not by themselves make the outcome of a game unfair, even if they involve bad calls made by officials, since officials are a necessary part of the game.

To return to the case of Scottie Pippen and Hubert Davis, it's hard to blame the referee who called the foul on Pippen in that situation, because it looked like a foul from his perspective, and allowing Pippen to unfairly hinder Davis in his three-point shot attempt would have given the Bulls an unfair advantage at this crucial moment in the game. So I think we should conclude that even if Pippen did not foul Davis, the result of the game was not unfair, because playing the game at all requires that a certain system of referees and officiating be in place. That system is never foolproof, so everyone must accept the lucky and unlucky breaks of the game that it generates.

The same analysis should be applied to the Bulls' victory over the Utah Jazz in the final game of the 1998 NBA finals, when Michael Jordan made a game- and championship-winning jump shot with 5.2 seconds left (and then retired from basketball for the second time, again temporarily, as it turned out). To free up space to shoot, Jordan drove the ball to his right, then pushed his defender (Byron Russell) in that direction, sending him sliding on the floor. This left Jordan with an open shot, which he made easily, freezing at the end of his follow-through for a few moments (as if to provide the perfect photo opportunity, of which many people took advantage).

Should Jordan have been called for an offensive foul in this situation? Applying the analysis developed above, it's hard to criticize the officials in light of the instant replays. From their point of view, and from the point of view of the instant replay, it is very hard to tell what difference Jordan's push made to Russell's defense. Did Jordan gain an unfair advantage through this contact? (Probably.) Would Jordan have had enough space to make the shot even if he had not pushed Russell? (We will never know.) The important thing is that there was in place a system of referees trying to enforce the rules, doing their best to make an instant judgment call on the basis of the information available to them. This is the best that we can do in basketball, the fairest situation that we fallible human beings can create. Even if the instant replays showed that Jordan did commit an offensive foul, we have to remember that similar judgment calls occur throughout the whole game. (Another interesting "no call," just a minute before Jordan's game-winning shot, involved Jordan's stripping the ball from Karl Malone under the Jazz basket, at the other end of the court, using a slapping technique for which Malone would become well known before the end of his NBA career.) Knowing that this is the best we can do and that the lucky breaks of the game even out over the long run, players, coaches, and fans alike should accept this kind of thing as an essential part of the game instead of complaining that the outcome is unfair.

At least that's how it looks to me, from my angle. You may come to a different view, based upon the information available to you. That's the way it goes, in life and in basketball.[11]

Notes

1. Daniel Dennett, *Elbow Room* (Cambridge, MA: MIT Press, 1984), 94. As Thomas Jefferson once said, "I'm a great believer in luck, and I find the harder I work, the more I have of it." Quoted in Pat Riley, *The Winner Within* (New York: Berkley, 1994), 159.

2. Dennett, *Elbow Room,* 95.

3. For example, see Linda Zagzebski, "Religious Luck," *Faith and Philosophy* 11, no. 3 (July 1994): 397–413.

4. The classical discussions of this idea, in recent philosophy, are Thomas Nagel, "Moral Luck," *Proceedings of the Aristotelian Society* 50 (supp. vol., 1976): 137–51; reprinted in *Mortal Questions* (Cambridge: Cambridge University Press, 1979), 24–38; and Bernard Williams, *Moral Luck* (Cambridge: Cambridge University Press, 1981). A helpful collection of excerpts from these works, together with responses to them, is *Moral Luck,* ed. Daniel Staman (New York: State University of New York Press, 1993).

5. For more on this question, see my discussion in Scott A. Davison, "Salvific Luck," *International Journal for Philosophy of Religion* 45, no. 2 (April 1999): 129–37.

6. Williams, *Moral Luck,* 20.

7. Dennett, *Elbow Room,* 96.

8. For a summary of postgame comments, see http://www.usatoday.com/sports/nba/02playoffs/games/2002–05–26-lakers-kings.htm.

9. Bill Bradley, *Values of the Game* (New York: Hyperion, 1998), 148.

10. For more on this episode, see Daniel Gallagher's chapter in this volume.

11. I wish to thank Gregory Bassham, Thomas Flint, William Cole, Layne Neeper, Timothy Simpson, Phil Krummrich, Kyle Macy, Bill Irwin, Wayne Breeden, and Randy Ross for helpful comments on earlier drafts of this chapter.

Peg Brand and Myles Brand

THE BEAUTY OF THE GAME

"IT'S BEAUTIFUL, BABY!" yelled Dickie V, as the unheralded junior dunked over his opponent, drawing a foul and tying the score with six seconds remaining in the championship game. "And one!"

"It wasn't beautiful," Billy said, struggling to be heard above the cheers of the crowd. "It wasn't pretty at all, but it got the job done, and that's all that counts."

The shooter bounced the ball, slowly and repeatedly, trying hard to loosen his limbs and lessen the stress that had fallen upon his shoulders. It was a hard foul.

"He's not the best free throw shooter on the team," Billy said, with considerable understatement. Forty-five thousand fans shifted in their seats.

The shooter knew what they were thinking, and *he* wanted to be responsible for the first and only loss of their opponent's perfect season. Feeling all eyes upon him, he prepared to shoot.

"Focus," he thought, as the crowd hushed and he raised his arms. Game sweat glistened on his muscles, deepening the colors of a tattoo acquired together with his teammates, celebrating their win in last year's Sweet Sixteen.

Swoosh.

"NBN, baby! Nothing but nylon!" Dickie yelled.

"It's not over yet," Billy grumbled, adding in a greatly lowered voice, "And just what did you mean when you said his dunk was beautiful? It was accurate, sure. But *beautiful?* Did we actually see the same shot?"

For several seconds, there was silence. Believe it or not, Dickie failed to respond. On-air time was ticking away. The television producer muttered to himself, "Talk, guys, talk!" He began to regret that Dickie had been hired as a guest commentator this year. The chemistry was all wrong.

"What do you mean what did I mean? I meant the shot was beautiful," Dickie finally said. "The player is beautiful. It's a beautiful game, baby. I oughta know! I've been doing this game since you were learning to dribble. . . . Hey, thirty-second timeout. What do you think the strategy will be, Billy?"

"Well, Dick, I don't think they're planning any *beautiful* shots, if that's what you're asking. Having studied the philosophy of art, particularly the birth of modern aesthetics in the eighteenth century, I'm not so sure I'm willing to take the judgment of an 'expert' about what counts as beautiful. Why not just admit it was a successful shot, satisfactorily executed, and leave it at that?"

The producer wished they had gone to a commercial. "What are you doing?!" he screamed into their earpieces. "Talk about the game, guys. Jim, cut in. Quick!"

"Billy," Jim interjected, "they say beauty is in the eye of the beholder. Who's to say that Dick's not right in his subjective response to what he saw on the court? He's a man of taste; surely he knows that the pleasure he feels in watching such a shot merits the highest praise. On the other hand, I can also understand your point; it was an awkward, off-balance shot—anything but beautiful. And I'll bet if we polled our television audience, nearly everyone would agree."

Panic was quickly setting in behind the camera as the opposing team prepared to inbound the ball. They needed a bucket to win, a free throw to send the game into overtime. The crowd cheered wildly; the roar was deafening.

The announcers, however, were so intent on their discussion of beauty that they missed the final play. With additional seconds of dead air and the producer at his wits' end, the instant replay appeared onscreen faster than lightning, prompting immediate comments about the missed shot and the fact that the game was over. Exhausted but animated, they agreed, in the end, that it had been a beautiful game. But now Jim wanted to know: What did they mean by that?

Hume Drives the Lane

Those in charge took a long commercial break—time to momentarily regroup—hoping that the postgame analysis would return to a focus on strategy, teamwork, and all the factors that led up to this unexpected result, this surprise ending. With a perfect record shattered, the year's dream team fell short.

Back on air, Jim was the first to speak. "Billy, Dick, let's talk about what we've just seen: a team nearly perfect in its execution, players toned to the highest levels of strength and stamina, a team—ranked number one all season—fails to complete its mission in the final seconds when the most intense pressure is on. How exactly was this a *beautiful* game?"

The camera crew gasped and looked at the producer. His jaw trembled; his lips moved, but no sounds could be heard. The crowd noise intensified as crews behind the scenes frantically started editing the footage that would be shown with the presentation of the national trophy. There was quite a bit of time to fill: fifteen minutes at least.

Dickie didn't miss a beat. "Hey, I'm an expert, baby. You're not the only one who studied those philosophers in England and Scotland intent on describing the typical aesthetic experience when a viewer looks upon beauty. I know what David Hume said in his famous 1757 essay, "Of the Standard of Taste." He was perfectly clear and unyielding about the subjectivity of a person's judgment of beauty, and his thesis is as true now as it was 250 years ago. As Hume said, 'Beauty is no quality in things themselves: It exists merely in the mind which contemplates them; and each mind perceives a different beauty.'[1] And that's how I know when a shot is beautiful and when to call a game beautiful!"

Jim unexpectedly jumped back into the conversation. "I can see Dick's point about knowing the game," he said slowly. "He does have long experience and what Hume would call a certain 'delicacy of taste' when it comes to seeing things an ordinary fan might miss, recognizing good moves, and making judgments about the artistry of the game.[2] Hume might as well have been speaking about our own Dickie V when he said, 'But though there be naturally a wide difference in point of delicacy between one person and another, nothing tends further to increase and improve this talent, than *practice* in a particular art, and the frequent survey or contemplation of a particular species of beauty.'[3] Few know basketball as well as our friend Dickie V."

"What makes *your* subjective experience the measure of all things beautiful?" shouted Billy, now wildly waving his arms. "This arena is filled with knowledgeable and devoted fans. There's no way to distinguish one expert from another, and shouting louder doesn't count. To say that an expert is the one who makes the right judgment call is circular, since your friend Hume also says that the right judgment is the one made by the expert.

"Look, Dick," Billy said, "an expert is someone who makes the right judgments about beauty. It is he—or she—who pronounces, who ordains that something is beautiful, whether it's a painting or a basketball game. But how do you define who counts as an expert? In the end, no matter what we say about refined taste or past experience, it comes down to making the right judgments. And that is circular! It doesn't help us at all in understanding the nature of beauty and which things are beautiful."

Dickie was stunned. His claim to expertise tottered on the shaky ground of circular reasoning.

Plato Goes Zone

Gaining momentum, Billy leapfrogged past Dickie's historical reference to travel back thousands of years to ancient Greece, the fountainhead of Western philosophy. "I know how to tell when something is beautiful," he said with growing animation, "and it doesn't rest on anyone's subjective judgment. There is an ideal of beauty—the Form Beauty—by which things and events in the world inherit their beauty and by which they are to be judged, and that dunk shot simply doesn't measure up to the ideal. The ideal is independent of any person, even purported experts. Beauty is objective. It doesn't depend on circumstances or context. As Plato (428–347 B.C.) wrote in the *Symposium:* 'This beauty is first of all eternal; it neither comes into being nor passes away, neither waxes nor wanes; next, it is not beautiful in part and ugly in part, nor beautiful at one time and ugly at another, nor beautiful in this relation and ugly in that, nor beautiful here and ugly there, as varying according to its beholders. . . . [The beholder] will see it as absolute, existing alone with itself, unique, eternal, and all other beautiful things as partaking of it.'[4] Saying something is beautiful, no matter the emphasis and no matter *who* says it is beautiful, carries no weight. Beauty isn't in the eye of the beholder! Beauty depends on copying, imitating, the ideal Beauty. Period!"

The producer feared that the viewing audience had long since switched channels or had left the room and were staring vacantly into an open refrigerator. Jim, looking more like Rodin's famous sculpture, *The Thinker*, than a postgame analyst, thoughtfully stroked his chin. He spoke up: "Billy is invoking a clear ideal of a particular kind of shot, Plato's famous theory of imitation, in which a good player strives to imitate, or copy, the ideal Form Beauty in his own play. Not satisfied with a merely adequate shot that lacks beauty, the skilled athlete tries—through inspiration and craftsmanship—to 'keep looking back and forth, to Justice, Beauty, . . . and all such things as by nature exist,' as Plato explains in the *Republic*—just as the best artists did in creating marble sculptures of powerful, dignified men."[5]

"Yes," said Billy, "the ancient Greeks gave us statues of exceptionally muscular, fit, and toned athletes; they wanted to imitate the athletes who imitated the Form and excellence of Beauty: men who embodied strength, courage, stamina, skill, and self-confidence."

"What are you talking about?" Dickie gruffly interrupted. "There's no such 'thing' as the ideal dunk shot. There are only the dunk shots we've seen and experienced over the years; there are only the games we've viewed and judged to be beautiful, all of which are based on a notion of beauty that resides in the eye of the beholder. It's a mistake to presume that there are ideals or Forms out there, somewhere in Plato's heaven, eternal and unchanging, that influence the way an athlete looks, the way his body is physically sculpted, the way he plays, and the level of skill he strives to perfect and implement. You're hypothesizing things—freestanding ideals—that just don't exist. Billy, I thought you were more sensible than that!"

The producer could feel a migraine coming on. "Guys, would someone *please* talk about the game? What's wrong with you? Get off this philosophy crap! Jim, help! Hurry up with the trophy presentation!" he said to no one in particular. "Come on!"

Jim looked at Billy and Dick, or rather past them. Deep in thought, he was considering his colleagues' contrasting views. Secure in his position—and his ironclad contract—he continued the discussion.

"We recognize that not only actual events, such as the game we just saw, are beautiful, but also works of art, such as paintings and sculpture, are beautiful. According to Plato, there is a tiered system of imitation, in which objects or events in the world imitate or resemble the Forms and inherit their characteristics from them. The game inherits its beauty from the Form Beauty by imitating it. Artists copy actual events or things, and their paintings and sculpture inherit the characteristics of those actual things they copy. So, for instance, a painting of a dunk would be beautiful if it copied the beauty of the actual shot.

"However, despite the attractiveness of this explanation, there are deep problems. In addition to Dick's point that there is no direct evidence that Forms exist independently of persons and their opinions, it's hard to see how these abstract ideals relate to actual things in the world.

"Look, guys, there's a dilemma here. Consider the ideal athlete, Plato's Form Athlete. Either this Form is itself an athlete or it's not. On the one hand, if the Form is an athlete, like the particular athletes we saw compete this evening, then there must be another Form, a third thing over and above the ideal athlete and the particular athletes, that makes them both athletes, from which they each inherit their natures of being athletes. Using the same reasoning, there is not only a third athlete, but a fourth one, and so on to infinity. But then we can never know what an athlete is, since to do so would involve knowing an infinite number of Forms, and no person can know an infinite number of things.[6]

"Suppose, on the other hand, that the Form Athlete is not itself an athlete, but an abstract ideal that doesn't exist in time and space. Then the problem is that the relationship between these abstract ideals and things in the world is mysterious. What sense could it make to say that an actual athlete, a person, 'copies,' 'resembles,' or 'imitates' the ideal? One is flesh and blood, and the other is an abstract, immaterial essence. The Form Athlete, then, has no apparent relationship to actual athletes and gives us no knowledge about them.

"So, Billy, even if the ideal Form Athlete exists, it can't help us at all in knowing what true athleticism is or in picking out excellent athletes.

The same goes for beauty. The Form Beauty provides no standard of what beauty is or what things are beautiful—dunks included."

Another awkward silence ensued. Billy, having been skewered on the horns of a dilemma, leaned back in his chair and looked pensively at the scoreboard. The only on-air sound was that of the producer exhaling.

Moments later, things finally looked like they were returning to normal. The winning team slowly mounted the hastily set-up platform at midcourt for the trophy presentation. Jim stood up and was gathering his notes when an urgent voice sounded in his earpiece: "Jim, hold the presentation! New York just called. The top brass! They say we can't leave it like this. Stop the confetti! Resolve the beauty argument! Now!"

Teamwork Wins, Once Again

Fortunately, Jim had thought through these issues before. In his long broadcasting career, he had seen chip shots head toward the hole as if they were drawn by magnets, tennis shots that buzzed like angry hornets as they kicked up chalk, three-pointers that arched high into the rafters and hit nothing but net—and philosophical arguments that were marvels of cogency and lucidity. And Jim knew beauty.

He interrupted Dickie and Billy, who had begun arguing again. "Of course, you're each partly right. Beauty isn't something merely subjective, but neither is it purely objective, based on some idealized, independent standard. Beautiful things in the world share some objective features and some subjective ones; or as I prefer to put it, they have both outer and inner beauty.

"The outer beauty is what is universally observable and follows a pattern of excellence for the type of object or event that it is. Take basketball. There is some similarity between music, dance, and athletics. Improvised jazz, like improvised but practiced dance, is similar to basketball. In them, beauty is to be found in the sequencing of the movements (or sounds), in the transitions between parts of the sequences, and especially in the interaction between participants. Just as a jazz musician must anticipate what others with whom he is playing will do and alternately lead and support them, so too must the basketball player anticipate where others will be on the court and either pass, dribble, or take the shot himself. The whole is beautiful when it works together seemingly effortlessly.

The beauty is on display for all to see and doesn't need an expert to translate it for us. This is beauty in the world.

"This is the beauty the fan sees and appreciates. It's satisfying to watch basketball when it's played beautifully. Like all improvised art, it flows in a way that anticipates what comes next and surprises at the same time. In large part, this objective, 'outer' beauty explains why the college game is so popular, and getting more so.

"But there is more to it than that. In addition to the motion, the fluidity, the coordination of individuals and teams, there's the strategy that makes it all work. This 'inner' beauty depends on what's going on in the players' heads, not just their bodies. The coaches devise the strategies that are internalized by the players during repetitious practice, and the players apply these strategies to rapidly changing events on the floor. Basketball, when played well, is a head game. It takes cognitive ability—smarts—to create a beautiful play and certainly a beautiful game. It's more than just what one sees on the surface; there is an inner beauty, a level of acumen and insight, to the game. It's what Plato called 'true excellence.'[7] This aspect requires expertise and experience to explain the strategies. Those who lack this expertise, or don't have an expert to explain it to them, miss much of the beauty of the game.

"Those who play know when they are in a beautiful game. The strategy unfolds, almost in slow motion. Teammates are where they are supposed to be, cuts are sharp, picks are set just at the right moment, and the ball arrives perfectly on time. For the knowledgeable basketball fan, there is a joy that is almost inexplicable in knowing the patterns in advance."

"Do you mean by 'inner beauty' the intelligence and excellence of execution that it takes for a player to be successful on the court?" Billy asked. "It's all coming back to me now. I recall Plato writing about the purpose of arts like music, poetry, and theater and their role in teaching people, especially the young, how to learn to recognize, love, imitate, and partake in beauty. Speaking of those artisans and craftsmen whose societal role was to create and promote the arts in his ideal republic, Plato wrote, 'We must seek out such craftsmen as have the talent to pursue the beautiful and the graceful in their work, in order that our young men shall be benefited from all sides like those who live in a healthy place, whence something from these beautiful works will strike their eyes and ears like a breeze that brings health from salubrious places, and lead them unawares from childhood to love of, resemblance to, and harmony with, the beauty of reason.'"[8]

"Excellent memory, Billy!" Jim exclaimed. "Yes, I like to think of the beauty of reason as an internal or inner beauty.

"Outer beauty and inner beauty," Jim continued. "There must be both. Physical movement by exceptional athletes for all to see, plus players acting with purpose, reason, and in concert with each other. These are the objective and subjective sides to beauty. Together, that's what made this a beautiful game!"

Beauty Rewarded

A voice spoke in Jim's earpiece: "New York says great job, Jim! Start the presentation!"

A dozen modern-day exemplars of Greek gods now began to file onto the platform: tall, well-proportioned young men donning championship caps and T-shirts, in the prime of their lives, physically and mentally. They had played the game of their lives. Unparalleled. Unprecedented. And unwilling to let the moment pass without looking into the camera and saying, "Hi, Mom!"

As the opening chords of "One Shining Moment" filled the arena, highlights of the winning team's season were shown. Magical moments from the Sweet Sixteen, the Elite Eight, the Final Four, and the title game flashed on the screen. Players were popping their game shirts and falling to the floor with joy. All the excitement, color, drama, and emotion of "March Madness" were relived, and the dark wooden trophy was handed to the winning coach, who hoisted it high in the air.

The announcers dabbed their eyes as the credits started to roll. Dickie and Billy thanked Jim, congratulated the winning team, each other, their viewers, their colleagues from the network, and, of course, their affiliates. They ended by thanking the student athletes, praising their skills and admiring their stamina, particularly their strength and grace under pressure. And finally, they agreed, "It *was* a beautiful game." And now they knew why. "There was both outer and inner beauty," Billy and Dickie said almost in unison.

As the music swelled and the singing began, Jim offered the last word.

"I consider 'One Shining Moment' to be the anthem to our coverage of this NCAA tournament."[9]

> In one shining moment, it's all on the line
> One shining moment, there frozen in time . . .
> [that] one shining moment, you reached for the sky
> One shining moment you knew.

Notes

Any similarity between the characters in this essay and real people is, of course, purely coincidental. Thanks to songwriter David Barrett for permission to reprint the lyrics to "One Shining Moment."

1. David Hume, "Of the Standard of Taste," in *Aesthetics: A Critical Anthology,* ed. George Dickie and Richard J. Sclafani (New York: Bedford / St. Martin's, 1989), 244.

2. Hume, "Of the Standard of Taste," 246.

3. Hume, "Of the Standard of Taste," 247.

4. Plato, *Symposium,* 210e2–211b5, in *Plato: The Collected Dialogues,* ed. Edith Hamilton and Huntington Cairns, trans. Michael Joyce (Princeton, NJ: Princeton University Press, 1961).

5. Plato, *Republic,* 501b1–4, trans. G. M. A. Grube (Indianapolis: Hackett, 1974).

6. Jim seems to have read Aristotle's *Sophistical Refutations,* 178b. Plato himself recognized the problem. See his dialogue *Parmenides,* 132a. Aristotle, *On Sophistical Refutations, The Basic Works of Aristotle,* ed. Richard McKeon (New York: Random House, 1941). Plato, *Parmenides,* in *Plato: The Collected Dialogues,* ed. Edith Hamilton and Huntington Cairns, trans. F. M. Cornford (Princeton, NJ: Princeton University Press, 1961).

7. Plato, *Symposium,* 212a3–5.

8. Plato, *Republic,* 401c4–d3.

9. Jim Nantz, CBS sports analyst, http://www.oneshiningmoment.com/lyrics/index.html.

SECOND QUARTER

Prime-time Players, Coaches, and Sages

Fritz Allhoff and Anand J. Vaidya

THE ZEN MASTER AND THE BIG ARISTOTLE

Cultivating a Philosopher in the Low Post

Philosophy, Bullshit, and Basketball

IT IS OFTEN HARD to see how esoteric philosophical speculations have anything to do with everyday practical concerns. The dense abstractions of Aristotle and the cryptic and poetical musings of Lao-tzu can easily seem irrelevant to our supercharged world of deadlines, day care, and cell phones. However, this conception of the relation between philosophy and everyday life is deeply mistaken, as the following analogy bears out.

As we write, philosopher Harry Frankfurt's book *On Bullshit* (2005) is a New York Times Bestseller. Although Frankfurt's book is a first-rate work of (semi-)serious philosophical analysis, many people probably buy the book only because they get a kick out of the title. Lots of people, in fact, think that that's exactly what philosophy is: bullshit.

Philosophers are happy to accept the unintended compliment. It's true that bullshit in itself is unattractive and useless—in fact, worse than useless if you step in it. But as third-world subsistence farmers know, cow dung fertilizes plants and can be used as fuel. Philosophy is much the same. Although it may initially seem useless and unappealing, philosophy promotes wisdom in our lives, nurtures the growth of the human spirit, and fuels our imaginations. Through engagement with the great thinkers of the past, philosophy opens our minds, disciplines our thinking, helps us overcome obstacles, fortifies us against adversity, and expands our sense of what is possible. Even philosophy that seems hopelessly abstract or esoteric may have surprising applications in other disciplines, as shown, for example, by advances in physics, mathematics, psychology, and linguistics by philosophers such as Aristotle, Descartes, Locke, Kant, Wittgenstein, and Russell. In addition, philosophy has led to extremely practical applications in fields such as computer technology, artificial intelligence, and democratic theory, not to mention Monty's Python's immortal "Philosopher's Drinking Song."

On the face of it, philosophy would seem to have little relevance to basketball. Unlike baseball, basketball isn't usually perceived as a "thinking person's game." Basketball is a relatively simple game with simple rules and a simple objective that stresses proper execution of a small number of basic skills (dribbling, shooting, passing, guarding, and rebounding). A fifth-grader can understand the fundamentals of good basketball. So what could tweedy philosophy professors possibly add that wouldn't be simply "bullshit"?

Well, as Kant and Dennis Rodman liked to say, appearances can be deceiving. Los Angeles Lakers coach Phil Jackson, often called the "Zen Master," actively uses philosophy to improve players' performance and to motivate and inspire his players and fellow coaches, both on and off the court. In fact, Jackson has so integrated philosophy into his coaching and his personal life that it's difficult to distinguish his role as a basketball coach from his role as a philosophical guide and mentor to his players. In this chapter we examine how philosophy has helped Jackson become a great coach and one of Jackson's star pupils, Shaquille O'Neal, become an MVP-caliber player.

Now and *Zazen*

Although Jackson was raised as a Pentecostal in a very religious family, the philosophical insights he brings to basketball mostly come from outside the religious tradition in which he was brought up. Among the philosophers Jackson has been most strongly influenced by are Aristotle, William James, Jiddu Krishnamurti, Pir Vilyat Khan, various Native American thinkers, and Carlos Castaneda. But the philosophical outlook that has most shaped his coaching style and personal life is Zen Buddhism. One work of particular importance is *Zen Mind, Beginner's Mind,* by the late Japanese Roshi, Shunryu Suzuki. Jackson has recommended this book to several of his players over the years.

Zen philosophy originates from the teachings of the Buddha (566 -
486 BCE), which are centered on the problem of human suffering. One
of the most basic truths of human existence, Buddha taught, was that
humans find themselves in a world of pervasive suffering. At a physical
level, humans can suffer because of physical injuries or unsatisfied bodily
desires, such as hunger, thirst, and desire for sexual pleasure. Socially,
humans suffer from the problems caused by social desires related to the
ego, such as status and attachment to material objects. Buddhism focuses
on how to eliminate the suffering that is due to frustrated desires. Zen is
a Japanese variant of the meditation branch of Buddhist philosophy, constructed out of a mix of Indian Buddhism and Chinese Taoism. One central element of Zen is the idea that religious dogmas and creeds are
irrelevant to learning the eternal truths of reality. Rather, one must di-
rectly experience these truths. The deepest truths of reality cannot be
grasped by the intellect or expressed in language. The best way to encounter these truths is not by relying on texts or rational thought, but by
practicing meditation under the guidance of an acknowledged Zen master, or *sensei*. In fact, words and concepts are more or less obstacles to
understanding the deepest truths of reality, including the ultimate truth
that reality is one.

One practice that Jackson often shares with his players is a type of
Zen meditation known as "zazen." In the form of zazen Jackson practices, a person sits completely still on a cushion with his eyes open and
focuses on his breath. The goal of this exercise is to achieve "mindful-
ness"—complete awareness of the present moment—by concentration on
one's breath and posture. By practice, one learns not only to relax, but
more importantly, to live in the present, empty the mind of limiting self-
centered thoughts, and simply *be*.

How is *zazen* important for Jackson and his players? For starters, the
ability to have a clear mind and relaxed state during moments of increased pressure allows one to execute the task at hand with complete
concentration. Imagine how much easier it would be to make a clutch
free throw in the closing moments of a championship game if one could
only block out such thoughts as: *I have to make this shot; everything is
on the line; I will lose my contract and the championship if I don't make
this shot; I wish the fans would just shut up and stop waving those ri-*

diculous things. . . . And what the *!#*! are those things, anyway? Blocking out thoughts like these would allow you to focus on the task at hand: making the shot.

In basketball, as in many other sports, too much thinking can interfere with maximum performance. As Jackson remarks:

> Basketball happens at such a fast pace that your mind has a tendency to race at the same speed as your pounding heart. As the pressure builds, it's easy to start thinking too much. But if you're always trying to figure the game out, you won't be able to respond creatively to what's going on. Yogi Berra once said about baseball: "How can you think and hit at the same time?" The same is true with basketball, except everything's happening much faster. The key is seeing and doing. If you're focusing on anything other than reading the court and doing what needs to be done, the moment will pass you by.[1]

Zazen also helps Jackson and his players relate better with one another, the referees, and the media. The images of a coach screaming from the sidelines at a referee and a player getting into a brawl with an opponent are iconic in the minds of sports fans. Jackson believes that the regular practice of *zazen* helps him and his players gain control of a situation, calm angry or egotistic thoughts, and concentrate on the immediate task at hand.[2]

Another aspect of Jackson's Zen-inspired philosophy is a focus on selfless play. Players are taught to put team goals ahead of purely personal ambitions. Perhaps the best example of this is the episode in which Jackson told Michael Jordan—then coming off one of the best offensive seasons in NBA history—that he would have to take fewer shots the next season in order to bring out the best in his teammates. Jordan agreed and became a consummate team player. He went on to lead the Bulls to six NBA championships—and in the process became the richest and most famous athlete in the world. Still, it can be asked: Why is unselfish play important in an era when high-scoring superstars get all the big sneaker contracts and mostly only acts of flashy individual showmanship make the ESPN highlight tape?

Jackson believes that NBA defenses are so good that no team with only a single dominant player can consistently win championships, and that selfish play leads to resentment amongst players and lower team morale. To win championships consistently, as the Celtics, Lakers, and

Bulls have done in recent decades, each member of the team must feel valued in a way that facilitates focus on the common goal: winning the game. As Aristotle would put it, what's important is for each player to understand his or her proper role or function (*ergon*) on the team, and work unstintingly to fulfill that role. Not only does selfless teamwork win championships; it also makes the game more fun. As Jackson writes: "The beauty of [team-centered basketball] is that it allows players to experience another, more powerful form of motivation than ego-gratification. Most rookies arrive in the NBA thinking that what will make them happy is having unlimited freedom to strut their egos on national TV. But that approach is an inherently empty experience. What makes basketball so exhilarating is the joy of losing yourself completely in the dance, even if it's just for one beautiful transcendent moment."[3]

In the case of Michael Jordan, Jackson's request for more selfless play on his part was crucial to the Bulls' spectacular success. In particular, Jordan's adjustment from point-maker to play-maker empowered his teammates to take on certain roles that they had turned over to his stunning abilities. With Jordan focused solely on scoring, his teammates didn't develop their own skills and often complemented Jordan more as spectators than as contributors.

A second example of Jackson's philosophy of selfless play comes from the kind of offense he has employed for many years: the triangle (or triple-post) offense. The triangle offense was first developed by Tex Winter in the 1950s and not used by the Bulls until Jackson became head coach. Jackson adopted the offense, which can take years to perfect, because it makes every player a threat and facilitates selfless, team-centered play. As Jackson says, the offense looks like a five-man *Tai Chi* performance and demands that all players work in unison, as a group. The point of the offense is not to attack the defense head-on, but to get it off-balance and overextended through a carefully orchestrated series of moves. For the offense to work, players must surrender the "me" of personal glory for the "we" of coordinated free-flowing team movement.

Two principles of selfless play lie at the core of the triangle offense: (1) the offense must give the player with the ball an opportunity to pass the ball to any of his teammates; and (2) the offense must utilize the players' individual skills. The first principle holds that by opening up more opportunities to pass the ball one can increase the probability that the defense will become unbalanced, leading to a better shot for the offense. The second principle expresses the sensitivity of the system to the skills of the players on the court. Each player must see for himself how best to function in the triangle offense, and what skills to employ to find weaknesses in the defense and take advantage of them. The obligation is partly on the player to see how he can contribute best to the offense. In some cases, this may require being a play-maker rather than a point-maker.

Jackson's involvement with his players goes well beyond his role as a coach. He also takes a genuine interest in their personal lives and fosters their growth as individuals. For some coaches, involvement in a player's personal life is thrust upon them. For instance, if a player has a drug problem and gets caught, the coach must become involved in the player's personal affairs. Some coaches no doubt wish that their interactions with their players ended with games and practices. But for those like Jackson who have taken philosophy to heart, it is difficult to neatly separate one's role as coach from one's role as spiritual mentor and friend. Jackson's approach to basketball flows from philosophical underpinnings that are foundational to his own life. They force him to take the needs of his players as individuals on and off the court into perspective, recognizing that basketball is only an extension of their lives, not the whole of it.

Jackson's Star Pupil

Philosophy has strongly influenced Jackson's coaching and personal credo, and Jackson, in turn, has powerfully influenced many of his players. Michael Jordan's transformation from individual superstar to team player is one prime example; another is the effect Jackson had on superstar center Shaquille O'Neal. Before Jackson arrived in Los Angeles, the Lakers had long underachieved. Despite having two of the most potentially dominant players in the NBA, O'Neal and Kobe Bryant, they were swept in the 1998–99 Western Conference Semifinals by the San Antonio Spurs. After Jackson's arrival, they promptly won three titles in a row (Jackson's third three-peat of his career) and cemented their legacy as one of the great teams in NBA history. How was Jackson able to effect such a change and help his players realize their potential?

Jackson's success centered on O'Neal, one of the most dominant big men in NBA history. While Kobe Bryant's talents were essential to the

Lakers' championship runs, there is no doubt that O'Neal was the true catalyst for the team. By Shaq's own admission, Jackson played a major role in establishing O'Neal's dominance, and much of that occurred off the basketball court. As every basketball fan knows, O'Neal has never been very good at free throw shooting.[4] In fact, he is one of the worst in NBA history, rivaling Wilt Chamberlain in this regard. Over the course of his career, O'Neal averages 53.1 percent from the free throw line, but during the 2002–2003 championship season he averaged an astounding (for him) 62.2 percent.[5]

What does any of this have to do with Jackson? Again, we return to the role that philosophy plays in Jackson's approach to coaching and his interaction with his players. One year Jackson gave O'Neal a copy of Aristotle's *Nicomachean Ethics* as a Christmas present. In this classic text, Aristotle argues that sustained excellence is achieved through habit and repetition. For Aristotle, this is the central dictum of moral education and personal growth. O'Neal has cited the mantra of habituation to explain his improved free throw shooting: by continuously practicing proper habits, he was able to internalize those techniques and perform better, especially under pressure, when the maintenance of subtle mechanics is more difficult. Indeed, he even went on to dub himself "The Big Aristotle" because of the influence of Aristotle's teachings.

Admittedly, even those of us who are not sports psychologists won't find this advice particularly novel: practice excellence and you are more likely to achieve it. But paying lip service to the dictum and truly owning it are completely different, and O'Neal was able to own it; Jackson certainly deserves credit for educating his star pupil in the ways of the philosophers. (Kobe Bryant, by the way, once said, "I don't know why Phil keeps giving me those books; he knows I'm not going to read them." As if we needed more reasons to favor O'Neal over Bryant!)

Further, the relationship between Jackson and O'Neal has always been characterized by warmth and mutual respect. In his most recent book, *The Last Season,* Jackson defends Shaq against his many detractors and notes that for "all his bravado, Shaq is a very sensitive, fragile soul who appreciates any sign of tenderness."[6] The mentoring relationship between Jackson and O'Neal clearly helped Shaq become a better team player and contributed greatly to the Lakers' three consecutive championships.

Giving Back

Surely there is life beyond the basketball court, and this is another way in which Jackson's coaching may have influenced O'Neal. As we noted earlier, one of the chief tenets of Jackson's philosophy is that of putting the team over the self; this was evidenced in his request that Jordan be willing to score less in order to make his teammates better (and, of course, to win those six championships). Today, O'Neal is unquestionably one of the most generous and unselfish professional athletes. Whether this owes more to Jackson's influence or the big man's big heart, we can't be sure; most likely it's a combination of both. Three recent events attest to O'Neal's generous spirit.

First, after being traded to the Miami Heat, O'Neal returned to Los Angeles on Christmas Day 2004 to play his former teammates. While this was certainly a big game, and all eyes were on his dramatic reunion with Bryant, O'Neal spent the morning giving to charity. Not only did he purchase presents for disadvantaged youth with his own money, he donned his Shaq-a-Claus outfit and handed them out personally. Then he went on to beat Bryant and the Lakers.

Second, following the 2004–2005 season, O'Neal's contract was up for renewal with the Miami Heat. He had been scheduled to make $30.6 million during the 2005–2006 season, but renegotiated his contract to make $100 million over the next five years or, on average, $20 million a year. Why would O'Neal leave $10 million (at least) on the table? In his own words: "This contract allows me to address all of my family's long-term financial goals while allowing the Heat the ability to acquire those players that we need to win a championship."[7] O'Neal certainly could have had more money, but he sacrificed personal earnings to give his team the chance to acquire the players that would give them the best chance to get past the Detroit Pistons and the San Antonio Spurs for the championship in 2005–2006. This extra money has allowed the Heat to acquire Antoine Walker, Steve Smith, and Jason Williams in the off-season. To be sure, O'Neal won't be struggling for money, but $10 million per year is a large concession and one that shows his commitment to his team, his teammates, and to winning championships. Again, this sort of selfishness is exactly what Jackson tried to instill in Jordan on the basketball court, and we now see it reflected in O'Neal's contract negotiations as well.

As a final example, in the summer of 2005 O'Neal took an active role in disaster relief for the victims of Hurricane Katrina. Along with his wife, Shaunie, he has personally lobbied the residents of South Florida for contributions, whether monetary or material, for those displaced by the hurricane.[8] O'Neal also challenged Heat president Pat Riley to make a contribution to the relief program, and Riley came through by announcing that all proceeds of the preseason game against the San Antonio Spurs would be donated to Katrina relief programs.

Again, the extent to which Jackson deserves credit for O'Neal's bigheartedness is open to question, though it is noteworthy that one heard far fewer of these stories during O'Neal's pre-Jackson tenures in Orlando and Los Angeles. At a minimum, Jackson brought Aristotle into O'Neal's life, and there is a suspicious connection between Jackson's advocacy of selflessness and O'Neal's displays of it.

In this chapter, we've explored how philosophical ideas can be translated into real-world success through the example of Phil Jackson's coaching and the play and character of Shaquille O'Neal. One of our targets has been the skeptic who thinks that philosophy can't be of practical value. This critic stands refuted in light of how philosophy has contributed to the winning of nine NBA championships by Jackson and Jackson's positive influence on both Michael Jordan and Shaquille O'Neal. Now anytime somebody asks Jackson what you can do with a philosophy degree, all he has to do is point to his trophy case. Nine NBA championship rings ain't bullshit!

Notes

1. Phil Jackson with Hugh Delehanty, *Sacred Hoops: Spiritual Lessons of a Hardwood Warrior* (New York: Hyperion, 1995), 50–51.

2. Jackson also regularly encourages team discussions of ethics centered on the Ten Commandments. Jackson, 124.

3. Jackson, 91.

4. For O'Neal's own take on his poor free-throw shooting, see Shaquille O'Neal, *Shaq Talks Back* (New York: St. Martin's Press, 2001), 87–91.

5. http://www.nba.com/playerfile/shaquille_oneal/index.html, accessed September 12, 2005. Since the 2002–2003 season, Shaq's free throw percentage has dipped below .500 every year.

6. Phil Jackson, *The Last Season: A Team in Search of Its Soul* (New York: Penguin Press, 2004), 79.

7. *Contra Costa Times* (online): http://www.contracostatimes.com/mld/cctimes/ 12279972.htm?template=contentModules/printstory.jsp.

8. http://www.nba.com/heat/news/shaq_hurricane_050907.html.

David K. O'Connor

WILT VERSUS RUSSELL

Excellence on the Hardwood

IN THE 1960S, professional basketball posed a great philosophical puzzle. Who is the ideal basketball player, Wilt Chamberlain or Bill Russell? My friends and I got our first taste of philosophizing by defending our answers to this question.

The competing ideals were sharply drawn. Supporters of Wilt pointed to his greater ability to dominate a game by himself, especially on offense. They also pointed out that he carried a heavier responsibility for his team's success than Russell, since he was always the focus of the action. Russell had better teammates, who could contribute more on their own. Everyone recognized that Wilt was preternaturally strong and fast, especially for a man who stood just over seven feet tall. Wilt had more points and more rebounds, and in one year more assists, than anyone else. In his 142 matchups against Russell's teams, Wilt outscored Russell 28.7 to 23.7 and out-rebounded him 28.7 to 14.5. Seven times Wilt scored 50 or more points against Russell, including a high of 62 on January 14, 1962. In that 1962 season, Wilt *averaged* over 50 points per game. Russell never scored 40 points in an NBA game.

Less quantifiable but maybe more important, Wilt became a mythic hero in a way Russell never did. If basketball has a Babe Ruth, it is Wilt Chamberlain. Wilt famously scored 100 points one memorable night against the New York Knicks, in a game played in Hershey, Pennsylvania. The achievement is so mythic that most people, including hundreds who told Wilt they had seen the game in person, have transplanted the game in memory to a better place for myths, Madison Square Garden. It might as well have been Mount Olympus.

Partisans of Russell thought Wilt's fans were silly to chatter on about how Chamberlain had less success than Russell just because Russell had better players around him. Surely it didn't *diminish* Russell that he played on better teams than Wilt did, they would say, and in fact it's part of what shows that he was a better player. Of the 142 matchups between Russell's Boston Celtics and Wilt's various teams, the Celtics won 85, as well as 7 of 8 playoff series. Russell's Celtics won the NBA championship eleven times in Russell's thirteen years. Wilt won one championship in those years, and one more after Russell retired.[1]

But most of Russell's supporters would have rejected the notion that all they cared about was that Russell's teams were more successful than Wilt's. Russell, they wanted to claim, was also a better player, regardless of the records, because he was a better *team* player, especially on defense. They would compare Russell's way of "making everyone around him a better player" with what they perceived as Wilt's selfish play, hogging the ball and generally stealing the spotlight. It wasn't only that Russell won more rings than Wilt, then. It's that Russell embodied a different and higher ideal of basketball excellence, an ideal of teamwork rather than of one-on-one domination.

Wiltonians, Russellites, and Aristotle

These arguments weren't merely theoretical squabbles. For us boys in the mid-1960s, the "Wilt versus Russell" question made a real difference in what standards we set for ourselves. If you were a "Wiltonian," you tried to live up to different ideals than those of your friends who were "Russellites." We had all the single-minded seriousness about sports typical of boys, so we focused on what the Wilt versus Russell question taught us about how to be athletes and teammates. That was the most serious part of our lives then. But the lessons about partnership and leadership weren't limited to sports. As other aspects of life have become serious to me, I've come to appreciate how those early debates with my friends are still important, even if they're being applied in the classroom, in marriage, or in the workplace rather than on the hardwood.

Though we didn't know it when we were debating the "Wilt or Russell?" question, my friends and I were continuing a philosophical conversation over two thousand years old, started by one of the giants of ancient

Greek philosophy, Aristotle (384–322 B.C.). At the beginning of his *Nicomachean Ethics*—still the most influential book on morality ever written—Aristotle makes the point that we study ethics to become good, not just to know what's good. He also understood something that children often understand better than adults: we look to heroes—now we call them stars—to figure out how to live. And that's what we were doing when we argued about Wilt and Russell.

More precisely, we were taking up a puzzle that Aristotle posed at the beginning of his *Politics*. "A man who by nature is outside a community is either a beast or a god," Aristotle says. Wiltonians and Russellites agreed on one thing. Something about Wilt's nature made him "outside a community." Wilt was much harder to make a part of a team than Russell. Did this mean Wilt was a sort of untamable animal, powerful and impressive, but lacking some essential human virtue that Russell had in abundance; or did it mean that Wilt surpassed Russell's merely human virtues, remaining in a splendid isolation from all other basketball players, including his teammates? Was Wilt a basketball beast who fell short of Russell's uncommon humanity, or did he transcend Russell in the direction of basketball divinity?

Wilt, Romantic Hero

Who was the bigger and brighter star, Wilt or Russell? It's already interesting, and philosophically important, that we're much more likely to call Chamberlain "Wilt" than to call Russell "Bill." One of the great philosophers of the last century, an eccentric Austrian named Ludwig Wittgenstein, said, "The limits of my language are the limits of my world." How we talk about something before we're trying to be smart about it is often the key to becoming smart about it. Why were we on a first-name basis with Wilt but not with Russell?

Some of the reason was their personalities, no doubt. Wilt was outgoing to a fault and had an opinion about everything, whether he knew anything about it or not. Russell cultivated an introverted, "angry young man" image, measured his words, refused to sign autographs, and kept the world, including his teammates, at a distance. But this is psychology, not philosophy. Was there something about the ideals they represented that went along with the difference in names?

Consider this: of all the great modern philosophers, the one most likely to go by his first name, even among stuffy academics, is Jean-Jacques Rousseau (1712–1778), J.-J. for short. J.-J. got along with no one and influenced everyone. He more or less invented romanticism and lived his life promoting the value of the great individual, fated always to be misunderstood and underappreciated by his or her ordinary contemporaries. We feel it's right to call him "Jean-Jacques" rather than "Mr. Rousseau" because it fits the romantic individualism he represented. When we're in a sympathetic mood, we take the fact that J.-J. was a social misfit as evidence that there was more to his individuality than society knew how to handle. He suffered, at least in his own estimation, from too much genius.

Wilt Chamberlain, Wiltonians argue, suffered from too much genius, too. The leading American voice of romantic individualism, Ralph Waldo Emerson (1803–1882), put this problem eloquently at the conclusion of his essay "Experience": "Patience, patience,—the true romance which the world exists to realize, will be the transformation of genius into practical power." Emerson's point is that romantic genius *should* be realized as practical power, but genius in itself doesn't guarantee its own success. The highest kind of genius, Emerson thought, couldn't be its own agent; it had to be patient, to wait passively for something it couldn't produce itself. Practical power, worldly success, is something genius longs for and feels it *deserves*. But it doesn't get it. The world, that poor and ordinary thing, doesn't cooperate. In Wilt's case, this ordinary world came in the form of teammates who envied his transcendent talent, and well-meaning coaches who never figured out how to get these relatively mediocre basketball players to serve Wilt, their natural king.

Wilt suffered with his genius in much the same way as a more recent first-name genius, Michael Jordan. Before his team started to win championships, Michael said, "I always wanted my teams to be successful. But I wanted to be the main cause." Did coach Phil Jackson make the Chicago Bulls successful by getting Michael to stop wanting to be "the main cause" (a pretty godlike motive, by the way)? Hardly. During their run to their first title, Bill Cartwright had this to say about Michael: "He's the greatest athlete I've ever seen, maybe the greatest athlete ever to play any sport. He can do whatever he wants, it all comes so easy to him. *He's just not a basketball player.*"[2]

Michael Jordan not a basketball player? Bill Cartwright was an un-
usually thoughtful and articulate professional athlete. When he made this
incredible statement, he was measuring Michael by something like the
Russellite ideal of teamwork, not the Wiltonian ideal of domination.
That is, he was noting the fact that Michael was not "just" any old player who depended on his teammates to do great things but, rather, a guy
with such singular talents that he could do amazing things on his own.
But suppose Cartwright had looked at himself and said, "If I and my
teammates can't figure out how to get along with this transcendent first-
name genius Michael, then *we're* just not basketball players." Why measure the great man by how he gets along with the lesser men, rather than
the other way around?

Aristotle faced this problem when he compared democracy to kingship in the third book of the *Politics*. Most of the time, he thought, democracy is better, because everyone gets a chance to use his talents. But
what if someone arises of truly superlative political talent, someone who
would do a better job for the community ruling by himself, as a king,
than the community could do by letting all citizens have a turn to use
their talents? Well, conceded Aristotle, "all that's left, as is after all natural, is for everyone gladly to obey such a person, and for such people to
be perpetual kings in their cities." But Aristotle realized that getting everyone to obey a natural king was no easy task. The other citizens, after
all, do have real political talents, just as Wilt's teammates had real basketball talents. Will these citizens really be better off by learning how to
obey a superlative ruler than they would by ruling on their own? Would
you rather be a servant who makes the great man's greatness possible, or
be the master of your own accomplishments, even though they fall short
of greatness?

Russell, the Consummate Executive

If Wilt was a romantic individualist, a suffering poet in high-tops, what
was Russell? Probably the best executive the game ever produced.

The ideal executive needs a very refined sensitivity and responsiveness to the particular strengths and weaknesses of his teammates. Like a
skilled member of a choral group, he exercises his talents in perfect harmony with his partners. The executive leads, but he also adapts his style

of play to the talent around him, so that as his teammates change, his play will change. He is a multipurpose chameleon, always blending in with his surroundings. This flexibility will show itself in a striking way if such a player is traded to a team quite different from his original one. He will be able "to fit in right away" and "find his niche" within the new style of play. He is just the player a coach might look for to turn a group of talented but young and selfish players into a cohesive team.

By contrast, the dominator like Wilt or Michael is relatively immutable. He doesn't adapt his style to his teammates; they adapt to him. From game to game, his contribution to the team doesn't vary nearly as much as the team player's, in either style or quantity. He is and expects to be the focus of the team's strategy. In short, a dominating star is a rock, and you do not trade for him unless you can say, "You are my rock, and upon this rock I will build my team." He is always and everywhere the same.

From the Russellite's perspective, the dominator's immutability is another aspect of his selfishness, since he makes others adapt to him rather than the other way around. The executive would think of the dominator's inflexibility as an impediment to his own self-expression. An executive violinist would take the same view of someone who is a fine soloist but never learns to play well in an ensemble. If you can only be a soloist, don't you fall short of the most accomplished musicianship? To be sure, this emphasis on responsiveness puts the team player more at the mercy of circumstance than the dominator. He depends much more on the high quality of his teammates for the exercise of his talent. But the Russellite may argue, in response, that the highest accomplishment is possible only under the rarest conditions.

The Dominator as a Selfish Player

Let's try a thought experiment to get a clearer view of what's at stake in the competing ways the Wiltonians and the Russellites see basketball excellence. Start by imagining that you are the coach of a professional basketball team, and you have two especially troublesome players.

Ed the Egoist is too worried about his own success for the team's good. He wants his contract to call for bonuses based on various individual statistics, stuff like minutes played, points scored, and postseason inclusion on all-star teams. He thinks of himself as an excellent basketball player when he piles up these numbers and awards, and the bankroll that goes with them. The result is that he isn't really focused on the team's success, and he grumbles about coaching decisions that take away from his numbers even when he realizes that they promote winning basketball. For example, he dislikes a switch to a more deliberate tempo that makes for lower-scoring games, even if the slower tempo helps the team win more often.

Don the Dominator is an extremely gifted athlete, easily the best player on the team. He is passionately committed to team goals, and he wants his contract to reflect this. His bonuses are for things like total wins and success in the playoffs rather than personal statistics. Unlike Ed, he receives precious little consolation from having a big night when the team loses. His conception of himself as an excellent basketball player depends to a large extent on how much he contributes to the team's success. Of course he doesn't identify *completely* with the team's success, any more than Ed is completely indifferent to it. Don takes some consolation in a big night during a loss, just not very much.

Ed and Don are both criticized by teammates and sportswriters for being "selfish." But a good coach will see that the underlying causes of their selfishness are different. Don identifies with team goals, not just personal ones, so he is clearly not excessively egoistic in the way Ed is. How then can he be called selfish?

Don's problem is that he expects to be the focus of his team's play, to dominate the action. Don is used to being the star, and he expects the team to be built around him and his talents. Unlike Ed, he doesn't care much about whether you coach a high- or low-scoring style of play, as long as he is at the heart of things, the "main cause," as Michael Jordan once said. He insists on being what sportscasters like to call the "go-to guy" when the game is in the balance. As a coach, you probably are relieved to have someone who wants to bear this responsibility. But other times your star's domination can upset the rest of the team. Don takes opportunities to excel away from the other players, and even if they realize he has the team's success at heart, they can still be irritated by being second bananas. (Jordan sometimes called his teammates his "supporting cast.") His very excellence can be disruptive to the team's chemistry. When his teammates criticize him for being selfish, they have in mind the way he seems to hog the ball and the spotlight, forcing them to adapt to him much more than he adapts to them.

Both of your problem players, then, can be called selfish. But Ed the Egoist is selfish because he's more or less indifferent to his teammates and their goals. Don the Dominator is very much committed to team goals, but the way he plays puts his teammates in the shadow. He takes away their opportunities to contribute as much to team success as they'd like. Sometimes both sorts of selfishness will produce the same behavior (for example, shooting too often), but they still have distinct underlying motives. In light of this difference, you as a coach will not be able to cure or mitigate the selfishness of Ed and Don, and so make them better basketball players, with the same treatment. Your cure must fit their distinct diseases.

With Ed, you might rewrite his contract to give bonuses for assists rather than points, or simply eliminate all personal incentives in favor of team goals like those in Don the Dominator's contract. But Don's selfishness requires another approach. As Don's coach, you need to teach him to open up more opportunities for his teammates, so they can excel and contribute to team success. But it would be a blunder to appeal to Don's unselfishness here. You don't want to treat Don like a grade-school boy, telling him to "give the others a chance to play" or asking him, "How would you like it if someone else dominated the game when *you* wanted to contribute more?" This is too much like asking him to hide his bright lamp under a basket to let the other dim bulbs shine. The point is not for Don to let his teammates have their turns, as if a basketball game were a series of solos and Don had stayed on stage too long, cutting down on the time the others had to perform. The game is more like a choral performance, with Don the strong-voiced singer who hasn't learned yet to blend in properly, spoiling the overall effect by sticking out too much.[3] You need to teach Don to exercise his basketball excellence in a more harmonious way, one that fits him more effectively into a partnership with his teammates and their talents.

You might do this by focusing Don on parts of his game that his current dominating style of play doesn't draw on. For example, you could work with him on finding the open man in situations where he now forces up a difficult shot. You can help him appreciate the specific kind of excellence required for this sensitivity to his teammates and their position on the floor. You might emphasize how rare this sensitivity is and hold up for his emulation great masters of these skills, like Magic Johnson, Larry Bird, Nancy Lieberman, or, more recently, Steve Nash. He can learn to take as much pride in this aspect of basketball excellence as he formerly took in shooting well.

Don shouldn't think of himself as sacrificing his own opportunities for his teammates when he makes this change. If you're a good coach, he'll also change the conception of basketball excellence by which he measures himself. Don will be pleased if his new style of play makes the team better, to be sure. But more importantly, you must also convince him that *he* will be a more excellent basketball player by developing this more team-oriented aspect of his game. In a sense, then, his game has become less selfish, and he shares the spotlight with his teammates more than he once did. But your educative role as Don's coach has not been to awaken altruism where once there was only egoism. You have done something more like changing his taste from concertos (with himself playing the lead, of course) to symphonies (where he enjoys his very ability to blend in).

Coaching a Real Star

So now you know how to turn a talented but dominating player into a team player. But is the ideal of teamwork *always* to be preferred to the ideal of domination? It's hard to think the answer is a simple yes when we honestly admit how impressive the leadership and independence of a dominating athlete can be. The very existence of a prolonged and spirited debate of the "Wilt or Russell?" question shows that there's more than one side to the issue.

Suppose you're coaching a basketball team of grade school boys. One of your players has far more natural talent than the other players. He is taller, jumps higher, runs faster, has quicker reflexes, and also possesses outstanding skills specific to basketball, such as dribbling, passing, and shooting. You have a difficult choice between building the team around him and letting him dominate or making him fit into a more team-centered style of play where he is not the focus of the action.

At this low level of competition, your team is quite likely to win more games if you subordinate everyone else on the team to this one player. Let him rebound, drive the length of the court, and fire away whenever he can, and you will score more often than if he passes to his less skilled teammates and tries to stay within the confines of a team offense. If your primary goal as a coach is to win as many games as you can, this is the strategy you will adopt. You will develop in your star those aspects of his game that are especially important for a dominator.

But you may well be uncomfortable with this if the price of winning more grade school games is that you stunt the long-term basketball development of your best player. You may decide instead to train him in the more team-oriented kinds of excellence, even if this will make the team less successful, in order to make *him* a better player. Ironically, this may also make the whole team better in the long run.

But for now, your star's inept teammates may not be able to exploit his team-centered excellences very well. They may fumble his artistic passes or fail to take advantage of the picks he sets for their shots. But you may be looking ahead to his high school career and beyond, when his teammates will be better able to appreciate and utilize the excellences you are developing in him now. At these higher levels of competition, with more-talented teammates and opponents, your star would be at a disadvantage if you had let him be a dominator rather than a team player back in grade school.

It is precisely with a view to this higher level that you can judge that you are making him a better player, training him in a higher degree of basketball excellence, by focusing on team goals rather than on individual excellence. You congratulate yourself on having the boy's long-term interests at heart, as well as his teammates, as you help him live up to the ideal of Bill Russell rather than Wilt Chamberlain.

But what if your star is a *real* star? Suppose, for example, he is a boy like Wilt Chamberlain. Now there is no level of competition so high that this athlete will not be able to dominate, even in the rarefied world of professional basketball. So no matter how far you look ahead, you see that this athlete will always contribute most efficiently to his team's success when the team is built around him and his teammates are forced to adapt to him. The basis for your judgment in the previous case, that you were making your star a better basketball player (even if you were making your grade school team worse) by emphasizing the excellence of a team player rather than a dominator, is now gone. Can you still congratulate yourself if you get your star to model himself on Bill Russell rather than Wilt Chamberlain? Once we remove the possibility that the dominator will harm his team with selfishness, can we still prefer the team player?

This is the situation that brings out most clearly the tension between the ideals of domination and teamwork. Even here, many basketball fans (especially coaches and sportswriters, I suspect) will prefer the excellence of the team player.[4] They will feel that the skills required for adapting to one's teammates and responding to them effectively represent the highest, most refined level of achievement in basketball. In effect, they see the Russellite ideal as a higher ideal than the Wiltonian ideal, *even in cases where the dominator ideal might bring more victories than the team-oriented ideal.* With all due respect to Vince Lombardi, winning is *not* the only thing. Russell was not merely more successful than Chamberlain. He also "played the game the way it should be played."

Wilt, Russell, and the Logic of Idealism

Recall how you justified coaching your grade school star in team-centered rather than dominating excellences. You looked beyond his actual level of competition toward a higher, future level where his future teammates would be more talented. At that future level, he would be a better *basketball* player by being a team player, not a dominator.

The Russellite could argue that we should extend this reasoning. Why not consider an *ideal* level of competition, rather than just a future level, with ideally talented teammates? If we want to understand the fullest flowering of basketball excellence, we must consider what it would be under the most favorable circumstances. Perhaps in real life, with its imperfections and distortions, circumstances arise in which a star will in fact make his team more successful by dominating than by becoming a team player. But this, Russellites could argue, is only a second-best situation, a compromise, even if those circumstances can in rare cases be present even at the highest actual level of competition. The conditions that make domination appropriate exist much more often as we move to lower levels of competition and perfection, evidence that the dominator is a creature of necessity, not the peak of full basketball development. (Aristotle makes a similar point in the *Politics,* arguing that kingship was more justifiable when humans lived in more primitive conditions.) The dominator, they could say, may do as well as he can under the conditions he is in. But he lacks the opportunity and the equipment for the highest exercise of excellence, as Aristotle says in the *Ethics*.

Wiltonians could respond that an idealization shouldn't make things too easy. The ideal circumstances to show your talent aren't the circumstances in which you are surrounded by help. They could reject the style of basketball of a star on the ideal team for demanding too little of the talents of the individual player. Individual excellence shows itself most clearly, they could argue, only when it overcomes difficult obstacles.

Think of the way sports fantasies work. We often set up extreme adversity to be overcome heroically by the fantasist. The clock is running out as you take a desperate final shot in the seventh game of the NBA championship; you limp into the batter's box in the bottom of the ninth at the World Series; the pass rush breaks through as you look for a receiver in the Super Bowl. In all of these cases, the fantasy idealizes to the extreme case precisely to isolate the highest exercise of talent.

To make an un-Aristotelian point in Aristotelian language, the Wiltonian could say a star can sometimes have *too much* equipment for his own happiness. Shakespeare realized this when he constructed a patriotic fantasy for King Henry V on the eve of the battle of Agincourt. The English are badly outnumbered, and a subordinate wishes they had more troops. "Wish not a man from England," says Henry, "I would not lose so great an honor as *one man more* would share from me." Henry, like Michael, wants team success, but he also wants to be its main cause.

This is not a wholesale rejection of the Russellite's idealism. The Wiltonian agrees to judge between the ideals of domination and teamwork from the perspective of an ideal case. But now the issue becomes whether it is more appropriate to idealize to the best circumstances or to the most extreme circumstances in looking for the fullest expression of excellence. This issue must be fought out and settled before we rank one ideal over the other.

This is the fight my friends and I found worth fighting. There is a different sort of response, though, that rejects either idealization. Some people think this sort of idealism is silly on both sides. For them, there simply isn't any "way the game should be played." They claim the only real question is which way of playing wins the most games. This is what some people like to call being a realist. These people tell us "to stick to the actual truth of things rather than to imaginings. Many visionaries have imagined teams and leagues that have never existed. But the way people *do* play is so far from the way they could or should play that anyone who abandons what *is* for what *should be* pursues his own failure rather than his success. A star who strives always to be a good team player is sure to fail, since there are so many players who are not good enough to actually help their team win. The ideal case provides no meaningful standard or guidance. Ideals are no more than a figment of the imagination, fit for the idle chatter of boys, but not for the strivings of *grown men and women.* Real princes can never be charming."

This so-called realist response to "idealism" is nearly five hundred years old and was stated most forcefully by Machiavelli in his diabolical little book *The Prince,* still the most influential book on immorality ever written. The paragraph above is just a paraphrase in basketball lingo of what Machiavelli said about politics. But such people, dear readers, are bad people. They aren't "realists" unless ideals aren't real. They are merely cynics who lack any sense of beauty or grandeur. Avoid them. The philosophical beauty of the "Wilt or Russell?" question can never be appreciated by people who can't feel how real an ideal is.

Notes

1. For a fascinating account of the early years of the Wilt-Russell rivalry, see John Taylor, *The Rivalry: Bill Russell, Wilt Chamberlain, and the Golden Age of Basketball* (New York: Random House, 2005).

2. Sam Smith, *The Jordan Rules* (New York: Simon and Schuster, 1992), 66, 249 (emphasis added).

3. Compare Aristotle, *Politics,* bk. 3.

4. It is noteworthy in this context that in 1980 Russell was voted Greatest Player in the History of the NBA by the Professional Basketball Writers Association of America.

Jerry L. Walls

THE WIZARD VERSUS THE GENERAL

Why Bob Knight Is a Greater Coach than John Wooden

DURING THE SUMMER of 2005, a remarkable movie entitled *The Great Raid* was released. The movie is remarkable primarily because the extraordinary events it depicts really happened. In 1945, during the Second World War, more than 500 U.S. prisoners of war were under the threat of imminent death in the infamous Cabanatuan Japanese POW camp in the Philippines. The movie recounts the story of how 121 men in the Sixth Ranger Battalion undertook a daring, against-all-odds mission to liberate those POWs.

This task was daunting not only because these men would be far outnumbered by the Japanese but also because they would have to travel, undetected, thirty miles behind enemy lines to reach the camp and would have to rely heavily on a strategic plan of attack and the element of surprise to have any chance of success. Despite the unlikely odds, this most audacious raid was a spectacular triumph. Nearly all the captives were rescued, and only two of the Sixth Ranger Battalion lost their lives.[1]

For my money, *The Great Raid* is a great movie.[2] But for now, I am more interested in the question of why the raid itself is worthy of being labeled as great. The broader issue of how greatness is measured is an inherently philosophical issue, especially since it involves judgments of value. Standards of greatness usually are not obvious or set in stone. They often depend on *contestable* judgments of comparative value.[3]

So what makes a military operation like the one described above deserve to be called great? I would suggest that there are at least two factors involved in this assessment. First, the mission was impressive because it was accomplished by a relatively small group of men who defeated a larger and better-situated group of enemies. This was not a victory of superior strength and numbers overwhelming an outmatched opponent. Rather, it was the triumph of an undermanned group that succeeded by virtue of a strategy that was carefully thought out, planned, and executed. But there is another factor as well. This raid also required outstanding courage and commitment on the part of those who carried it out. So in addition to the strategic brilliance of the mission, it demonstrated the sort of heroic valor and sacrifice that makes for greatness. The character these men displayed demands our honor and respect even more than their skill and savvy in executing their ingenious plan of attack.

In this chapter I want to explore what makes for greatness in coaching. This is admittedly not as important an issue as what makes a military operation great. However, I think our discussion thus far gives us some clues that may be pertinent to measuring greatness in basketball coaches.

This issue, I have discovered, incites considerable passion among fans. In my many years of engaging in basketball arguments, some of the most spirited disputes I have participated in have involved the question of who are the truly great coaches of the game. My choice for the top of the list is admittedly controversial. In fact, for many people he embodies the very idea of controversy more than any other figure in all of sport. I refer, of course, to Bob Knight, the man whom hoops fans also know as "the General." I can hardly recall the number of times people have reacted with surprise, if not indignation, when they learn that I am an outspoken fan of the General.

Part of the reason some find it surprising that I love the General is that I teach at a theological seminary. Some apparently see it as incongruous that a guy who teaches philosophy to students preparing for the ministry can be a fan of a guy whose most notorious moment in the public eye came when he threw a chair across the gym in protest of what he took to be a bad call in a game. The chair is only the most famous episode in a whole litany of incidents in which Knight's volatile temper has gotten the best of him.

But my appreciation for Knight is not the only thing that evokes surprised reactions from my fellow hoops fans. I have gotten similarly strong reactions from a number of people when they learn that I am *not* a big fan of another coaching icon, namely "the Wizard of Westwood," John Wooden. Several times people have brought his name up when they have learned I am a basketball fan who also teaches in a seminary. Surely, they assume, I must be a fan of one of the great statesmen of the game, a man known for his famous "pyramid of success" and who is so much a gentleman that he wouldn't even tolerate swearing in practice.[4] When they hear that I am not, they are often flabbergasted and sometimes even seem to be offended. Usually, an explanation is demanded. Here it is.

In a discussion of human greatness, the philosopher Ralph Waldo Emerson (1803–1882) writes: "I admire great men of all classes. . . . I like rough and smooth, 'Scourges of God,' and 'Darlings of the human race.'"[5] While Emerson would likely find reasons to like both the "rough" General and the "smooth" Wizard, I will argue that Knight, the scourge of the modern media, if not of God, is a decidedly greater coach than Wooden, a darling of the media. In the process it will become clear why I admire the General but have much less enthusiasm for the Wizard.

My argument will hinge on two fundamental points that seem to me to be obviously true, points that are suggested by my discussion of *The Great Raid*. First, it is more impressive to succeed if one does so with comparatively fewer resources at one's disposal than it is if one has more. Second, success is greater if it is achieved in a way that is morally honorable than if one resorts to, or tolerates, something unethical or dishonest in order to succeed. I will say more in defense of these two points later, but for now I will take these two claims as intuitively obvious. The more controversial issue is how these points apply to Knight and Wooden.

Two Hall of Fame Careers

Before we proceed, it is worth taking a moment to recall the achievements of our two coaches. Both are in the Hall of Fame and both would be in the top five of almost anyone's list of the greatest college basketball coaches of all time. Wooden's fame is due primarily to an unmatched run of national championships he won at UCLA. Although he became head coach at UCLA in 1948, he did not win his first national championship until 1964. He went on to win a total of ten national championships in twelve years, including seven in a row; both of those statistics are still records that no one has come close to breaking. He also had four seasons in which his teams went 30–0. During one stretch, his teams won eighty-eight consecutive games, including thirty-eight straight NCAA tournament games. The annual award for the outstanding player in college basketball is named the John R. Wooden Award.

Knight's fame is due mainly to his years as head coach at Indiana University, where he won three national championships, the first of which was in 1976, when he was thirty-five, and the most recent in 1987. His 1976 team was the last to go undefeated in college basketball. In 1984 he became one of only four coaches in basketball history to win an NCAA championship, an NIT championship, and an Olympic gold medal. Currently at Texas Tech, he led his teams there to at least twenty wins his first three years, thereby becoming the first coach at that university to have three consecutive twenty-win seasons. At the time of this writing, he is only a few wins away from passing Dean Smith as the coach with the most wins in the history of men's college basketball.

Doing More with Less

Now, let us consider my first proposed standard for measuring coaching greatness, namely, that it is more admirable to succeed if one does so with fewer resources than one's opponents. This essential point was made centuries ago in ancient Greece by no less than Aristotle. He observed that we must take into account such factors as fortune and misfortune in our assessment of a man's life. The noble man will always do the best he can, "as circumstances permit," Aristotle says, "just as a good general makes the most strategic use of the troops at his disposal, and a good shoemaker makes the best shoe he can from the leather available, and so on with experts in all other fields."[6]

Translating the point into hoops lingo, this means that it is more impressive if a coach can win with players who have less natural talent than the opponents. To see more clearly the force of this point, let's consider another area where this principle applies, namely, education. This comparison is particularly apt since many leading coaches conceive of themselves primarily as teachers, including Knight and Wooden.

A great coach is a great educator who teaches his players not only how to play the game of basketball but also how to succeed when the clock runs out on their basketball career. A great teacher must be able to discern the potential of each of his players and to develop that potential as fully as possible. Not all students are equally gifted, so the success of a teacher must be measured not only by what his students learn but also by the ability they had to begin with. One of America's most noted educators, the philosopher Mortimer Adler, who also served as the chairman of the board of editors of the *Encyclopedia Britannica,* made the point by saying that not all students can be expected to move the same distance down the track. "The measure or standard of accomplishment cannot, therefore, be based on the expectation of a single arithmetical equality of results. It must be based on a proportional equality of results—a mastery of what is to be learned by all to the extent that is proportional to the individual measure of their capacity for achievement."[7]

Now if this point is correct, a coach's success cannot be measured simply in terms of how many games or championships he has won. Before we can gauge the level of his success, we must first ask how talented his players were in comparison to his rivals. In comparing Wooden and Knight, the question is whether the players they have coached have been roughly equal in talent or whether one of them had a decided advantage in this regard.

Fans who are reasonably informed about hoops history will see this as a no-brainer. Beginning with his first championship team in 1964, each of Wooden's championship teams had at least one player who went on to become an NBA all-star. Among those players were two of the most dominant players in the history of the game, Lew Alcindor (later known as Kareem Abdul-Jabbar) and Bill Walton, who between them led UCLA to five championships.

With such exceptional talent at his disposal, Wooden's winning was only to be expected. Television sports show host Summer Sanders made this observation rather pointedly on an episode of *The Sports List* that listed the top college basketball players of all time, a list topped by the two guys just mentioned. Sanders concluded the show by saying something like, "No disrespect to Mr. Wooden, but do you really have to be a wizard to win with Walton and Alcindor?"

Other notable UCLA players from this era who went on to become NBA all-stars are Gail Goodrich, Sidney Wicks, Jamaal Wilkes, and Marques Johnson. At least fourteen of the players who played for Wooden during his championship run went on to play in the NBA for at least four years, and eleven of these averaged eleven or more points over their professional careers. One of these was Swen Nater, whose role at UCLA was to be Walton's backup. From the 6'1" Goodrich, who starred on Wooden's first two championship teams, to the 7'1" Alcindor, who led the Bruins to three championships, Wooden had exceptional talent every year his team won it all. Alcindor's extraordinary NBA career is well known, but many of today's fans will be less familiar with Goodrich. This unlikely-looking NBA star averaged 18.4 points over his fourteen-year professional career and was good enough to lead the great 1971–1972 Los Angeles Lakers team—a team that included all-time greats Wilt Chamberlain and Jerry West—in scoring with 25.9 points per game.

By comparison, Knight's teams have been significantly less talented. This is not to deny that Knight has had many excellent basketball players. Indeed, one cannot win championships without good players. But the issue here is a matter of degree. Whereas all of Wooden's championship teams had at least one NBA all-star, Knight has had only one player who achieved that distinction: Isiah Thomas, who was the star of his 1981 NCAA championship team. Thomas played at Indiana for only two years, turning pro after his sophomore year. During the years in which Wooden coached, it was uncommon for players to leave early for the NBA. Moreover, freshmen were not eligible until 1973, near the end of Wooden's career. So he had the advantage of coaching his stars during the best years of their development as college players, an opportunity that today's coaches who have exceptionally talented players seldom enjoy.

Knight's 1981 team was certainly a talented group, as was his 1976 team. Indeed, each of the starting five of the 1976 team played in the NBA for at least five years. None, however, was an all-star, and only two averaged double figures for his NBA career, a little more than ten points a game. My point is that Knight's 1976 championship team was a great *team,* a group of guys with less-than-spectacular individual talent who played together to achieve the maximum of their potential.

But the most impressive example of Knight's ability to win without NBA-level talent is his 1987 championship team. What is remarkable about that team is that none of the players were first-round draft picks in the NBA. Typically, the team that has won the NCAA championship in the past has had at least one first-round pick, if not several, usually lottery picks. A recent example is the 2005 champion North Carolina Tar Heels, which had four players taken in the first fourteen picks of the 2005 draft, including the number two pick, a player with great NBA talent who did not even start at Carolina due to the number of experienced upperclassmen on the team! The most notable NBA career of Knight's 1987 team was that of Dean Garrett, a junior college transfer who played overseas before making it in the NBA, where he averaged 4.8 points over a six-year career. The star of that team was Steve Alford, an underwhelming physical specimen who was a jump shooting specialist. In Knight's system, he averaged enough points to be a two-time first-team All-American. But he was not big enough or quick enough to be a first-round draft pick.

Some of Knight's most impressive coaching victories have occurred in years when he didn't have championship-caliber teams. In 1984, Alford's freshman season, Knight's team won an upset victory in the NCAA tournament over one of the most talented teams ever assembled, Dean Smith's North Carolina team that included future NBA all-stars Sam Perkins, Brad Daugherty, Kenny Smith, and a guy every hoops fan knows as simply "Michael." Apart from Alford, there is not another name on that Indiana team that anyone outside of Indiana is likely to remember.[8]

Now, some might object to this argument that development of talent is one mark of great coaching and the fact that Wooden had so many NBA all-stars is a credit to his skills in player development. Surely there is something to this point. Some of Wooden's better players at UCLA, such as Jack Hirsch, who played on his first championship team with Goodrich in 1964, were not particularly touted in high school. Nevertheless, the fact of the matter is that most players who end up becoming stars in the NBA are players with great natural talent. As the old saying goes, size cannot be coached. Nor can speed and quickness and vertical leap. And most of Wooden's players who went on to become NBA all-stars had these in abundance.

The more telling cases of player development occur when players who are not expected to do great things grow into players who end up doing so. Several of Knight's players could be cited as examples, but consider two of his recent players at Texas Tech, Andre Emmett and Ronald Ross. Neither of these players was a high school All-American or highly recruited nationally. In fact, Ross first joined the team as a walk-on. In the season before Knight arrived at Texas Tech, Emmett averaged 7.7 points a game for a team that went 9–19. In Knight's first year at Tech, Emmett averaged 18.7 points a game and became an All-Conference player as Tech won twenty-three games and went to the NCAA tournament. Emmett graduated as the leading scorer in Big Twelve history. The year after Emmett graduated, Ross became an All-Conference player, averaging 17.5 points a game, and led Tech to the Sweet Sixteen in the NCAA tournament.

It might also be argued that recruiting is part of coaching, so Wooden's recruitment of great players is an integral component of his greatness as a coach. There is also something to this point, but it should not be exaggerated, for a number of reasons. First, recruiting is not a distinctively basketball skill. In many ways, recruiting is a matter of salesmanship, and part of what makes one a good recruiter is the same whether one is recruiting for basketball, football, or the U.S. Marine Corps. The ability to evaluate talent *is* a basketball skill, and some coaches have the ability to recognize talent that others overlook. But recruiting as it is usually understood is not so much a matter of talent evaluation as it is a matter of persuading those who are widely recognized as the top prep players to attend one's school.

Recruiting is certainly a vital and legitimate part of the game, but unfortunately it has become part of the sordid underbelly of college athletics. All too often, recruiting is less about convincing a student that he will gain an education and grow as a person than it is about pandering to the egos of immature young men who have an exaggerated sense of their self-importance, not to mention their talent. Moreover, recruiting has been heavily influenced by shoe companies, television exposure, and other factors that have little to do with the development of athletic skill or higher education. Worst of all, recruiting has been corrupted by the involvement of boosters who have provided inducements to recruits in the form of cars, money, and other benefits that violate NCAA rules.

Integrity, Greatness, and Success

This brings us to my second criterion for measuring true greatness, namely, that success is greater if it is achieved in a morally honorable way than if one resorts to, or tolerates, something unethical or dishonest to accomplish one's goals. Indeed, I would argue that true success cannot be achieved in a dishonest way. Unethical success is a contradiction in terms.

Now this is hardly a novel idea; rather, it is a matter of broad moral consensus. This point was stated with classic precision by the Greek dramatist Sophocles, who has one of his characters say, "I would prefer even to fail with honor than win by cheating."[9]

The reasons that cheating is viewed with such disdain are easy to see. Cheating is not only a lie, but it is also a form of stealing. It is a lie because the one cheating typically presents himself as competing honestly when in fact he is not. It is a form of stealing because the cheater unfairly takes for himself honor and recognition that rightfully should have gone to someone else, someone who competed according to the rules, who would have received the honor of winning if the contest had been fair. Likewise, the joy of winning is stolen from the fans of teams who compete honorably, according to the rules. And ironically, the cheater ends up cheating himself. This point was made recently by baseball great Cal Ripken in reference to the much-publicized use of steroids by some of the biggest names in his sport. Ripken remarked: "Ultimately, at the end of the day, you couldn't say you were better than the other person because you knew you had a secret. You knew you had cheated."[10]

No doubt the enormous pressure to win, to be recognized as a "winner," is a major reason that cheating is not only so prevalent but even widely accepted. What is even more troubling is that the "win at all costs" mentality reflects a fundamental shift away from traditional moral values. Noted public philosopher Tom Morris observes: "How we get there is as important as where we go. This seems to be a nearly forgotten truth in our highly competitive society. Everybody wants to be a winner. Nobody wants to be a loser. It was once the worst kind of insult and severest kind of condemnation to be called . . . a liar, untrustworthy, unscrupulous, unethical, immoral. . . . In more recent days, the most dreaded affront and reproach seems to be 'loser.' A label to be avoided at all costs."[11]

At the heart of what makes Knight great as a coach is his rejection of this mind-set and his unwavering commitment to honesty and fair play. One of the things that positively leaps off the pages of his recent autobiography is that a central driving force of his career is a burning passion to show that winning need not come at the price of cheating. In the early pages of his book, he expresses this point eloquently in describing the terms on which he wanted to succeed at Indiana.

I wanted to win those games and build those championships the way some
people, primarily in the press, were saying could not be done anymore—by
following NCAA rules; by recruiting kids who could and would be genuine
students and four-year graduates as well as excellent basketball players and
teams. I wanted to make the INDIANA they wore across their chests an
identifying symbol that meant to people throughout the state, the Big Ten,
and the country that inside that jersey was a kid who would compete like
hell and represent his school on the court and off it, during his college years
and after them, in a way they would make the most important judges of all,
that kid's parents, as proud as they could be.
   To do all that and win was the goal.
   To win without doing all those things would have been to fail.[12]

Several pages later, he reiterates that as badly as he wants to win as a
coach, and as much as he hates to lose, he utterly rejects the notion of
winning at any cost. "No. Absolutely not. I've never understood how
anybody who cheated to get a player, or players, could take any satisfac-
tion whatsoever out of whatever winning came afterward."[13]

Knight's record matches his word. Over his many years of coaching
there has never been any sort of cheating or rules violations involving his
program. Moreover, he has been staunchly committed to the idea of *student*-athletes, demanding that his players attend class regularly and consistently maintaining one of the highest graduation rates in the country.
His record stands as a monument to the fact that it is possible to win,
even at the highest level, without compromising academic standards or
breaking the rules that define fair play and honesty.

The Tarnished Wizard

Can the same be said for Wooden? Apparently not, though this will likely come as a surprise to many fans, even well-informed ones. A number
of noted basketball insiders claim that it is widely acknowledged in basketball circles that Wooden's run of championships was made considerably easier by wealthy boosters who rewarded recruits with financial
inducements that are forbidden by the NCAA. I first learned of these allegations several years ago and was quite surprised when I read them.
While I will cite some representative writers who claim these allegations
are common knowledge among basketball insiders, my concern is not to
try to prove the charges, which would take us far beyond the scope of this

essay. I am concerned here primarily with the implications if these charges are in fact true and widely recognized within the hoops fraternity, as a number of writers insist they are.

Obviously, the implications for the sport are enormous. For a start, it means the man who rewrote the record book in NCAA basketball coaching, setting records that seem completely out of reach in today's era of greater parity in the game, made his indelible mark on the history of the sport in a less-than-honorable fashion. It means that the most famous dynasty in college basketball history was built on corrupt foundations.

One sportswriter who takes the allegations as common knowledge, Earl Cox, cites them in response to a column by another writer, Rick Bozich, who was discussing which college basketball program should be considered the greatest of all time. Bozich opts for UCLA over Kentucky because of Kentucky's repeated NCAA probation, despite the fact that Kentucky has been dominant over a much longer period of time than UCLA. Cox's reply states the essence of the allegations.

Fair enough, but if anyone is going to mention UK's problems in relation with UCLA, I have two words for Bozich and anyone else who wants to blast UK and say nice things about UCLA. Those two words: Sam Gilbert, the sugar daddy of all sugar daddies. For some strange reason, John Wooden never won big at UCLA until his friend started attracting the finest high school basketball players in the nation, most formidable of whom was named Lew Alcindor. For some strange reason, few people have chosen to write about Gilbert's relationship with UCLA, but former Bruin players weren't bashful about standing up in front of ESPN cameras and telling what he did for them. This was in the all-century shows that ESPN presented five years ago. All I am saying is, be fair and tell the truth, not just one side.[14]

Cox's concern to be fair and tell both sides of the story with respect to Wooden has also been expressed by a number of sportswriters in reference to Knight. A few years ago, during the controversies surrounding the events that eventually led to Knight's firing at Indiana, Wooden's name was often invoked as an example of a perfect gentleman, a role model to be emulated, in contrast to the more volatile Knight. One of the writers who saw this as an unfair comparison was Dave Kindred of the *Sporting News,* who cited the following lines from Kareem Abdul-Jabbar's autobiography as evidence that Wooden tolerated repeated violations of NCAA rules in order to build his dynasty at UCLA: "Sam [Gilbert] was a very valuable and influential friend to me. He never did anything illegal; all he did was ignore the NCAA's economic restrictions about helping athletes. He was like everybody's grandfather, got us stuff wholesale, knew where to get inexpensive tires for your car or a cheap apartment.... Sam steered clear of John Wooden, and Mr. Wooden gave him the same wide berth. Both helped the school greatly. Sam helped me get rid of my tickets, and once the money thing worked out, I never gave another thought to leaving UCLA." Kindred concluded his article with what he called a "scruples question: Would you rather have a coach who throws a vase against a wall or a coach who turns a blind eye to the buying of players in his behalf?"[15]

For one final piece of testimony that Wooden's cheating is widely acknowledged in basketball circles, consider the observations of sportswriter Dan Wetzel in a column for ACCToday.com: "Most people in the game believe it, believe it so much that the specter of Bruin booster Sam Gilbert has always cast a quiet shadow over Wooden's legacy. Even the Hall of Famer's most ardent backers grow mum when asked about Gilbert, the millionaire fan who for years doted on the recruits and then players that delivered title after title to Westwood."[16]

It is important to note that these allegations were never investigated by the NCAA and consequently never formally or legally proven. Of course, as all philosophers are aware, some things can be known even if they have never been proven. Whether cheating at UCLA during Wooden's tenure is one of those things depends on what information insiders who claim to know have access to. At any rate, what is a matter of public record is that UCLA was placed on probation in 1981 under Larry Brown, and UCLA was ordered to disassociate Gilbert from the recruiting process.[17] Moreover, Gilbert was later charged with laundering money for a known drug runner, but he died just two days before federal officials went to his home to arrest him.[18]

Now what is curious is just how quiet the "shadow" of Gilbert has remained in the consciousness of sports fans. Although Wooden's cheating appears to be widely recognized among sportswriters and other basketball insiders, his image remains untarnished in the larger public. Anyone who watches college basketball regularly will hear numerous references to Wooden and his extraordinary legacy, with not so much as a hint about the rules violations that fueled his accomplishments. Moreover, he is typically depicted as the epitome of class, a man whose contributions to the game deserve the highest respect and admiration. The shadow simply disappears in the sunny picture that is painted of Wooden's gracious personality and singular achievements.

In fact, in numerous conversations on these matters, I have found that few basketball fans, even very knowledgeable ones, have even heard of Gilbert. Many have reacted with utter disbelief, and in a few cases with something bordering on angry denial, when I told them about Gilbert and his alleged role in UCLA basketball. Their image of Wooden was such that it seemed completely unthinkable to them that he might have cheated or tolerated cheating in any way.

So here is an interesting irony. Everyone who knows anything about basketball knows about Knight's chair-throwing incident, but hardly anybody seems to know about Gilbert outside of sportswriters and basketball insiders. Moreover, while the chair and the litany of associated incidents gives Knight a negative image in many people's minds, the shadow of Gilbert has done little to tarnish Wooden's image.

Lord Chesterfield and Cheating

Well, as Andre Agassi said in the famous commercial, "image is everything." In a society inclined to accept this notion, cheating may seem like a relatively small matter. One can cheat while being a very likable person, the sort of person who is "like everybody's grandfather."

This point was made very memorably centuries ago by James Boswell, the biographer of Samuel Johnson. His famous biography recounts many conversations he had with Johnson and their friends, conversations that sometimes dealt with questions of moral philosophy. In one such conversation, a certain Mr. Hicky asserted that "gentility and morality are inseparable." Boswell, however, insisted otherwise. "By no means, Sir," he replied. "The genteelest characters are often the most immoral. Does not Lord Chesterfield give precepts for uniting wickedness and the graces? A man, indeed, is not genteel when he gets drunk; but most vices may be committed very genteely: a man may debauch his friend's wife genteely: he may cheat at cards genteely."[19] And, I would add, a man may cheat at recruiting genteely.

Boswell goes on to tell us that Johnson joined the debate with Mr. Hicky by drawing a distinction between honor and exterior grace, noting that a man who displays exterior grace may not necessarily be honorable. I suspect that this distinction is one that has become obscured in our society, which places so much emphasis on image. Indeed, I am inclined to think that the difference between Knight's and Wooden's public image is due to the fact that our society values certain personality dispositions and social graces more than it values core moral virtues like honesty and fair play, or even assumes that they are one and the same. But those who accept Samuel Johnson's distinction will see things differently. Faced with Kindred's "scruples question" mentioned above, I suspect Johnson would choose the man who throws vases over the man who turns a blind eye to cheating.

This is not to defend throwing vases or chairs, nor is it to deny that Knight deserves some of the criticism he has received. Knight's failings should not be whitewashed, nor should it be denied that some of his failings have detracted from his greatness as a coach. Indeed, even some of his best friends and most loyal fans sometimes find themselves reduced to silence by his behavior. And most would agree that the General apparently has a considerable way to go before he will be a candidate for sainthood.

But keeping in mind that I am concerned here with the more modest issue of what makes for coaching greatness, I would nevertheless contend that Knight's shortcomings do not detract from his legacy nearly as much as the shadow of Gilbert detracts from Wooden's achievements. At the heart of the issue here is nothing less than the integrity of the game that has made both Knight and Wooden famous and allowed both of them many opportunities they would not otherwise have enjoyed. Knight's foibles and flaws do not undermine the very integrity of this great game, but cheating clearly does.

In conclusion, the General is well named because his place in coaching history is due to his extraordinary skills as a tactician, strategist, teacher, and motivator. As one would expect from a great leader, he has been uncompromisingly committed to winning with honor. The Wizard was also a teacher, strategist, and motivator of uncommon skill. But his magic is less dazzling when one takes into account the overwhelming talent advantage he had at his disposal. The enchantment is further diminished when one learns of widespread allegations that his magic was performed with multiple assists from the dark art of NCAA rules violations. Measuring coaching greatness by the two criteria I have identified, the General wins by a slam dunk over the Wizard.

Notes

1. Several Filipino guerrillas who assisted in the raid also lost their lives.

2. Though the movie got "two thumbs up" from Ebert and Roeper, it was largely panned by critics and received little attention or publicity.

3. For more on this point, see the chapter by David O'Connor in this volume.

4. Ironically, according to sportswriter Charley Rosen, Wooden had a "not-so-secret habit of viciously cursing opposing players during the course of ball games." http://msn.foxsports.com/nba/story5505042?print=true.

5. Ralph Waldo Emerson, "Uses of Great Men," available at http://www.emersoncentral.com/greatmen.htm.

6. Aristotle, *Nicomachean Ethics,* trans. Martin Ostwald (Indianapolis: Liberal Arts Press, 1962), 1101a.

7. Mortimer J. Adler, *The Paideia Program* (New York: Collier Books, 1984), 3.

8. Well, fans from North Carolina may also remember some of these players. The name of Dan Dakich, for instance, may ring a bell for Tar Heels fans. This game, incidentally, provides support for the recent observation of sportswriter Gregg Doyel: "There's a reason Knight has one more national championship than Smith with less than half the Final Four appearances. Smith was a better recruiter and a brilliant coach, but Knight's the best tactician in college basketball history." Gregg Doyel, "Take It to the Bank: Knight Will Pass the Dean," http://cbs.sportsline.com/print/collegebasketball/story/9035497.

9. As the play unfolds, the character who speaks this line succumbs to dishonesty and as a result suffers a deep sense of disgust with himself. For an insightful discussion of the play and its practical moral implications, see Tom Morris, *If Aristotle Ran General Motors* (New York: Henry Holt, 1997), 40–43.

10. Associated Press, "Ripken 'in a State of Denial' over Palmeiro's Test," http://sports.espn.go.com/mlb/news/story?id=2130301.

11. Tom Morris, *True Success: A New Philosophy of Excellence* (New York: Grossett/Putnam, 1994), 219.

12. Bob Knight with Bob Hammel, *Knight: My Story* (New York: Thomas Dunne Books, 2002), 6–7.

13. Knight*, Knight: My Story,* 24.

14. Earl Cox, "Earl Cox on Sports," http://www.voice-tribune.com/2_10_05/earlcox2_10_05.html.

For details of how Gilbert flagrantly and frequently violated NCAA rules during the latter years of Wooden's tenure at UCLA, see Mark Heisler, *They Shoot Coaches Don't They? UCLA and the NCAA since John Wooden* (New York: Macmillan,

1996), 44–62. According to Heisler, Gilbert did everything from paying for abortions for players' girlfriends to scalping their tickets. For another account of Gilbert's role in UCLA basketball, see Jim Savage, *The Encyclopedia of the NCAA Basketball Tournament* (New York: Dell, 1990), 710.

15. Dave Kindred, "Indiana's Decision No Whitewash," http://www.sportingnews. com/voices/dave_kindred/20000518.html.

For more on Gilbert's relationship with Abdul-Jabbar, see Heisler, *They Shoot Coaches Don't They?* 54–56. Heisler cites another vivid example to illustrate Wooden's tolerance of Gilbert: "'I remember we were on a road trip in Chicago,' said Greg Lee, 'and five guys all got on the bus together wearing matching coats with fur-lined collars. It was pretty conspicuous. It's not like Coach was an ostrich about Sam but he wouldn't confront the problem'" (56).

16. Dan Wetzel, "An Old Hoops Battle," http://www.acctoday.com/Dan_Wetzel . . . =6869&author=76&subject=2&school=0.

17. Apparently, Gilbert ignored the NCAA and continued his involvement with UCLA until his death in 1987. See Heisler, *They Shoot Coaches Don't They?* 60–62.

18. http://www.english.ucla.edu/ucla1960s/7071/austin12.htm. For an insightful analysis of some pragmatic and self-serving reasons why the NCAA may not have investigated UCLA during Wooden's tenure, see Brian Seel, "Time to Be Honest about Wooden's Legacy," http://www.sportspages.com/content/blog.php?p=461&more=1. See also Heisler, *They Shoot Coaches Don't They?* 57.

19. James Boswell, *The Life of Samuel Johnson* (New York: Modern Library, 1952), 521. The entry is for April 6, 1775.

THIRD QUARTER

Shooting from the Perimeter

Dirk Dunbar

THE DAO OF HOOPS

The Dao does nothing, yet leaves nothing undone.

—*Daode jing* (v. 37)

THE DAO ("THE WAY") permeates popular culture. The yin-yang symbol is a media icon, visible on car bumpers, TV commercials, T-shirts, surfboards, you name it, while books such as *The Tao of Pooh, The Tao of Physics,* and the Tao/Dao of almost anything imaginable can be found in most bookstores.[1] The reason is simple: the Dao and its related notions offer a model of balanced and harmonious action that can enhance all kinds of ways of being and doing, including the art of playing basketball.

For me, basketball is the ultimate sport: to play it well requires teamwork, instantaneous decision making, spontaneous hand-eye-foot coordination, patience, intensity, dedication, concentration, and selflessness. All these elements are emphasized in ancient China's earth-wisdom tradition, particularly in Daoism. Key Daoist concepts such as *wuwei, qi,* and *ziran* not only integrate the most significant qualities of the sport but also demonstrate how basketball can serve as a microcosm of a balanced, meaningful life. I am not just writing theoretically but also speaking from experience. Both in basketball and in life, Daoism has helped point me in the right direction. While I excelled in hoops, admittedly, I'm still trying to navigate the rest.

I started playing basketball before I can remember. With help from my older brother, I learned the fundamentals on a small court with a four-foot basket in our basement. I could dribble equally well with each hand and shoot layups and laybacks and even make an occasional free throw on a regulation basket by the time I entered kindergarten. At the YMCA, on the court in our backyard, and in school gyms all over town, I spent countless hours in pickup games or alone, pretending to be (or to be playing against) Oscar Robertson or Jerry West. Anytime anyone asked me what I wanted to be when I grew up, my answer was immediate: a professional basketball player.

All through my youth, I lived and breathed the game, carrying a basketball with me wherever I went. "If a basketball had hair," a reporter quoted my coach, "he'd marry it." Following a fun-filled high school career (during which I was selected to all-state and All-American teams, led the nation in scoring, and was recruited by over two hundred colleges), I attended Central Michigan University and was the third-leading scorer as a freshman in the Mid-American Conference. I was contacted by a number of NBA scouts and agents and felt confident that I had a future in pro basketball. I watched film, worked endlessly on fundamentals, and continually broke down every aspect of my game in an effort to become a complete player. Only later, however, when I discovered Daoism, could I truly understand and fully appreciate the game.

Balancing Yin and Yang

Daoism is an ancient Chinese wisdom tradition that is more an evolving way of life than a system or a philosophy. Many Daoist practices have developed over thousands of years and have a variety of practical applications that relate to balancing yin and yang, such as proper breathing, martial arts, fengshui, art, acupuncture, and healthy eating. Rooted in an animistic worldview, the Dao patterns nature's interconnected cycles, displaying and celebrating creative diversity by guiding the interplay of yin and yang. "All beings carry yin and embrace yang, and blending the vital force of each creates harmony," the *Daode jing* teaches (v. 42).

Yin is a dark, ecstatic, receptive, feminine force that represents the earth, coldness, wetness, softness, spontaneity, and nature's chaotic yet creative power. Yang is a light, rational, assertive, masculine force that reflects the sun and heavens, warmth, dryness, hardness, control, and order. The interdependence of yin and yang is based on the principle that whenever a thing reaches an extreme, it reverts toward its opposite. Day peaks and turns toward night, it rains when clouds absorb too much moisture, hot fires burn out more quickly, gravity counterbalances to harmonize planetary orbits, and animals breathe in rhythm with plants. From the origins of Chinese earth wisdom to the peak of Daoist thought in the writings of Laozi (sixth century B.C.) and Zhuangzi (fourth century B.C.), the Daoist tradition evolved from myths, rituals, and fortune-telling into poetic and practical expositions of how that way could inform a myriad of activities, including, as it turns out, basketball.

To balance yin and yang on the basketball court requires a blending of seemingly conflicting opposites such as competition and surrender, strategy and spontaneity, aggression and patience, and self-sufficiency and teamwork. Basketball, like every other sport, involves yang traits associated with competition and winning. While winning has become far too important in our culture, even to the point of being the supreme measure of "success," being competitive and goal oriented helps ignite creativity and heighten focus. However, as former Nebraska football coach Tom Osborne has noted, if victory becomes the sole purpose of playing, that can actually get in the way of winning. As the classical Daoist philosopher Zhuangzi states:

> When an archer is shooting for nothing
> He has all his skill.
> If he shoots for a brass buckle
> He is already nervous . . .
> He thinks more of winning
> Than of shooting—
> And the need to win
> Drains him of power.[2]

To perform at the highest level possible, our goal cannot be any external reward; rather, one must be so immersed in the action that the playing becomes an end in itself, free of distraction and desire. Competition, when balanced with a yin perspective, isn't focused on defeating the "other," but on overcoming the obstacles that suspend the sort of mindful surrendering necessary for optimal performance. The same is true of strategy: if one concentrates solely on which play to run, which trap to set, which pass to make, then the potential for a spontaneous response to a particular situation is lost and so is the ability to counteract the other team's defense or offense. Having a plan is important, but not as important as cultivating the ability to react. That includes, of course, the need for individual skills to shine within the context of the team. A good offensive player should have the freedom to freelance, to take a risk and make a move that is not part of a designed play. Basketball is a process, not something that can be controlled, diagrammed, or mechanically executed. In nearly all cases, a balance must be found, for whenever an action is forced or agenda-driven rather than allowed to happen, the opposite of the intended outcome may well occur.

Wuwei, Practice, and Disciplined Surrender

"The zone" is a common term among athletes. It refers to the special state in which the body's instincts, due to muscle and nervous system motor training, transcend ego-consciousness in ways that Michael Murphy, cofounder of the Esalen Institute, calls "extraordinary" or "metanormal." Murphy, who has cataloged thousands of extraordinary experiences in sport, calls the zone "a space beyond ordinary space that is intimately connected with both body and mind."[3] I have been in that space many times, particularly at the height of my basketball career. I can bear witness to many of the elements Murphy designates as extraordinary: a unique sense of illumination, altered perceptions of time and space, and exceptional feats. I scored sixty-five points in a high school game, forty-one in a college game, and seventy-four in the European professional league, and I can attest that there were phases in each game when I experienced the zone, moments when time and action seemed to slow down and play became effortless, not guided by me per se but by a kind of "flow" in which I sensed my "self" and all action as one. That flow was not confined to moments in games but was activated daily in a regimen of practice and playing. Although I cannot presume to know how one initiates flow, I am comfortable describing it in terms of the Daoist concept of wuwei.

Wuwei enacts the Dao, rhythmically balancing the orderly yang and chaotic yin. Literally translated as "no action," wuwei does not mean passivity, but a natural, unstructured, playful, and egoless mode of action that is quite different from the socially regulated activity emphasized in the Chinese Confucian tradition. By embodying wuwei, the person of the Dao is as effortless as flowing water. Gracefully guided by gravity to the lowest places and powerful enough to cut through rock, flowing water is a common Daoist analogy of how one can—by being humble, unassuming, yet effective—mirror the Dao. As the *Daode jing* (v. 78) declares:

> In the world is nothing
> so soft and gentle as water.
> Yet nothing hard and inflexible
> can withstand its power.

Wuwei does not mean that one is merely reactive or content to avoid obstacles to personal development; rather, wuwei means acting in such perfect accord with the environment that you become so completely absorbed in what is happening that your sense of self is not limited to a locality, but is part of the process or field of action. As verse 48 suggests:

> By not forcing things,
> you embrace wuwei.
> When nothing is forced,
> nothing is left undone.

As Alan Watts points out, we use many phrases to characterize wuwei, such as "going with the grain, rolling with the punch, swimming with the current, trimming the sails to the wind, taking the tide at its flood, and stooping to conquer."[4] "Practice wuwei, and everything falls into place," the *Daode jing* says (v. 3). To learn to go with the flow is not a matter of will but requires thousands of hours of training and a ceaseless practice of disciplined surrender. Only when motor memory has been thoroughly ingrained can one activate the unconscious processes that transport one into the zone. As LA Lakers coach Phil Jackson notes:

> Basketball is a complex dance that requires shifting from one objective to another at lightning speed. . . . The secret is *not thinking.* That doesn't mean being stupid; it means quieting the endless jabbering of thoughts so that your body can do what it's been trained to do without the mind getting in the way. All of us have had flashes of this sense of oneness . . . when we're completely immersed in the moment, inseparable from what we're doing. This kind of experience happens all the time on the basketball floor; that's why the game is so intoxicating.[5]

Watts calls wuwei a means of "taking the line of least resistance in all one's actions" by exercising the "unconscious intelligence of the whole organism and, in particular, the innate wisdom of the nervous system."[6] In other words, while it takes years of discipline to cultivate instinctive bodily wisdom, only when one surrenders the ego to the process can the highest level of performance be attained. As Abraham Maslow explains, the key to peak performance lies "in the Taoistic feeling of letting things happen rather than of making them happen, and of being perfectly happy and accepting of this state of nonstriving, nonwishing, noninterference, noncontrolling, nonwilling. This is the transcendence of ambition, of efficiencies. This is the state of having rather than of not having. Then of course one lacks nothing."[7]

Whether dribbling through a press or double-pumping a jump shot to avoid getting it blocked, the most effective acts are not conscious choices but instinctive reactions based on years of practice and moments of disciplined surrender. The trick is to string a number of those moments together when it counts. I'll never forget the feeling of hitting eight long-range jump shots in a row against Eastern Illinois en route to scoring thirty-three in the second half (and that was before the three-point line); or scoring nineteen points in the last four minutes against Frankfurt to help my team win a tournament game by one point; or constantly breaking down the defense, scoring twenty-nine points, and dishing out a career-high twenty-two assists in the Icelandic championship game (which we won by three). One of the most meaningful compliments I received after a well-played game was, "You were unconscious!"

Qi, Meditation, and Mastery

The art of shooting free throws mirrors the game of basketball in that it involves unending practice and a ritual of preparation, such as setting oneself, taking a couple of dribbles, taking a deep breath and slowly exhaling, and focusing on the rim—all before releasing the shot. While all elements are important in preparation, nothing is more vital than breathing and imaging. Proper breathing helps relax and focus the mind, while visualizing the ball going into the basket is paramount in creating confidence. Both are vital to the rhythm of the force, the *prana* or "primal breath," that Daoists describe as *qi*. Another key concept in China's earth-wisdom tradition, qi is the energy that moves through patterns of varying degrees of yin and yang intensity. The mythological origins of qi involved ancestor spirits, but in later Daoist thought qi became identified as the force that runs through the "dragon veins" that connect the sky with the mountains, valleys, and rivers. Through stars and rocks to hearts and fingers, its movement is harmonious when flowing and balanced, and unhealthy when blocked and unbalanced. An elemental manifestation of Dao, qi is the vital force that, when engaged, makes wuwei the natural response to anything—beginning with the act of breathing.

Balancing the in and out of breathing was called *Tu na* by Huangdi, the legendary Yellow Emperor. *Tu* refers to exhaling and *na* to inhaling, and the two were inevitably equated with yin and yang, respectively. Daoist breathing exercises are designed, to paraphrase Zhuangzi, to let out the old, bring in the new, and find "the still point of Dao." Originally used to exorcise demons and channel the vital energy associated with gods of the body, breathing exercises were eventually recognized as expelling poisons and germs and revitalizing qi. Allied with breathing techniques, meditation practices may have started as an attempt to contact gods or spirits, but "just sitting," as Zhuangzi calls it, serves as a means to balance emotions, quell desire, invigorate mental and physical health, and harmonize with the Dao. In basketball the ability to meditate, to quiet the mind and visualize, to breathe deeply and balance qi, can dramatically improve one's game. Effectiveness, as verse 10 of the *Daode jing* notes, requires a kind of mastery that centers all "pure" action:

Can you still your mind
and embrace the original oneness?
In harmonizing qi,
can you return to infancy? . . .
Acting without expectations,
leading without dominating,
this is called the supreme virtue.

To embrace the original oneness, to act without desire, to harmonize qi are all tied to a process of disciplined surrender that comes only from countless hours of practice and the willingness to relinquish the ego to unconscious powers. "When compulsion controls qi, energy is misdirected," according to the *Daode jing* (v. 55). The practice of surrender is, perhaps, nowhere more important or more difficult in hoops than on the free throw line. Standing alone with the action stopped, it becomes imperative to yield and let pure concentration and confidence take over, regardless of the score or how late it is in the game. As George Leonard—a cartographer of levels of athletic prowess—points out, "The courage of a master is measured by his or her willingness to surrender."[8] Or, as Laozi puts it, "Surrender begets perfection" (v. 22). Although I'm older, slower, heavier, and far from perfect, I can still surrender enough to hit over a hundred straight free throws.

Ziran and "Letting Go"

It is no secret that many great athletes possess inner calm, superior improvisational skills, and the ability to know when to do what. To be comfortable in all situations, regardless of the score, the pressure, the opposition's strength, is to have what Bill Bradley calls "a sense of where you are."[9] You not only know where you are on the court, but you also sense who you are in relation to your abilities, your opponents' skills, and your potential to perform spontaneously, without fear or anxiety. To achieve this requires a harmony of self and surroundings, a unity that is captured in the Daoist concept of ziran. Literally translated as "self-so," ziran means both nature and spontaneity and is illustrated in the endlessly unique configurations of snowflakes, in the meanderings of rivers and biological evolution, and in patterns of waves and seasons. Ziran implies a sort of planned randomness that allows action to unfold spontaneously pure and chaotically ordered. The action is unwilled, but driven; it is aimed, but goal free. The *Daode jing* advises, "Embrace the great formless form and let things go their way" (v. 35).

To embody ziran on the basketball court would entail, for instance, aiming a shot, releasing it, and instead of trying to will it in, simply letting it be. By recognizing yourself as a partner to the action as opposed to being the source of it, the ego is transcended and the counterproductive potential of willing something to happen is avoided. If, on the other hand, one is focused on what one is "trying" to do to make the shot, thereby separating oneself from the surrounding field of action, "analysis paralysis" can result as thinking interferes with unconscious muscle memory. As Zhuangzi expresses it:

> The Unconsciousness
> And entire sincerity of Tao
> Are disturbed by any effort
> At self-conscious demonstration.[10]

To be "self-so," or to embrace ziran, is to recognize the innermost self beyond the ego, freed from attachments and open to anything. Even the Dao, according to Laozi, flows in accordance with the "law of ziran" (v. 25). That law, as Michael Murphy explains, includes wuwei and qi: "The cultivation of *i* [wholeness] and *chi* [qi] are complemented in Taoist practice by *wu wei*, disciplined flow and surrender to deep nature, and *tzu jan* [ziran], disciplined spontaneity. The doctrine of *wu wei* leads its practitioners to refrain from contention, to remain silent and aloof, while *tzu jan* prompts them to respond naturally and spontaneously to attacking forces."[11]

To sense ziran is to be aware that we are part of nature and that nature is not completed by human consciousness. That awareness, which reveals nature as perfectly complete, encourages a reverence for all being and teaches the value of balance. To find the Dao is to find ways to counteract anger, to feel that we are our relationships, and to be content in the search that is life by embracing its dynamic and ever-changing nature. This helps explain why the Daoist sage is renowned for being joyous as well as humorous. Always careful not to take anything too seriously, including loss, regrets, or even death, the sage recognizes the transitory nature of existence but sees it as the Dao in endless states of transformation. Aware of the relativity of all positions, including his or her own, the person of the Dao warns of the fallibility of not seeing the limits of goals, distinctions, and convictions. Free of separation and able to abandon the ego, the sage transcends the competitive, dominating attitudes that breed pride, hostility, and senseless aggression. As the *Daode jing* (v. 30) puts it:

The sage does what is necessary then stops.
Using strength without coercion
The master ventures on the path,
Able to achieve without pride . . .
Able to achieve without possessing
Able to achieve without force.

By trusting natural processes associated with ziran, from sunsets to healing, we are more apt to release fear, anxiety, and worries that are obstacles to growth and compassion.

Basketball and Philosophy

Basketball has played an extraordinarily important role in my life. It not only merged my childhood dreams and day-to-day reality but also helped guide, mold, and transform me. Ten games into my sophomore year of college, I blew out my knee and had total reconstruction. In the following three years I had four more operations, changed my major from religion to philosophy, and took a deep interest in Eastern thought. I had an injury-free senior year in the Sunshine State Conference and was the nation's seventh-leading scorer in Division II. Following a series of NBA tryouts, I signed with a team in Iceland, where I led the European League in scoring (we lost to Barcelona in the European Cup). After two years in Iceland (long enough to make it into the Icelandic version of the Trivial Pursuit game), with the motto "Have jump shot, will travel," I played and coached seven years in Germany, where I met my wife, attended various universities, and started making up for all the years that I didn't drink beer. Besides studying foreign languages, cultures, and philosophies, I made enduring friendships. No question, basketball has helped engender in me a cross-cultural awareness that, like the sport itself, transcends race and nationalities. The game has taught me discipline, self-mastery through constant mental and physical nurturing, and a viable approach to living life—one nicely captured by a fellow student of Eastern thought, coach Phil Jackson: "Like life, basketball is messy and unpredictable. It has its way with you, no matter how hard you try to control it. The trick is to experience each moment with a clear mind and open heart. When you do that, the game—and life—will take care of itself."[12] As the *Daode jing* avers, "When the supreme Dao is present, action ignites from the heart" (v. 18).

Over millennia the Chinese have discovered practices that allow the seeker to get in touch with and enact the principles of the Way. Those practices include dance, meditation, alchemy, acupuncture, fengshui, and martial arts, all of which aim at harmonizing the bipolar aspects of the qi force. By balancing the in-and-out of breathing, the meridian points of the body's energy system, the intake of nourishment and medicines, the arrangement of objects in the physical environment, and the movement of the body through space, practitioners are led toward the Dao. In a similar fashion, basketball can serve as a path toward the Way. It can open the door to action that is selfless, masterful, and completely embedded in the here and now. The secret is to surrender to an inner force that can be trained but not controlled and to a way of being that embraces a Self beyond the self. In other words, there is more to a good hook shot than meets the eye.[13]

Notes

1. With help from a variety of translations, my former Chinese instructor, John Lu, and two of my colleagues, Li Ping Zhang and Sari Cinnamon, I have freely translated the verses from the *Daode jing*. In concert with a scholarly movement aimed at authenticating Daoist thought in contemporary terms, I have chosen the pinyin as opposed to the older Wade-Giles system of transcribing Chinese characters into alphabetical form. Hence, the more familiar transcription of "Tao" is rendered as "Dao," "Lao Tzu" as "Laozi," and *"Tao Te Ching"* as *"Daode jing."*

2. Quoted in Thomas Merton, *The Way of Chuang Tzu* (New York: New Directions, 1969), 107.

3. Michael Murphy, *The Future of the Body: Explorations into the Further Evolution of Human Nature* (New York: Tarcher/Perigee, 1993), 218.

4. Alan Watts, *Tao: The Watercourse Way* (New York: Pantheon, 1975), 76.

5. Phil Jackson, *Sacred Hoops: Spiritual Lessons of a Hardwood Warrior,* 2nd ed. (New York: Hyperion, 1996), 124, 115–16.

6. Watts, *Tao: The Watercourse Way,* 76.

7. Abraham Maslow, *The Farther Reaches of Human Nature* (New York: Viking, 1975), 277.

8. George Leonard, *Mastery: The Keys to Success and Long-Term Fulfillment* (New York: Plume, 1992), 81.

9. Quoted in John McPhee, *A Sense of Where You Are,* 3rd ed. (New York: Farrar, Straus and Giroux, 1999), 1.

10. Merton, *The Way of Chuang Tzu,* 134.

11. Murphy, *The Future of the Body,* 455.

12. Jackson, *Sacred Hoops,* 7.

13. My journey into the Dao of basketball continues, as I am seeing the sport through new eyes, not as a player or coach, but as an impassioned spectator who is "trying hard" to practice wu wei in fan-filled audiences. My son, Jeremy, loves to play and, if you ask me, he's got game.

Bernard Jackson Jr.

HOOP DREAMS, BLACKTOP REALITIES
Basketball's Role in the Social Construction
of Black Manhood

BASKETBALL IS AN institution that can play a pivotal role in the construction of black manhood, and the philosophical dimensions of such a construction are quite complex. Philosophers of sport owe a debt of gratitude to feminist theorists, for they have done a great deal of important work in this area. Feminist theorists have convincingly argued, for instance, that "manhood" is not something that biological males are simply born with. No one doubts that men are male human beings, and their maleness is a biological given. But this notion of "givenness" obscures the process of identity formation in a dual-gender system. Naomi Zack, a leading feminist philosopher, makes this point clearly.

No child would be capable of inventing and creating its identity as a man or a woman on its own, or even capable of typing itself as male or female, from its earliest days. [Female/male] identity starts out as a primary item of the social equipment of infant care, external to the child and imposed on her as instruction and management of mind, body, and behavior. Human infants are designated male or female at birth, and individual identities as men or women develop after that designation in a dual-gender system. The designation itself is merely a matter of words: "It's a boy!" or "It's a girl!" However, the words do more than note a biological fact. The words announce and direct the trajectory of the individual's psychological and social development. A child that remained an "it" following birth could not become a recognizable social agent in a dual-gender system.[1]

Gender, of course, is not the only component that goes into the social construction of black male manhood. Race and class also play important roles, as do a host of other social and cultural factors. In this chapter, I focus upon the vital roles of love and toughness in this process. I shall argue that while love is critical to this construction, toughness is not.

The Role of Love in Black Male Basketball

Except in soaps, female mud-wrestling venues, and bad rollerball movies, the love that women have for one another is evident in all parts of our society. Despite this, however, the belief is widespread that there is a great deal of hate among women, that they are jealous and hypercompetitive with one another, especially when a man is involved. Fortunately, this characterization—reinforced by films such as *Mean Girls* (2004) and a spate of recent books such as Rachel Simmons's *Odd Girl Out: The Hidden Culture of Aggression in Girls* (2002)—is a caricature, for it masks what is quite obvious: women often have a great deal of affection for one another, and they are not afraid to show it. They kiss one another in public, hug warmly, and hold hands. No one sees this as problematic. In fact, our society has acknowledged that it is valuable for women to have "girlfriends." And women who hang out with men exclusively are often derided by other women. In short, love among women is widespread, accepted, and encouraged in America today.

Love among men, on the other hand, is a very touchy subject. While "hanging with the boys" is a ritual that is practiced and oftentimes encouraged—as long as "hanging'" doesn't interfere with one's duties, especially as a spouse or parent—few would think of this as "love." We often refer to this activity as "male bonding," but we typically have no idea what this bonding entails. Bonding involves more than just watching a game, getting drunk, ogling women, and seeing who can piss the farthest off a bridge: it involves sharing one's most intimate thoughts and feelings. But men are still not encouraged to engage in this "real sharing"—at least with other men. Professor Thomas McLaughlin comments that there is rarely any "explicit, verbal sharing of personal information and emotion" among the noontime regulars he plays with at his university. Although he feels affection for his hoops buddies and knows them intimately *as players,* he admits: "I don't know much about their lives off the court, and we don't tend to socialize, even though we live in a small community. In some cases, I don't even know the last names of men I have played with for many years."[2] Today, taking on the persona of the

distant male who doesn't share his feelings is discouraged. Not only is
such a stance difficult for all kinds of relationships, but "holding everything in" is also stressful to the person himself. But once again, such sharing is not encouraged among men; instead, hanging with the boys is
referred to as bonding. And the use of the term is quite interesting, for we
know that real bonding doesn't take place. We know that men *should*
engage in real bonding, but this makes us uncomfortable. Thus, we use
the term "*male* bonding": men are not supposed to bond the way women
do—that is, men are not supposed to *really* bond. Unfortunately, this
suits most men just fine.

This difference in the way men and women relate to members of their
own gender raises two interesting philosophical questions. One is the
classic nature/nurture debate: are these differences due mainly to "nature" (the basic biological differences between men and women) or to
"nurture" (the way men and women are brought up and socialized in
contemporary American culture)? This question is partly conceptual (i.e.,
philosophical) and partly scientific. The second question is straightfor-
wardly normative: should men be encouraged to be more open and expressive in their relationships with other men? That is, should there be
more real sharing and genuine bonding between men, as opposed to mere
hanging?

Most philosophical questions are notoriously difficult to answer, but
these, I suggest, are easy. The fact that intimate and expressive male
friendships are commonplace in many cultures around the world today,
as well as in many past cultures, shows conclusively that our society's
unease with such friendships is not due to nature.[3] The normative question is equally easy to answer. Studies show that people with intimate,
supportive relationships tend to be both happier and healthier than those
who lack such relationships.[4] Why, then, should men limit their intimate
relationships to members of the opposite sex?

Brothers in/at Arms

The world of sports presents males with both hopes and challenges in
constructing their masculine identities. In sports, *real* bonding does take
place. Both teammates and adversaries treat one another as brothers. It
may be strange to think of adversaries treating one another as brothers,

but a little reflection will help make my point. If you are a man who has engaged in competitive sports all your life, think back to your childhood. Recall the times when you were most competitive. Weren't the most intense battles waged between you and your brother or brothers or those very close friends you considered brothers? During these battles, your goal was not just to defeat your opponent but to beat him soundly. Human beings are animals, and as in other animal species, one of our goals is to establish dominance, especially among those closest to us. This struggle for dominance doesn't necessarily include the need to eliminate the opponent. One of the goals may simply be to show "who's boss," to establish what are called "bragging rights." However, the established dominance usually ends with the conclusion of the competition. The brothers go back to being brothers, to taking care of each other, to loving one another. These battles constitute an integral part of real bonding and are part of the process of attaining manhood. As McLaughlin notes, basketball "is one of many places where men learn to negotiate their masculinity, right down at the level of the body, movement, and emotion."[5]

We know that athletes engage in such battles, but what evidence do we have that they resume their roles as brothers? Many basketball fans will remember the 1990–1991 Eastern Conference championship series between the Chicago Bulls and the Detroit Pistons. The Pistons were the two-time defending NBA champions, and the Bulls swept them in four games. With this victory, a new dynasty was inaugurated in professional basketball—the Bulls went on to win six championships in eight years—and the Pistons were not pleased that their reign had come to an end. The Pistons, led by future Hall of Famer and self-anointed leader of the "Bad Boys" Isiah Thomas (even though Bill Laimbeer, Dennis Rodman, and Rick Mahorn were "badder," Thomas was their leader), stormed off the court, ignoring the Bulls and failing to shake hands or congratulate Chicago on its victory. The Pistons were known for their boorish behavior, so their failure to be congratulatory wasn't a big surprise. But in basketball, and in football, the other professional sport dominated by black men, such a failure is rare. The conclusion of an NFL or NBA game is usually a "love-in": opposing players embrace, discuss family issues, and make plans for later in the evening. This is, of course, what brothers do. Players treat one another as family members. In sports, there is the opportunity for real bonding to take place.

The Role of Toughness

Unfortunately, such public displays of affection aren't always appreciated by coaches, owners, league officials, or the media. As McLaughlin points out, "sport is often presented in the media as a hypermasculine practice, focusing on its fierce competitiveness and its displays of male dominance. Think of the extremely photogenic high-fives, chest bumps, and sexualized dances of victory that seem to accompany any televised sports event."[6] And it's no surprise that most coaches, owners, league officials, and media moguls are white men. For many white men, to engage in sports is to engage in war. In a recent film depicting the early years of Paul "Bear" Bryant's reign as head football coach of the University of Alabama Crimson Tide, Bryant calls football "war." Pat Riley, former head coach of the Los Angeles Lakers and current coach and general manager of the Miami Heat, made a similar comment about basketball. In fact, Riley was one of the earliest supporters of the infamous "hard foul," instructing players to prevent opposing players from scoring at any cost. To Bryant and Riley, two white coaches often referred to as geniuses, the opposition was the enemy, and it was important that their players understood this. Those players who didn't exhibit the requisite warrior mentality were scolded and punished, usually by being labeled "soft."

No player wants to be known as soft. David Robinson, a gentleman, an active participant in the life of his community, and one of the nicest guys you'll ever meet, was often stuck with this label. When the San Antonio Spurs continually failed to advance past the Western Conference championships (things changed when future first-ballot Hall of Famer Tim Duncan joined the team), Robinson was always blamed for the failure. Never mind that he was one of the leading scorers in the league, that he was one of the greatest defensive centers of all time (in my opinion, only Bill Russell was better), and that his team won only 25 percent of its games when he was lost for the year to injury. Robinson was not considered a physical player, and the soft label followed him throughout his career. For this reason, Robinson may never receive his due credit, although he, like Duncan, is a future first-ballot Hall of Famer.

I believe that most black players have internalized the idea that a great basketball player must be tough. The mantra often reiterated in basketball circles is that "defense wins championships," and it so happens that good defense is characteristically physical and tough. Tough-ness, however, has an ambiguous place in the formation of black manhood. For white men, the message is clear: a real white man is a tough man. Whether he's at home, in the boardroom, in the gym, or driving his truck "off-road," it's imperative that he be tough. This toughness often spills over into violence, and the violence is accepted. One need look no further than at the way hockey is now played. Once a beautiful game that show-cased speed, grace, and skill, hockey has become a haven for bullies. And it may not be a coincidence that hockey is a sport dominated by white men. But the most disturbing aspect of this violence is that it is accepted, even encouraged. Hockey fans like to see their warriors battle it out; after all, hockey is war. For black men, the message is mixed. Tough defense wins championships, but it's clear that the marquee players are those who make the game look pretty. No-look passes, crossover and behind-the-back dribbling, the beautiful finger roll (George Gervin, the Ice-man, "rolleth"), and pretty 360 dunks—that's what people pay to see. The huge popularity of the *Streetball* phenomenon is a testament, not to the glory of toughness, but to the reverence accorded flashy play. One must be tough to survive in "the Hood," but even the toughest gangsters give basketball players respect.

"Coolness" is another aspect of the black masculine ideal of tough-ness. As former New York Knicks great Walt Frazier remarks: "Coolness is a quality admired in the black neighborhoods. Cool is a matter of self-preservation, of survival. It must go back to the slave days, when often-times all a black man had to defend himself with was his poise. If you'd show fear or anger, you'd suffer the consequences. Today, the guy re-spected in the ghetto is the guy who resists the urge to go off—who can handle himself in a crisis."[7] Don't get me wrong. I'm not denying the value of toughness or poise, or the importance of these qualities in the development of black men; nothing could be further from the truth. This is where the dynamics of a simple game like basketball become quite complex. Nowhere are these dynamics revealed more vividly than in the 1994 movie *Hoop Dreams*. This award-winning documentary follows the lives of two young, black, inner-city basketball players, Arthur Agee and William Gates, from their early teens to their early twenties. While sociologists will undoubtedly find the film fascinating, philosophers should pay attention to the film as well. (In fact, it is a fine film that everyone should see.) Because my concern is with the film's philosophical import, chronicling the entire film is not necessary. I'm especially interested for the moment in what one of the players, Arthur Agee, learns about the costs of a success-driven, "commodifying" culture.

It doesn't take long for the people around Agee and Gates to notice that these two kids have superior basketball talent. Both are taken out of their black inner-city schools and offered financial aid to attend St. Joseph's, a predominantly white Chicago suburban high school known for its powerhouse basketball teams. Agee struggles academically and fails to meet his coach's high expectations on the court. When Agee's father is laid off work, his family can no longer afford to make tuition payments, and Agee is forced to leave school. He returns to his neighborhood high school, plays spectacularly during the state tournament in his senior year, and earns a scholarship to a community college. At the film's conclusion, Arthur is still "chasing the dream," although it's obvious he doesn't have NBA talent. Agee never fully comes to grips with the extent to which he is being used. For him, the dream lives on.

It is the other player, William Gates, who learns the deeper philosophical lessons. William suffers a serious injury during his junior year of high school, and he is never the same player again. Nevertheless, he is talented enough to have a stellar high school career and earn a scholarship to Marquette University, an institution that boasts impressive athletic as well as academic credentials. The injury sustained in high school hampers his college career, and he eventually decides to quit the team. However, William's institution honors its commitment to his education and doesn't revoke his scholarship.

One might think that William had the more successful career: he didn't flunk out of his first high school, he had a fine high school career, and he earned a college degree. However, this "success" didn't come without a high price. He was a fierce competitor, and he often played hurt. Players are often encouraged to play hurt, to "suck it up." But when they are unable to perform to the best of their abilities—and of course, most injured players are unable to play their best—they are frequently criticized for coming up short.

Often this criticism comes from the very persons who encouraged them to make the attempt in the first place. Gates was harshly criticized both by his coach, Gene Pingatore, and by certain members of his family.

He knew his importance to his team, and he was determined to give it everything he had. When he performed well while playing hurt, he was called "tough," "brave," a "warrior." When he performed poorly while playing hurt, his coach described William—William *the person*, not simply his play—in terms that are better left unprinted. Coaches want families to believe that they are second fathers to their children, that their children can come to these coaches for advice. William wasn't lucky enough to have such a coach. When Gates asked for advice concerning a problem he had with a friend, Pingatore told him to forsake the friend. Pingatore's thinking was transparent: anything that could distract William from his performance on the basketball court was to be discarded, including other people.

Why is this brief analysis of *Hoop Dreams* included in a discussion of toughness? Both Gates and Agee were being used: by the "playground recruiter" who led Agee to believe that he was the second coming of Michael Jordan; by Coach Pingatore, who lured both away from their neighborhoods with the promise of a better "educational" experience; and by their families, who burdened them with the belief that success in basketball—and the "new house for Mama" that comes with it—is a form of repayment for all their families have done for them. However, these experiences have toughened these players—and I don't mean that they are now ready to go out and fight someone with a club.

Agee holds on to the dream that will never come true. He never made it to the NBA. But now in his early thirties, he continues to play and promote basketball, has started his own clothing line, has moved his family out of the projects, and is actively involved in many charities. Not everything has gone smoothly in his life. He is the father of four children, each with a different woman.[8] He knows it's hard to be successful when one is a product of the inner city, but it's harder to survive when one is not doing what one loves. To continue to dream and do what one loves when the possibility of failure looms large is a measure of toughness.

Gates is tough as well. He has reinvented his life. After graduating from Marquette, he became a minister. Much like Plato's enlightened prisoner in his famous allegory of the cave, Gates has chosen to return to the projects, where he now serves as a minister in the Living Faith Community Center in Chicago's Cabrini-Green. In 2001 he made a renewed attempt to achieve his dream of playing in the NBA. After practicing with

Michael Jordan for five hours a day, Gates was invited to tryouts with both the Chicago Bulls and the Washington Wizards. As before, however, his dream ended when he suffered a serious injury.

Although Gates's love for basketball has waned, he now realizes that there is more to life than basketball. It's difficult for some people to deal with the fact that those who purportedly love you are really using you. I believe that William has learned another valuable philosophical lesson: as Karl Marx (1818–1883) noted, it is natural for human beings, especially in capitalist societies, to use and exploit other human beings. So often in big-money sports, players are "looked upon as a supply of a commodity like any other."[9] Gates, in fact, was bluntly cautioned about this by the famous film director Spike Lee when Gates attended the prestigious Nike All-American Basketball Camp the summer before his senior year of high school. Lee told the mostly black players at the camp: "You have to realize that nobody cares about you. You're black, you're a young male—all you're supposed to do is deal drugs and mug women. The only reason you're here is because you can make their team win. If their team wins, these schools get a lot of money. This whole thing is revolving around money."[10] Fortunately, the good Jesuits at Marquette University refused to commodify William, honored their commitment to him, and helped him prove to the world that he had much more than "use value."

At the end of the documentary, William expresses the hope that the people in his life will continue to love him even though he is not a successful basketball player. In other words, he hopes that although he is treated as a means to an end, he is not treated *merely* as a means but always at the same time as an end—that is, as a person with intrinsic dignity and worth, who should be loved and valued for his own sake and always treated with respect. As the great German philosopher Immanuel Kant (1724–1804) said, persons must be valued *as persons,* never as mere "commodities" or things. In *Hoop Dreams,* we see both the false allure of a mercenary culture and the courageous spirit needed to overcome it.

At one point in *Hoop Dreams,* Agee and Gates embrace—a real embrace—and they express their feelings of love for one another in words. Yes, two young black men tell each other, "I love you." Black men love the game of basketball because we love the stuff of our dreams. So where does the love between Agee and Gates come from? Certainly it comes from being part of a shared struggle, from recognizing that this simple game can raise one from the miserable conditions in which too many black citizens of the United States are mired. However, I believe that it goes deeper than that. Black men want to see each other succeed. I know this sounds strange: most of the crime committed by black men is directed toward other black men. But bear with me for a moment. Nothing makes me prouder than seeing black men succeed, seeing black men *make it,* and I know from long experience that I am not the only black man who feels that way. Unfortunately, it's rare to hear of such success outside the realm of basketball. (The stories of black male success are there, but they don't make good copy.) For many inhabitants of our inner cities, the *only* successful black men they know are basketball players. So the love between Agee and Gates is similar to the love between brothers: it is a love that is a source of strength, of support. It is a love that says you can make it, although the odds are against you. If black men love one another, they can make it.

Notes

1. Naomi Zack, *Inclusive Feminism: A Third Wave Theory of Women's Commonality* (Lanham, MD: Rowman and Littlefield, 2005), 41.

2. Thomas McLaughlin, "'Man to Man': Basketball, Movement, and the Practice of Masculinity," *South Atlantic Quarterly* 103, no. 1 (2004): 186.

3. See C. S. Lewis, *The Four Loves* (New York: Harcourt Brace, 1960), 87. Think, for instance, of Tennyson's *In Memoriam* or Plato's *Symposium.*

4. David G. Myers, *The Pursuit of Happiness* (New York: Avon, 1993), chaps. 8 and 9.

5. McLaughlin, "'Man to Man,'" 171.

6. McLaughlin, "'Man to Man,'" 183.

7. Quoted in David Shields, *Black Planet: Facing Race during an NBA Season* (New York: Crown Publishers, 1999), 73–74.

8. Mike Wise, "Looking Back at Broken 'Dreams,'" *Washington Post,* July 5, 2004, D1.

9. Karl Marx, *The Economic and Philosophic Manuscripts of 1844,* trans. Martin Milligan (New York: International Publishers, 1964), 120.

10. Robert Paul Walker, *Hoop Dreams* (Atlanta: Turner Publishing, 1995), 99–100.

Deborah A. Wallace and James M. Wallace

SHE GOT GAME
Basketball and the Perfectly Developed Woman

If you want to see the best basketball in the world, watch a women's basketball game.

—John Wooden

Women's basketball sucks.

—Stacey Pressman

DISCUSSIONS OF WOMEN'S basketball often divide into these two opposing assessments of the game: either it is celebrated as the purest form of basketball, played gracefully by competitive athletes in a spirit of cooperation and a devotion to teamwork, or it is condemned as the slowest, dullest form of basketball, featuring participants who seldom demonstrate the individual athleticism and wizardry that make modern men's basketball so entertaining. Both camps reason from the same set of evidence: compared to the men's game, the women's game is played "below the rim," "on the floor," with more cutting and passing, less one-on-one jousting, less power and aggression, fewer slam dunks, and absolutely no alley-oops. For fans like John Wooden, the legendary coach who led the UCLA men's team to ten national championships in the 1960s and 1970s, this less-flamboyant display makes the women's game the best basketball in the world, played the way the game was designed to be played. While Wooden, known for his humility, patience, and gracious demeanor, might serve as the old-fashioned voice for the old-style game, Stacey Pressman, writing for the *Weekly Standard*, summarizes the argument for the bored modern fan in her colloquial evaluation of the worth of women's basketball: it sucks. Pressman speaks for many detractors of women's basketball who blame the very qualities that Wooden admires—teamwork and the lack of athleticism—for the dullness of women's basketball. "Watching 40 minutes of underhanded lay-ups isn't exciting," she complains.

Like most debates over taste, this one has no resolution. Some people enjoy watching the slower, less aggressive women's game; some don't. Some people enjoy watching golf or bowling, and some don't. And those who find women's basketball unexciting aren't likely to be tempted by Wooden's promise of seeing basketball at its best. But the argument over women's basketball is more significant than a mere disagreement over whether the sport is worth tuning in to on a rainy Saturday afternoon. Pressman's real aim is not so much to denigrate women's basketball as to argue that the game's defenders are part of a "girl-power publicity machine" that runs on political correctness and a reluctance to admit the truth (that the game is boring) for fear of appearing sexist. Most collegiate women's programs fail to turn a profit, she reasons, and "no one watches women's basketball," yet the game survives on ESPN and NBC as a politically motivated endorsement of mistaken notions of equality. For Pressman, women's basketball is "jam[med] down your throat" by television, not because the game is exciting, pure, or traditional, but simply *because* it is played by women. "Sports programming," she concludes, "should be about entertainment, not waging the gender wars on our television sets." Pressman intends, it seems, to return fire. She has no fear of appearing sexist since she believes she speaks the truth. But she *is* defending a sexist position.

One could argue that Pressman bases her evaluation of women's basketball on standards borrowed from the men's game: by comparison, women's basketball is not aggressive enough or fast enough; consequently it is not popular or profitable. It is, therefore, not good enough. Ironically, Pressman, a woman, dismisses women's basketball using evaluative standards common in patriarchal societies, in which positions of power are usually held by men. Such societies tend to privilege reason, independence, physical strength, toughness, and competitiveness (traits associated with "masculinity") over compassion, emotion, gentleness, passivity, care, and cooperation, which are usually associated with "femininity." Pressman disparages the women's game, not on principles of athletic competition in which well-trained, dedicated, hard-fighting opponents play by the same rules, but for its failure to live up to standards drawn from the men's game. It might be argued that Pressman finds the game boring only because she views the women's game through the lens of patriarchy. Granted, she is entitled to her boredom, but she defends her judgment of the game by comparing it with a completely different game, the one played by men. Hers is a judgment by opposition. Had men's basketball not existed to set the standard, would she, without that point of comparison, have found the women's game so dull or have described it in the same language? If men were to master the balance beam, would we start complaining about Olga Korbut's fragility, petiteness, and low vertical leap?

Those, like Wooden, who praise women's basketball for its lack of stereotypically masculine features, it might be suggested, also exhibit a patriarchal attitude toward the game, since the compliments frequently come by way of comparison to the men's game: women are admired for not betraying the supposed best traits of their gender, including the deep sense of community that leads to such commendable teamwork. On this basis, Wooden has frequently praised the women's game and criticized the men's in interviews with sports commentators and analysts. His attitude might best be summed up by Jean Strouse, writing in the *New Yorker:* "John Wooden . . . said a couple of years ago that the best pure basketball in the country was being played by women's collegiate teams because the women relied on fundamentals—playing below the rim with grace and finesse—while the men had grown sloppy and showboaty, with too much traveling and wrestling under the basket, and too much emphasis on the highlight-reel dunk."[1]

Although it may seem uncharitable to place Wooden's appreciative comments in the same class with Pressman's, his remarks can be seen as similarly patriarchal. In fact, on the basis of such comments, one could conclude that men are to be congratulated for having developed such passivity and compassion in women as to make their game more interesting and enjoyable now that the men's game has become so excessive. Whereas Pressman argues, in essence, that the game is boring because its athletes don't play like men, Wooden admires the game because its athletes don't play like men.

Many devotees of women's basketball, however, do not see the game as the corrective to the modern men's version. Fans of women's basketball (and there are many) enjoy the game for what it is and find that to-day's game provides a chance to value modern womanhood without comparisons to men. In fact, we will argue in the remainder of this chapter that while a patriarchal society has done all it can to shape the game of women's basketball to promote a sexist and idealized image of women and, in fact, to prevent women from playing like men, the game as it is currently played can deepen our understanding of gender relations and the modern condition of women.

We Don't Want to Marry Amazons

In her essay, "Foucault, Femininity, and the Modernization of Patriarchal Power," philosopher Sandra Lee Bartky provides a good foundation for our examination of the way in which women's basketball has been shaped to reflect a masculine worldview. Bartky takes as her starting point Michel Foucault's revolutionary notion that modern institutions such as the army, the school, and the prison create a form of discipline intended to restrict and regulate the movements and operations of the human body. Bartky argues, however, that Foucault failed to recognize that discussions of the body must take sexual differences into account. Foucault, she writes, "treats the body . . . as if it were one, as if the bodily experiences of men and women did not differ and as if men and women bore the same relationship to the characteristic institutions of modern life."[2] Starting with a central tenet of feminist thinking—that we are born male or female and that our identity as "masculine" or "feminine" is constructed by social and cultural forces—Bartky examines "those disciplinary practices that produce a body which in gesture and appearance is recognizably feminine."[3] She includes among these disciplinary practices, for example, the diet and exercise programs promoted in mass-circulation women's magazines, which are intended to restrict the size and shape of a woman's body. Other disciplinary practices limit a woman's range of acceptable gestures: women are usually expected to maintain a reserved posture (especially while seated), smile more than men, avert their eyes when speaking to men, and gesture less broadly than men. Perhaps the most recognizable disciplinary practice that women have learned to master in their quest for the feminine body is what Bartky calls "ornamentation," the use of cosmetics, jewelry, and the selection of clothes.[4]

In all three categories—shape, gesture, and ornamentation—discipline over the female body is maintained through surveillance. Again, Bartky takes her cue from Foucault, who showed how the actions and movements of prisoners and students are controlled through constant surveillance by wardens and teachers. A prisoner who knows that he is being watched (or even that he might be watched) will discipline himself by practicing only those movements that are permitted and avoiding those that are forbidden. Women, likewise, learn disciplinary practices under the watchful and unrelenting eye of men. There is nothing naturally feminine, in other words, about the woman who has managed to become the slender, graceful, ornamented reflection of the model in a magazine. Such a woman has merely disciplined herself; she has learned to alter her female body to meet the demands and expectations of her beholder. In a patriarchal society, the individual woman's identity—and her value as a woman—is determined by standards established by men. Femininity, implicitly a term of approval, is nothing more than an idea, a social construct, and the perfectly developed woman is merely one who has achieved a level of social conformity and sexual desirability.

Historically, female athletes living in a male-dominated society have keenly sensed the scrutinizing gaze of men who reduce women to their shape, gestures, and ornamentation. For a woman to use her body in sweaty games that require speed, strength, and aggression is to invite commentary on her supposed lack of traditionally feminine qualities and looks. Daniel Ferris, secretary-treasurer of the AAU (Amateur Athletic Union) in the mid-twentieth century, crystallized the point in an article he wrote for *Parade Magazine* in 1952: "Many U.S. men do [say], 'We like our women beautiful and feminine. We don't want to marry Amazons.'"[5] It has long been a powerfully effective sentiment. Surveying women in the 1950s for her doctoral dissertation, Laura Kratz found that the most common reasons women gave for avoiding participation in sports were the fears of developing muscles and of looking masculine.[6] Such fears have a deep history in the United States, where, before the late nineteenth century, women's participation in sports was generally limited to nothing more strenuous than footraces and horseback riding, which they could participate in "as long as they maintained their grace and femininity."[7] In the second half of that century, as Patricia Vertinsky shows, adolescent girls interested in sports heard conflicting messages, often from women who directed physical education programs, concerning the effects of participation in athletics: "On the one hand, definitions of femininity and menstrual disability theory encouraged girls to accept limits on their actions, including athletic limitations, as the price for having a female body. On the other hand, the development of physical strength and health was a necessary attribute of a robust, productive mother. Some resolution was required to support the training of strong and healthy girls for the demanding responsibilities of motherhood within the boundaries of social respectability and the domestic realm."[8] The focal point of this double vision is the female body and its use by patriarchy: a woman was supposedly limited in what she could or should attempt, but she needed a strong body to become a good mother. What was a girl to do?

The answer arrived, in part, in the form of basketball, which in the 1890s was the country's fastest-growing sport for women.[9] Within a few years of its introduction, however, the women's game came under criticism from both men and women who worried about women's capacity to handle the game's physical demands without damaging their delicate reproductive systems, and from those concerned that the intensely competitive nature of the game could make women too masculine. Senda Berenson, who oversaw basketball at Smith College in the 1890s, noted, "Rough and vicious play seems worse in women than in men: . . . [and] the selfish display of a star by dribbling and playing the entire court, and rough-housing by snatching the ball could not be tolerated."[10] If stealing was unladylike, fighting for a loose ball was worse: girls "become 'scrappy,'" wrote one commentator, "lose their tempers, and often go so far as to make a complete spectacle of themselves."[11] Such competitiveness, noted a Wellesley teacher in 1903, was unhealthy for anyone, but especially for women since "the qualities they tend to develop are not womanly."[12] Such women are perilously close to becoming Amazons.

A No-Win Situation for Women

Rule changes were introduced almost immediately, and the game was modified in various leagues and at various times over the next forty years to prevent intense play and excessive strain. One of the most widespread rule changes involved dividing the court in half. Teams were composed of six players, and three players from each team were restricted to one half of the court, limiting the amount of running any one woman would have to do. Her range was further limited by restrictions on the number of times she could dribble the ball, two or three depending on the league. It was illegal for two defenders to trap an offensive player, and touching another player or attempting to steal the ball was forbidden. Such regulations would ensure that participants maintained some measure of feminine decorum. To aid the cause, rules often included helpful advice. In one set of rules, players were cautioned that passing the ball with two hands "tends to cultivate flat chests and round shoulders" and "no woman can afford to be flat-chested."[13]

Whether the rule changes had the desired effect is a matter of opinion. According to a male physician in 1931, women who play basketball "develop ugly muscles and scowling faces and the competitive spirit. As an inevitable consequence your girls who are trained in Physical Education today may find it more difficult to attract the most worthy fathers for their children."[14] On the other hand, the chair of the AAU's Basketball Committee reported to his committee after seeing a woman's game in 1930: "I will admit I too was skeptical and fully expected to see fainting girls carried away in ambulances, others laced in straight jackets after severe cases of hysteria and some in complete collapse after extreme cases of melancholia, the air permeated with smelling salts, etc., but I was agreeably pleased that none of these things happened."[15] Must have been the one-handed passes.

The history of women's basketball is filled with examples of players trying courageously to thrive as both athletes and "feminine" women, including participating in beauty pageants during tournaments, altering uniforms to make them more revealing, openly discussing their heterosexual relationships and motherhood, and fielding teams, like the Red Heads, who acted out coquettish scenes in exhibition games with men's teams.[16] Early commercials for the WNBA assured fans that off the court, women athletes shopped for shoes and got manicures. In 2001 *Playboy* offered Lisa Harrison, of the Phoenix Mercury, half a million dollars to pose nude. Such deference on the part of female athletes and the constant focus on the female body proves, of course, how impossible the female athlete's position has often been: she must promote her femininity to avoid being denigrated while at the same time fighting off suggestions that her femininity disqualifies her from being taken seriously as an athlete. If she's too pretty, she can't possibly be any good; if she's too good, she can't possibly be a real woman until she shows us in some conventional way that she is. The problem lies, of course, not in women but in the assumptions themselves and in patriarchal attitudes about the female body.

Patriarchal notions of femininity, as they are described by Bartky and other feminist philosophers, reveal that in a male-dominated society, women are equated with their bodies. Told that they must maintain some physical measure of desirability and femininity, women are also told that feminine traits are less respected than masculine ones and that the body is less valued than soul, mind, reason, and intellect. In an influential essay, philosopher Elizabeth Spelman lays the creation of this trap at the feet of Western philosophy, arguing that the traditional dualistic view of mind/body, the devaluing of the physical part of our existence, and the "assumption that woman is body, is bound to her body, or is meant to take care of the bodily aspects of life" have "deeply contributed to the degradation and oppression of women."[17] The notion that our minds are separate from our bodies is not in itself sexist or oppressive, but when mind is equated with men and body with women, as Spelman contends, oppression results, and the oppressed have a difficult time liberating themselves. Women who reject the body and its associated values or aspire toward purely intellectual goals merely confirm the existence of a mind/body split and show tacit support for the notion that mind has primacy.

As athletes, women face a similar irresolvable contradiction: play as women are expected to play—with restraint, cooperation, teamwork—and they will appear to have resigned themselves to their weaker side of the feminine/masculine dichotomy; they will seem happy to have inherited a game whose slow pace and frequent passing of the ball were created by rules designed to limit women's physical movement, and they will lose the attention of fans who, conditioned by men's sports, want to see a more exciting game. Imitate men—play harder, faster, more aggressively, with more flash and athleticism—and they again give credence to the feminine/masculine split, this time suggesting that real accomplishment means acting like men. Either way, it's women: 0, patriarchy: 1. The solution is the creation of a new game: a game that undermines old categories of masculine and feminine, that evolves with the increasing talents of female athletes, and that is not altered to reflect the demands of patriarchy or evaluated on patriarchal standards. If the strong female athlete challenges conventional social categories, create a new category.

The Modern Woman's Game

Observing the current game through a clear lens, one with no refractive ideology, may be nearly impossible, but suppose that a visitor to planet Earth watched only women's, and no men's, basketball. What would such a visitor discover in a few selected women's games? In the first WNBA game, in 1997, Los Angeles Sparks center Lisa Leslie unsuccessfully attempted a slam dunk. In 2001 Michelle Snow, of the Tennessee Lady Vols, successfully dunked the ball (the first in a women's game since 1994), and Leslie followed one year later with the first dunk in the WNBA. Nearly half the points scored by the winning team in the first championship game in the WNBA were scored by one player, Cynthia Cooper, whose ball-handling athleticism would thrill even our intergalactic visitor, as would any game in which our traveler had the opportunity to see the slashing drives of Teresa Weatherspoon, the shot-blocking ability of Margo Dydek, or the shooting skills of Katie Smith, who scored forty-six points in one WNBA game. In the third season of the WNBA, Debbie Black's battle for a loose ball included a choke hold on one player and an attempt to punch another. The confrontation ended with an opponent slapping Black. Last year, the Phoenix Mercury's Diana Taurasi lowered her shoulder and leveled DeLisha Milton-Jones, of the Washington Mystics, in a game that saw four technical fouls and an ejection. A few weeks later, Seattle Storm forward Iziane Castro Marques was suspended for one game for throwing a punch at a player's head. Watching Phoenix's Jennifer Gillom play in Italy in her pre-WNBA years, our visitor would see the full power of women on display: "You saw bruises after every game. No blood, no foul—that's the way they play over there."[18] When Duke beat Louisiana State to advance to the NCAA final game in 2006, the Associated Press ran a photo of two Duke players celebrating with a jumping chest bump.

Slam dunks, individual showmanship, superstar statistics, determination, power, aggression, violence, bruises, blood, chest bumps—women can, if they want, play forcefully, powerfully, "above the rim," with intensity, determination, and flashes of individual brilliance. More or less than men? Who's to say, and what's the point in asking? Any comparisons to the men's game will privilege one game over "the other." Our visitor might be cautioned not to generalize from the few examples given above, but he (turns out it's a he) could justly conclude that women are capable of playing with intensity and standing out individually. Because the athletes are getting faster and better, not because the game needs to live up to a standard established by men, the WNBA will institute rule changes in the 2006 season. A new shot clock, for example, shortened from thirty to twenty-four seconds, will aid today's faster, more athletic players. In the past, rules changed to reflect gender stereotypes and paternal attitudes; today's changes respond to the increasing talents of women.

There's no denying, however, that our visitor would also come away from an experience of women's basketball believing that the game involves passing the ball around and running plays to get an open shot, and that these plays occur more often than one-on-one drives or attempted dunks. Indeed, reflections on basketball written by female players often comment on the sense of togetherness, camaraderie, teamwork, compassion, and concern that women athletes share. Rather than choosing to believe that camaraderie is simply a defensive result of patriarchal treatment of women, or that cooperation is an essential quality of femininity, we choose instead to see the emphasis on teamwork as a conscious choice made by women in an effort to win games and to make basketball more enjoyable for those who play and watch it. Michelle Snow, the slam-dunking Tennessee player, told a reporter for *South Coast Today*, "Our game isn't about somebody coming out, going one-on-one and taking it coast-to-coast. It's about being team-oriented, about passing to someone who's open. That's what I love about the game. If it was one-on-one all the time, it wouldn't be any fun."[19]

Snow's well-considered approach to teamwork may have been reinforced by her coach at Tennessee, Pat Summitt, who begins with the assumption that teamwork is not an inherent value in any athlete and teaches cooperation as a means toward achieving team and personal goals.[20] Other coaches, like Ole Miss's Ron Aldy, have made similar comments: "The athleticism [in today's female athletes] has made the game better, but women are still more receptive to the team concepts of passing, cutting, ball-handling and pure shooting. We need college coaches who keep demanding those things."[21] Aldy and Summitt and coaches like them don't preach teamwork and fundamentals to their women's teams as a message to ego-driven men's teams. Teamwork and fundamentals—foul shooting, cutting, passing, picking, dribbling, shooting—are how basketball games are won.[22] Here John Wooden's comment about the "purity" of women's basketball is correct: the essence of basketball is to help each other move to the other side of the court and put the ball in the net. The woman's game can remain "pure" because women's teams can decide to play it that way, to help each other win games. Conscious control over their destiny—the decision to *deliberately* play the game in a manner that balances individual and team-centered concerns and that is enjoyable and rewarding to the women who play the game—is how women's basketball best answers the demeaning and contorting demands of patriarchy.

If Pressman and Wooden were our standard-bearers for both the negative and positive views of women's basketball that result from comparison to the men's game, Lisa Leslie and Michelle Snow are co-captains on this new team, composed of women who *can* dunk but don't necessarily always want to, who can shoot and pass, drive the lane or dish off, act independently and cooperatively, defend and explain the game, and celebrate all the power and strength in the female body without deference or apology. Where the strong female athlete once seemed a contradiction, especially to men accustomed to labels such as "masculine" and "feminine," women's basketball players today seem to cut across cultural, social, and ideological lines. Leslie, perhaps the best WNBA player yet, a woman who once told *People* magazine that her motto was "Go for the jugular," is a runway model for the Wilhelmina agency.

Certainly, women's sports, and women's basketball in particular, have not solved the gender wars. Women's basketball is still struggling with how far it will go in breaking down barriers and crossing fault lines, such as those regarding sexual orientation. And equality and respect have not been won simply because Michelle Snow can dunk a basketball or because Lisa Harrison turned down *Playboy*'s offer to pose nude. Indeed, the oppressive purveyors of body image can easily convince young women that the muscular female body has replaced the wafer-thin body as the feminine ideal. But female basketball players today, less molded than before in the image of patriarchy's ideal woman, can teach us much about the capacity and integrity of women. What women's basketball has become, despite early efforts to contain and control it, reflects the gain in society when individuals are liberated from forms of dominance. Equality lets individuals grow and express themselves, and society can learn from new ideas and approaches. Freedom from social expectations means freedom to reveal the depth and range of one's talents and distinctiveness. And basketball, perhaps all sport, is where that depth and range might be best revealed. We'll give the last word to an anonymous high school student who tried a century ago to say the same thing:

> In this age of women's movements, few people have realized yet that the movement which is doing most for womankind is centered in our High Schools. A new type of girl has sprung up in our country. A girl more perfect mentally, morally, and physically, than the girl of twenty years ago. This is the basket ball girl. Many are her detractors; numerous are her critics, but her champions and supporters see in her the future greatness of American womanhood.
>
> . . . From the High school basket ball girl is being developed that strong, self-reliant woman, that woman who is cool and keen in her judgment, quick and sure in her action, calm and unselfish in her dealings. Altogether the perfectly developed woman.[23]

Notes

The second epigraph is drawn from Stacey Pressman, "Slam-dunk: Why is it that women's basketball is always on television even though no one is watching it?" *Weekly Standard,* online edition, April 8, 2003. Accessed March 3, 2006. Available at http://www.weeklystandard.com/content/Public/Articles/000/000/002/515gdyfj.asp.

1. Jean Strouse, "She Got Game: Women's Basketball Is Getting Intense," *New Yorker,* August 16, 1999, 37.

2. Sandra Lee Bartky, "Foucault, Femininity, and the Modernization of Patriarchal Power," *Feminist Philosophies,* ed. Janet A. Kourany, James P. Sterba, and Rosemarie Tong, 2nd ed. (Upper Saddle River, NJ: Prentice Hall, 1999), 120.

3. Bartky, "Foucault, Femininity," 121.

4. Bartky, "Foucault, Femininity," 123–25.

5. Quoted in Mary Jo Festle, *Playing Nice: Politics and Apologies in Women's Sports* (New York: Columbia University Press, 1996), 43.

6. Festle, *Playing Nice,* 43.

7. Patricia Vertinsky, "Women, Sport, and Exercise in the 19th Century," in *Women and Sports: Interdisciplinary Perspectives,* ed. D. Margaret Costa and Sharon R. Gutherie (Champaign, IL: Human Kinetics, 1994), 64.

8. Vertinsky, "Women, Sport, and Exercise," 69.

9. Joan S. Hult, "The Story of Women's Athletics: Manipulating a Dream, 1890–1985," in Costa and Gutherie, *Women and Sports,* 86.

10. Quoted in Hult, "Story of Women's Athletics," 86. Ellipses and brackets are hers.

11. Quoted in Festle, *Playing Nice,* 30.

12. Quoted in Festle, *Playing Nice,* 31.

13. Quoted in Festle, *Playing Nice,* 31.

14. Quoted in Festle, *Playing Nice,* 30.

15. Quoted in Lynn Emery, "From Lowell Mills to the Halls of Fame: Industrial League Sport for Women," in Costa and Gutherie, *Women and Sports,* 115.

16. See esp. Festle, *Playing Nice,* 44–52, and Emery, "Lowell Mills to Halls of Fame," 113–16. Both authors provide extensive examples of what Festle calls, following Jan Felshin, "apologetic behavior," behavior intended to demonstrate that women could be both feminine and athletic. As dramatized in the popular film *A League of Their Own* (Columbia Pictures, 1992), similar tactics were employed in women's professional baseball leagues in the 1940s.

17. Elizabeth V. Spelman, "Woman as Body," *Feminist Studies* 8, no. 1 (spring 1982): 127.

18. Quoted in Ken Rappoport and Barry Wilner, *Girls Rule! The Glory and Spirit of Women in Sport* (Kansas City: Andrews McMeel, 2000), 64. Lisa Leslie told *USA Today* something similar when discussing preparations for the Athens Olympics in 2004: "We have to come out ready to go to battle. It's going to be very physical. The rules are different, and they get that extra step. In international play almost anything goes. If you don't have the ball, away from the ball you could be out there swinging." "U.S. Women Hold Court," *USA Today,* online edition, August 25, 2004. Accessed March 8, 2006. Available from Academic Search Premier, Ipswich, MA.

19. Ron Higgins, "Women's Game Is Changing before Our Eyes," *South Coast Today,* online edition, March 31, 2001. Accessed March 21, 2006. Available at http://www.s-t.com/daily/03–01/03–31–01/c04sp119.htm.

20. See Gregory Bassham and Mark Hamilton, "Hardwood *Dojos:* What Basketball Can Teach Us about Character and Success," in this volume.

21. Quoted in Higgins, "Women's Game Is Changing."

22. Currently, 18 percent of NBA players are foreign born, and the percentage is rising rapidly. Is it merely coincidence that international players, schooled in a team-first, back-to-basics style of play, are increasingly outpacing flashier but less fundamentally sound American players? When Team USA lost to Greece in the semifinals of the 2006 World Basketball Championship, several analysts blamed the U.S. team's lack of fundamental skills and overdependence on one-on-one play. One reporter put it succinctly: "The U.S. has dazzling skill; the Greeks are a dazzling team." "USA Basketball: Greece Carves Up Team," *Detroit Free Press*, online edition, September 2,

2006. Accessed September 6, 2006. Available at http://www.freep.com/apps/pbcs.dll/
article?AID=/20060902/SPORTS13/609020360/1051/SPORTS.

23. "The Value of Girls' Basket Ball," in *Whatever It Takes: Women on Women's Sport,* ed. Joli Sandoz and Joby Winans (New York: Farrar, Straus an Giroux, 1999), 78. The authors wish to thank Jennifer McClinton-Temple and Louis Rader for their assistance in preparing this chapter.

FOURTH QUARTER

Metaphysical Madness

Kevin Kinghorn

SHOOTING WITH CONFIDENCE

THE HISTORY OF basketball is full of three o'clock superstars you've never heard of. They consistently hit nine out of ten shots from outside the three-point arc, and it's not unusual for them to have made their last fifty free throw attempts. Absolute superstars they are. But they do all this at three o'clock—during team practices and pregame shootarounds. Once the eight o'clock tip-off comes, they're completely different players. In games they suddenly become shaky free throw shooters, and their three-point percentage plummets toward single digits.

Ever hear of Josh Carrier? He played for the University of Kentucky from 2001 to 2005. During his senior year alone, Kentucky played on national television over a dozen times. But if you've never heard of him, it's understandable: he was rarely on the floor. Although he was a highly recruited three-point specialist, and although from all reports he consistently torched the nets in practice, his shooting prowess never transferred to game-time situations. In limited playing time, he finished his career shooting 26 percent from the three-point line, 29 percent from the field, and a dismal 42 percent from the foul line.

Many college teams have their own Josh Carrier: a player who lights it up in practice and sometimes dominates team scrimmages. A player whom fans see in summer pickup games and then run off to hype to the skies in Internet chat rooms. But all these hopes end in disappointment. In the tense atmosphere of game situations, their confidence evaporates into thin air, and with it seems to go their talent as well.

Why the Dramatic Drop in Performance?

This kind of drop in a player's performance is obviously linked to his emotions. We all have experiences on a daily basis that illustrate the truth that our emotions can greatly impact our physical bodies. Our hearts race and our palms sweat when we anticipate a first date. When we're nervous about speaking in public, our mouths become dry. When we're making a sales presentation to an important client, our hands shake. When we're scared, we feel sick to our stomach and weak in the knees.

Athletes of all kinds know all too well the physical effects of emotions like nervousness and anxiety. Celtics great Bill Russell routinely used to throw up before big games. Billiard players talk about their arms feeling as though they weigh fifty pounds each when a crucial frame is on the line. For basketball players, it's not difficult to imagine how the involuntary physical effects of emotional pressure might throw off their jump shot.

But what exactly is the source of these negative emotions for basketball players? And, more important, is there any way for a player to control these emotions? Is there any hope that three o'clock superstars can learn to channel the confidence they feel in practice to big games, where it really counts?

Let's begin our diagnosis by noting that there are two different sources for such detrimental emotions. The first source doesn't involve the player's beliefs, but the second does.

Oh My! What Was He Thinking?!

Emotions can arise in us even before we're aware of how stressful our situation is. Sometimes the sheer scope and unfamiliarity of an environment are enough to send emotions rushing through us, even before we've had time to reflect on what's happening. Consider the special feel of a play-off game at tip-off time, or the deafening noise of a hostile crowd, or the confusion of a last-second scramble to try to run a play when the game is on the line. These things can cause a player to go into emotional overload. And with these acute emotions come the physical effects we fans have come to recognize. The player feels his head spinning. He loses his bearings on the court. We speak of a player getting "rattled" or looking like a deer caught in a car's headlights.

The classic example of getting rattled in this way has to be George-town's Fred Brown, who gave North Carolina the 1982 NCAA champi-onship when he passed the ball to James Worthy in the closing seconds of the game. Of course, Fred was nearly outdone eleven years later when Michigan's All-American center Chris Webber made repeated efforts in the closing moments of the game to ensure another Carolina victory, in-cluding calling a timeout that Michigan didn't have.[1] These are times when the emotions of the moment interfere with the brain's ability to process information as it normally would, times that allow Dick Enberg to utter his trademark, "Oh my, what *was* he thinking?!"

Sports psychologists sometimes teach relaxation techniques to play-ers. The players might be told to imagine themselves in a familiar or "safe" place like their practice gym. The players are taught to breathe deeply and slowly. These are techniques for combating the first kind of detrimental emotion: the kind that arises simply from the pressure and unfamiliarity of the moment. Sometimes these techniques work. But if you take a freshman point guard, and put him in a Final Four game televised around the world, and throw a full-court press at him that his coach didn't have time to go over at the pregame meeting . . . well, I don't care *what* breathing techniques he's been taught, he's going to get rattled!

Shaky Beliefs = Shaky Jump Shot

The second source of choke-producing emotions is more widely experi-enced than the first and is therefore of even more interest to us. This second source involves a player's beliefs.

Everyday examples make clear the connection between beliefs and emotions. If you're speeding on the highway and believe you see a police-man on the shoulder of the road holding a radar gun, you experience a rush of emotion. If you believe your child might have wandered off at the mall, you feel a sudden jolt of panic. If you're a guy at the arena and you suddenly realize there are no urinals in the restroom you absentmindedly walked into, again there's a rush of emotion.

In each of these cases, you want things to be a certain way. You desire not to get a speeding ticket; you desire not to lose your child; you desire that you not be caught in the ladies' room. And when you believe that these desires might not be fulfilled, you experience a rush of blood and adrenaline and the corresponding emotions of fear and anxiety.

So it is in basketball. Every player wants to do well, to be a hero instead of a goat. Every player desires to make his next shot. But when a player starts to believe that the next shot might not go in, then the emotions of fear and anxiety start to surface. And we've already seen how such emotions can throw off a player's shooting.

The interesting question now becomes: is there a way for a player to control her beliefs? When fans sense that one of their home players is playing tentatively, they sometimes yell, "C'mon! Shoot it!" They're urging the player to trust in her ability, to believe in herself. But can a player *choose* to believe that her next shot will go in?

You've Gotta Believe, Son, You've Gotta Believe

Our everyday language suggests that we can sometimes choose what we will believe. We say things like, "I refuse to believe that," "Why won't you believe me?" and "I've decided that such a course of action would be a mistake." Despite what this language suggests, however, there is a big looming problem. Philosophers have offered powerful arguments that no one is capable of *deciding* to believe *anything*.

To see the philosophical problem inherent in the idea of choosing to believe something, consider the difference between *believing* something to be true and *wanting* it to be true. Suppose I told you that Dennis Rodman was in a local bookstore signing copies of his latest book, *A Wallflower in the NBA*. You might take my word for it and believe that he's in the bookstore. Wanting to let Rodman know what you think of his rapacious rebounding and shameless exhibitionism, you might also want him to be in the bookstore. So, as you hop in your car and head for the bookstore, you both *believe* and *desire* that he's there signing books.

As you enter the store, you see that there is no book signing and that I was only pulling your leg. What happens to your desire? Well, nothing. You can still *desire* that Dennis Rodman be in the bookstore. You can even choose to *imagine* that he's in the store. But you won't be able to *believe* that he's in the bookstore. And this is because our beliefs have a certain connection to the truth that our desires and imaginings do not.

Our beliefs—unlike our desires and imaginings—are *representational* in nature. They represent what we think is already true of the world. As the philosopher Bernard Williams (1929–2003) puts it, our beliefs "aim at truth," that is, "purport to represent reality."[2] In other words, to hold a belief is to think that the belief represents some fact about the actual world. Now, if I could somehow choose to believe something, Williams points out, then I would realize that my belief stems from my own free *choice*, and thus doesn't necessarily have any connection with facts about the actual world. But now we have a big problem. For, if I realize that my belief doesn't necessarily have any connection with what's true about the actual world, then it's not a belief in the first place!

Another way of putting this is to say that our beliefs are our "maps" of the world. Just as a map represents what's true of the actual world, so, hopefully, do our beliefs. Imagine if a mapmaker were to *choose* where to put the borders of the fifty states. Suppose he says to himself, "I think I'll put Florida up here today, and I'll put Kansas on the East Coast, and I'll make Wyoming the shape of an oval." If a mapmaker realized that the map before him was simply the product of his own choices and didn't therefore necessarily represent the actual borders of the fifty states, then he couldn't consider it a genuine map. Similarly, if a person knows that his belief is merely the product of his own choice, then it simply cannot be an actual belief.

He's Sure Cocky, but It Works

So the underconfident basketball player is in a real bind. Unless he can believe that his next shot is going in, his emotions will have detrimental effects on his performance. Yet, a player can't believe such a thing simply by choosing to believe it, because our beliefs aren't within our direct voluntary control.

Still, there are strategies that are available to the player who wants to shed the self-limiting effects of underconfidence. To understand these strategies, we first need to consider what it is that separates the underconfident player from the player who is brimming with confidence.

One characteristic of truly great players is that they all seem to have a ridiculously high level of confidence. I remember one postgame interview with Larry Bird in which the reporter noted that Bird tended to be a streaky shooter. He asked Bird if, after missing a few shots in a row, he ever doubted his ability to take the final shot at crunch time. Bird replied that he *always* believes his shots are going in and that he is always surprised when one of them misses. He went on to say, "If I miss nine in a row, I expect the tenth one to go in for sure."

Bill Walton tells another story about Bird's unflappable confidence. One night Bird made a three-point shot against Phoenix, but the officials didn't count it. When Celtics coach K. C. Jones began drawing up a play during the next timeout, Bird interrupted him: "To heck with the play," he said. "Give me the ball and tell all the rest of the guys to get out of the way." Walton recalls:

> K. C. wasn't in the mood to have his authority challenged.
> "Shut up. Larry," he said. "I'm the coach here."
> And then he started diagramming his play. "All right, now, Dennis, you take the ball out and get it to Kevin. Kevin you throw it to Larry and then everybody get the hell out of the way."
> The game was in Phoenix and Bird walked out of the huddle and went straight to the Suns' bench. He stood in front of the Phoenix bench, turned to their players and said, "I'm getting the ball right here and I'm gonna put it in the hoop. Watch my hand as I follow through."
> D. J. threw the ball to Kevin. Kevin threw the ball to Bird and Bird made the shot.[3]

The reason this kind of confidence is remarkable is that our beliefs generally tend to develop from *evidence* that is presented to us. Just as a jury considers evidence and renders a judgment as to whether the defendant is guilty, so we, too, form most of our beliefs on the basis of what we think the evidence suggests.

Suppose we're at a game where Larry Bird has missed nine shots in a row. (Of course, Bird probably never missed that many shots in a row in his life, but let's assume this for the sake of argument.) Surely, we wouldn't be confident that his next shot was going in. Based on the evidence of nine straight misses, we'd reckon that he's just having a really, really bad day. Certainly we wouldn't be confidently expecting his next shot to go in. Yet, Bird stated that he *would* confidently expect his next shot to go in. And I have no doubt that this is true in the case of Larry Bird.

Confident players like Bird seem to be unaffected by any evidence that would suggest that they aren't shooting well and could very well miss their next shot. How can this be? Philosophers who study psychology have a ready explanation.

The Power of Wishful Thinking

Studies have shown over and over that a person who strongly *wants* something to be true will often come to *believe* that it is true. Everyday experiences also bear this out. Consider the heated rivalries in basketball over the years, like Duke versus North Carolina, Kentucky versus Louisville, or the Celtics versus the Lakers. Have you ever watched one of these games on TV with fans from each team in the same room? It's amazing how each set of fans will scream at the referees throughout the game. Each side is absolutely convinced that the majority of the referees' missed calls are going against their own team.

What's behind this phenomenon? Well, both sets of fans strongly desire that their team win, and this subconsciously affects what they believe about the referees. Each side may even insist that they are "setting their biases aside" and are just describing what is "objectively" going on in the game. But we know better. Philosopher Francis Bacon (1561–1626) put his finger on the problem when he said, "Whatever a man wishes were true, that he more readily believes."[4]

High school and college coaches will probably be the first to agree with Bacon's statement. Coaches must often deal with parents who are convinced that their son is destined for stardom and can't understand why he isn't getting more playing time. Parents can also be among those who encourage their son to enter his name into the NBA draft, when the rest of the world can see he isn't anywhere near ready. What's going through the minds of these parents? Francis Bacon's statement says it all.

Players like Larry Bird want to win and want to succeed so much that they can be oblivious to anything that would suggest that they somehow *shouldn't* take the last shot of the game. Again, this confidence serves them well on the court. But what of the player who lacks confidence? If desiring something to be true tends to lead a person to believe that it is true, does this mean that underconfident players really don't desire to make their next shot or to be the star of the game?

Well, of course they desire these things. However, there is another factor that affects a person's beliefs. Bacon was right to point out that our desires often affect our beliefs. However, it's also true that *fears* can have a powerful, opposing effect on beliefs. Consider the case of a child who fears that there might be monsters lurking under his bed. Such fears may be so acute that he comes to believe that there actually *are* monsters under his bed. And this belief arises, of course, despite the fact that he desires all monsters to be kept well away from him.

So, just as wishful thinking can lead us to believe something we wish were true, so our fears can make us believe something we wish were *not* true. A basketball player undergoing a crisis of confidence desires—like Larry Bird—to make his next shot. But his self-belief will be hindered by the fear of failing, of losing the game, of being the goat.

He's Not Just My Coach, He's My Therapist

As we saw earlier, the underconfident basketball player cannot simply *choose* to believe that his next shot is going in. But there are two broad strategies that can be adopted in an attempt to counteract the detrimental effects brought on by lack of self-belief.

The first strategy is to increase the player's *evidence* that he will make his next shot. Again, a person's beliefs will follow involuntarily from his assessment of the evidence. He cannot simply choose to believe something when he thinks the evidence points in another direction. But if a player somehow acquires more evidence suggesting that he will hit his next shot, then his beliefs would naturally tend to follow in that direction.

Both coaches and sports psychologists have recognized the benefits of setting goals in practice. The goal might be to make a winning basket in a simulated last-minute situation, to make two free throws so the team won't have to do extra running, or to make a certain number of shots in a row in a shooting drill. Indiana's Steve Alford used to set the goal of "hanging the net," and he wouldn't end his shooting drills until he swished one in such a way that the net would hang. Fortunately, the baskets he practiced on didn't have metal nets.

Coaches are wise to end practices when such goals are met. That way, the shooting successes from practice tend to stick in a player's head more than the failures. Coaches also encourage players to visualize themselves nailing jumpers over and over. They encourage players to act confidently, to remember past successes in games, and to engage in positive self-talk. When these strategies work, they have the effect of bombarding the player with evidence on top of evidence that she is a great shooter. When the player then thinks about her next shot, there is so much positive evidence fresh in her mind that she naturally forms positive beliefs about the prospects for her next shot going in.

The success of these strategies varies considerably. Some people have an easier time brushing aside past failures than others do. But when these strategies work, they succeed because they increase the evidence a player has that his next shot will go in.

The second strategy doesn't seek to increase a player's evidence or even change his beliefs. Instead, it seeks to decrease the *negative effects* of a player's beliefs. Specifically, the strategy seeks to lessen the impact of a player's beliefs on his emotions.

A player's underconfident beliefs about his next shot can cause performance-diminishing emotions like fear, anxiety, and tension. Players know that there may be serious consequences if they miss. Again, no player wants to be the goat, to let down his team and the fans. But coaches can make this situation better or worse.

Fans easily pick up on the fact that some players are on a short leash. The coach puts them in, but he's quick to pull them out as soon as they commit a silly foul or miss a defensive assignment. Fans see that some players shoot hesitantly because they're looking over their shoulders, afraid that a single miss will find them sitting on the bench—and staying there. And so they yell at the coach, "Give him a chance!" or "Leave him in to see what he can do!"

One big reason why this kind of "quick hook" from a coach is detrimental to a player is that the negative consequences of a single missed shot are too great. The player has too much riding on the shot going in. If a player believes that his next shot might not go in, intense feelings of fear and anxiety may arise. For often there is simply so *much* to fear.

Now, contrast all this with the attitudes of players who mount great comebacks. One of the frequent accompaniments of great comebacks is that, at some point, the coach gives a speech to the players along the following lines: "O.K., forget about what's happened. Go out there and shoot. Just shoot the ball, then keep shooting it, then shoot it some more."

It's amazing what players can do when all the pressure is taken off. We say that the team is playing like it's got "nothing to lose." And this is a pretty accurate description. For there is no longer much to fear from a single missed shot. The coach has removed the bad consequences—and thus the fear—of missing.[5]

A great example of this strategy comes from coach Rick Pitino and player Kenny Walker, when both were with the New York Knicks. The Knicks' half-court offense was essentially to throw the ball in to Patrick Ewing, who would either try to score from down low or kick it out to a guard. If neither of these things worked, and if the shot clock was winding down, they'd swing the ball around to the weak side, and Kenny Walker, the small forward, would usually have an open twenty-footer. The problem was that Walker wasn't making very many of these shots. He was undergoing a crisis of confidence.

Pitino told Walker, publicly, that the day he *stopped* taking that shot was the day he would cease to be a New York Knick. This wasn't an attempt to create evidence for Walker or get him to believe that his next shot was going in. Instead, it was an attempt to take away the negative consequences of a missed shot—and thus to lessen the effects that Walker's underconfidence had in producing emotions like fear.

Pitino's strategy didn't produce a miracle. Walker was always going to be a slam-dunk champion, never a pure shooter. But the strategy was right on the money. My guess is that it had as positive an effect on Walker's jump shot as any shooting drill ever did.

Job Security for the Sports Psychologist

In the end, underconfident basketball players will never be able to overcome the philosophical problem that they can't simply *choose* to believe that their next shot is going in. In the long term, as philosopher Tom Morris reminds us, the best strategy to build confidence is to build competence. "Great confidence," he says, "is rooted in great preparation."[6] But in the short term, as we've seen, there are strategies that can be adopted by players, coaches, and sports psychologists alike. First, they can try to increase a player's evidence that he *will* make his next shot. Second, they can try to lessen the negative impact of a player's beliefs on his emotions.

Because strategies do exist to help the underconfident player, there will always be a market for sports psychologists. And this is good news for all of us. After all, sports presenters will need experts to interview when the next Fred Brown or Chris Webber makes a bonehead play and we all want to find out, "What *was* he thinking?!"

Notes

1. Since Dean Smith won both of his championships in these extraordinary circumstances, conspiracy theorists might want to examine this. Did someone at Carolina invent some sort of device or substance that discombobulates opposing players in the waning moments of really big games?

2. Bernard Williams, "Deciding to Believe," in *Problems of the Self* (Cambridge: Cambridge University Press, 1973), 136, 148.

3. Bill Walton with Gene Wojciechowski, *Nothing but Net* (New York: Hyperion, 1994), 103. Readers may also recall the dramatic final scene in the movie *Hoosiers*—recently named the best sports movie of all time in an ESPN poll—when the championship hopes of the Cinderella Hickory Huskers are down to one last shot, and star player Jimmy Chitwood confidently says to his coach, "I'll make it," and proceeds to do so.

4. Francis Bacon, *Novum Organon* (Oxford: Oxford University Press, 1855), bk. 1, sec. 49.

5. A similar strategy is widely employed in male-impotence therapy—so I hear.

6. Tom Morris, *The Art of Achievement* (Kansas City: Andrews McMeel, 2002), 59.

Steven D. Hales

THE HOT HAND IN BASKETBALL
Illusion or Reality?

ANY BASKETBALL FAN or weekend warrior knows what it means to have a hot hand. It's the feeling that you are in the groove, that you can't miss your shots, that everything you do is the right thing. "If only I could play like that all the time, I'd be starting for the Lakers," we lament. The pros feel the same way. Purvis Short, of the Golden State Warriors, has said, "You're in a world all your own. It's hard to describe. But the basket seems to be so wide. No matter what you do, you know the ball is going to go in."[1] Dean Oliver, a statistician on the staff of the Seattle Supersonics, writes: "In the first round of the NCAA Tournament a few years ago, I began to sense my own hot streak. Every shot seemed to hit the mark. Every pass of mine was converted and returned later. The game felt completely natural."[2] Familiar territory, right?

Well, maybe not. Some psychologists and statisticians have recently argued for a very surprising thesis: despite nearly universal beliefs to the contrary, there is no such thing as streak runs of success in basketball; no one has ever been on a roll or had hot hands. According to the late Harvard scientist Stephen J. Gould, "Everybody knows about hot hands. The problem is that no such phenomenon exists."[3] Psychologists Thomas Gilovich, Robert Vallone, and Amos Tversky write, "probably . . . most players, spectators, and students of the game believe in the hot hand, although our statistical analyses provide no evidence to support this belief."[4] Psychologist Robert M. Adams concurs: "Even though virtually any basketball player, fan, or commentator would scoff at the notion that the 'hot hand' is only an illusion, the present data confirm that."[5]

Before taking a look at the reasoning behind these claims, we would do well to ask why a *philosopher* should have anything to say about the matter. One of the most ancient philosophical specialties is epistemology—the theory of knowledge—and one of the core epistemological issues is skepticism. Do we in fact know the things we all think we know? Skeptics argue that, for one reason or another, the answer is no. Hot hands deniers are a sort of epistemological skeptic; they maintain that in fact we don't know something we all think we do. We don't know that basketball players have hot hands despite widespread beliefs to the contrary. In this chapter I will defend the view that there are hot hands in basketball, that they are ubiquitous, and that players and observers are often right in identifying them. The skeptics do have a point worth considering, but they misunderstand the force of their own reasoning.

The Success Doesn't Breed Success Argument

Stephen J. Gould writes, "We believe in 'hot hands' because we must impart meaning to a pattern—and we like meanings that tell stories about heroism, valor, and excellence, . . . and we have no feel for the frequency and length of sequences in random data."[6] While this may be true at some deep level, it is certainly not the reason sports participants give for the reality of hot hands. Anyone who has ever played a sport will cite internal, *felt* experience in favor of hot hand phenomena. When you are hot, it feels like you can't miss, that every shot is just an easy layup. When you're cold, it feels like no matter what you do, no matter how much you concentrate, every shot you take is a brick. A plausible way of expressing these attitudes is that a player has a better chance of making a shot after having just made his last two or three shots than he does after having missed his last two or three shots. Ninety-one out of one hundred basketball fans polled believe this statement; that is, they believe that success breeds success.

The success-breeds-success idea is the driving force in the first argument against hot hands, an argument endorsed by all the skeptics. Call this the Success Doesn't Breed Success Argument:

1. Someone has a hot hand only if he or she is performing in such a way that success breeds success.

2. Studies show that success does not breed success in basketball.

3. So, there are no hot hands in basketball.

In a classic study of the hot hand phenomenon, Thomas Gilovich and his colleagues found that players on the Philadelphia 76ers believed that success breeds success, just as the fans did. In interviews, the 76ers often said that after making a few shots in a row, they "knew" that they were going to make their next shot, that they "almost couldn't miss." This has a plausible psychological explanation: when a player realizes that he is hot, his confidence in his subsequent shots increases; he relaxes and doesn't overplay his shots; he just gets in the groove and shoots smoothly and cleanly. Regrettably (and remarkably) the data fail to bear this out. In fact they show a slight negative correlation between a hit and the following shot. The 76ers were just a little bit likelier to miss after hitting three in a row. The converse is true too—they were likelier to hit after a cold period of zero or one hit in the last four attempts than they were to continue missing. Moreover, this finding held true for both field goals (shot under defensive pressure) and free throws (shot without such pressure), and in similar studies of the New Jersey Nets and the New York Knicks. Knowing this, we can refit our psychological explanations: when a player realizes he is hot, he tends to push the envelope and attempt more difficult shots, believing that he can do anything he wants. Such a strategy then leads predictably to failure. How wonderfully malleable psychological explanations are!

One might conclude that the empirical results show that the internal sensation of being hot is unreliable. As one group of researchers puts it, "The sense of being 'hot' does not predict hits or misses."[7] Other critics have intimated even more strongly that since one's own felt experience is not wholly trustworthy, it adds nothing to the statistical study of the hot hand.

This is not the best explanation of the data. A more plausible interpretation is that the 76ers were mistaken in thinking they could tell when their streaks of success would end. That is, either they mistakenly believed that their prior success had a causal influence on the future, or they reasoned that having made several shots in a row was good evidence that they would make the next one. It is of course interesting that neither form of reasoning turns out to be reliable, but this doesn't undercut the players' beliefs that they were hot. The problem isn't that their internal feelings of having a hot hand are wrong but rather that they have a misguided optimism about how long their streak will last and where they are in it. They believe that they are *toward the beginning*, or *in the middle of* a success streak. In fact, they may well be at the end of one, and their next shot will be a miss. The streak could be three successful shots in a row, or it could be ten. Upon sinking the third basket, a player may well feel confident about hitting the fourth, believing hopefully that he is at the beginning of a ten-streak instead of at the close of a three-streak.

In short, what the data show here is not that one's internal sense of being hot is wrong, but that there is no telling how long one will remain hot—the streak could end at any time, and induction from past success fails. Wilt Chamberlain couldn't feel a cold front coming in as he went for a field goal on February 28, 1967. In fact, maybe he felt pretty optimistic about sinking his shot. Who wouldn't, having not missed a single shot in the previous thirty-five attempts? Does this positive attitude, however statistically mistaken or unjustified, show that Wilt wasn't hot during his streak? Of course not.

The Predictable Streak Argument

The second skeptical argument tries a different tack—hot hands are not undone by the failure of streaks to cause or predict future success, but by the very predictable nature of the streaks themselves. Call this the Predictable Streak Argument:

1. Someone has a hot hand only if his or her streak of success is statistically unlikely.
2. Studies show that there are no statistically unlikely streaks of success in basketball.
3. So, there are no hot hands in basketball.

Supporters of this argument include Gould (1991) and Gilovich, Vallone, and Tversky (1985). There has been much debate over whether the second premise of this argument is true. Gould endorses it except for "one major exception, one sequence so many standard deviations above the expected distribution that it should never have occurred at all: Joe DiMaggio's 56-game hitting streak in 1941."[8] Debate over this "exception" has generated a small cottage industry devoted to computing the exact probability of DiMaggio's streak. The noteworthy thing about Gould's claim concerning the DiMaggio streak is that unless one accepts the first premise in the Predictable Streak Argument, there is no reason at all to take the streak's statistical unlikelihood as proof of hot hands. So it is the first premise that requires critical scrutiny.

Precisely how unlikely does a streak of success have to be before we are prepared to count it as a legitimate instance of hot hands? Gould sets the bar extremely high, admitting only what he calls "the most extraordinary thing ever to happen in American sports."[9] But why should we follow suit? It is not as if DiMaggio's streak was somehow so momentous that its description is beyond the reach of probability. *Every* success run will be more or less probable given the average skill of the player involved. Suppose someone achieves a sports success with only a 1 percent chance of occurring. The only reason to think that it does not have every bit as much of a claim to being a case of hot hands as the DiMaggio streak is the acceptance of Gould's arbitrarily high standards. Every sporting event will fall somewhere on the curve, whether it is four standard deviations from the mean, or only one.[10] It is nonsense to suppose that there is something "off the chart." There is no principled way of parsing the above-average portion of the curve into "hot hand" and "not hot hand" zones.

Thus, if the word "unlikely" in premise 1 is defined strongly enough, à la Gould, then the argument is bound to be right. Yet this smacks of thievery. On the other hand, if "unlikely" is weakened enough, then every positive deviation from the mean will count as a case of hot hands (some are just hotter than others), premise 2 will be false, and the conclusion will not follow. We could fix our improbability standard for hot hands at some precise level by fiat, but there is no principled way of doing so. The Predictable Streak Argument is therefore of little interest. It is sound only if we agree to a purely arbitrary account of how statistically unlikely a streak of success must be to count as an instance of hot hands.

The Chance Argument

A third argument offered by skeptics against hot hands is the Chance Argument:

1. Someone has a hot hand in basketball only if his or her number of success streaks exceeds that predicted by chance.

2. Studies show that there are no success streaks in basketball whose frequency exceeds the number predicted by chance.

3. So, there are no hot hands in basketball.

Defenders of this argument maintain that a run of successful shots "can be properly called streak shooting only if their length or frequency exceeds what is expected on the basis of chance alone."[11] Each sequence of hits (successful field goals in basketball, for example) or misses (unsuccessful ones) is counted as a "run." In any random process there will be such runs. For example, suppose I flip a fair coin a dozen times. Despite the fact that the probability of tossing heads is .5 (i.e., 50 percent), if I were to get exactly HTHTHTHTHTHT, this would be quite surprising, as the probability of this sequence is only .00024, whereas the probability that it is some other sequence is .99975. If I do the flipping and get a sequence other than strict heads/tails alternation, this should be completely expected, because it is so enormously likely that I get such a result. Suppose I do the flipping and get, say, HHHTHTHTTHHT. While this specific result is not so likely, it is very probable, as we have seen, that a result like this one is obtained. Such sequences are noticeably "clumpy," containing bursts of heads and runs of tails. In addition, the example just given shows more heads than tails. In the long run the number of heads and tails will approach equivalence, but not in short stretches like this.

In defense of the second premise of the Chance Argument, Gilovich and his colleagues studied field goals made by the Philadelphia 76ers during forty-eight home games in the 1980–1981 season, and also conducted a controlled study of twenty-six Cornell University basketball players. In examining these data sets, the question posed was whether any player had more such success runs than one would expect to get when flipping a coin. The answer was no.

Suppose the chance of making each basket is .5 (obviously this value has to be computed on a player-by-player basis). If a player shoots sixteen rounds of four shots per round, on average only one of these rounds will be a run of four hits ($.5^4 = 1/16$). The same is true of coin tossing—on average four heads will come up once every sixteen rounds of four flips. This does not mean that making baskets is nothing but chance. To bor-

row an example of Gould's, Michael Jordan will get more runs of four in
a row than Joe Airball because his average success rate is higher, and
Jordan's average success rate is higher because of his superior skill. Suppose Jordan shoots field goals with a .6 probability of success. About one
out of eight sets of four shots will be four hits in a row ($.6^4$). If Joe, on the
other hand, is only half as good from the field as Jordan, making .3 of his
field goal attempts, he will get four straight roughly only once every 125
attempts ($.3^4$). Nothing besides probability is needed to explain the pattern of runs. The conclusion of the Chance Argument is that therefore
there is no such thing as a hot hand.

While these are interesting empirical findings, the Chance Argument is
unsound. The problem is neither the way the study was conducted nor the
way in which the numbers are calculated. As in the second argument, the
error is in the first premise. There are a couple of problems with this premise. The first is that, at first glance, this is a strange requirement for a "hot
hand." One would think that what an unusual number of success streaks
shows instead is *streakiness*—a player who runs hot and cold. Gilovich
and his colleagues also conclude that, contrary to popular perception,
players are never streaky, but this is a different matter from having hot
hands. The other, more vital, problem with the first premise is that it in-
corporates the same arbitrariness that we saw in the Predictable Streak
Argument. To what extent should the number of streaks deviate from
statistical expectations in order for it to count as hot hands? There seems
to be no nonarbitrary place to draw the line. Do we draw it at statistical
significance? At three standard deviations from the expected distribution?
As with the "statistically unlikely" criterion of the Predictable Streak Argument, any number of streaks can receive a statistical modeling—some
patterns of success runs are just considered less probable than others. The
common thread in both the Predictable Streak Argument and the Chance
Argument is that essential to the hot hand is success beyond what is to be
expected from a chance process. This is the root error.

A Commonsense View of Hot Hands

The Predictable Streak and the Chance arguments are on the right path
in one sense: they correctly link having a hot hand with the nature of
streaks. My contention is that a hot hand just *is* a streak or run of shoot-

ing success, with no arbitrary restrictions on how rare or improbable it must be. If Shaquille O'Neal hits ten free throws in a row, he *does* have a hot hand, even if statistically this is a reasonably likely occurrence given his skill as a player and the large number of free throws he shoots. Even if, after hitting those ten free throws in a row, Shaq misses the eleventh, and empirical study tells us that his success with the first ten made it no likelier that he would make the eleventh, this is no reason to think that he didn't have a hot hand. Gilovich and his colleagues write, "Evidently, people tend to perceive chance shooting as streak shooting."[12] That is, people see statistically expected runs of success (chance shooting) as a hot hand (streak shooting). Gilovich is entirely right. There are then two possible conclusions to draw: (1) the skeptics are wrong to draw a distinction between chance and streak shooting; and (2) everyone else is wrong in thinking that there is such a thing as streak shooting. The skeptics, naturally, opt for the second. But I am arguing that there are good reasons for instead choosing the first, not the least of which is that such a view preserves and explains the widespread belief that players have hot hands.

The hot hand critics have to assume an error theory. They maintain that people are just uniformly mistaken in believing that they ever have a hot hand and always wrong in believing that others do. The skeptical view is not just that success makes people too optimistic about future success, or that the internal sense of being hot is sometimes wrong. Rather, the skeptics maintain that it is *always* wrong. This is a bitter pill to swallow. Sure, sometimes people are universally wrong about things that seem compelling—the history of science is replete with instances. The sun's motion in the sky and the evidence of design in the universe are familiar examples. Nevertheless, we should jettison widely held, intuitively plausible beliefs only if this is mandated by a clearly superior theory to the one in which our beliefs are embedded. The hot hand skeptics have not met this condition.

What of the feeling of hot hands? Does my analysis of hot hands give short shrift to the importance of the basket seeming wider or the sense of things slowing down? I don't think so. Unlike the skeptics, I take the sense of hot hands and the observation of hot hands in others seriously. When people believe that they have a hot hand, they may well usually be right. When they are right, their internal sensation of being hot represents the world: they *are* shooting above their norm, passing better than average, rebounding better than usual, deviating above the mean. This may all be within the bounds of normal statistical variance, but that only serves to explain the phenomenon. I am arguing that the *nature* of hot hands involves above-average success, whereas at best the sense of feeling hot constitutes *evidence* for having hot hands. Whether the sense of being hot is an all-or-nothing quality, whether it comes in degrees, and how well it correlates to actual success in performance are matters for further study. The empirical studies are right in taking hot hands to be an empirical, quantifiable matter.

There are also valuable practical lessons to be learned from the studies. For example, coaches who give instructions that a hot player be given the ball more or see more court time may be making a costly error. Statistically the hot streak could end at any moment. Thus the strategy of "give it to the hot player" is no better than that of a Vegas gambler who, having won her last three blackjack hands, bets the house on the fourth. However, the lesson the authors of these studies draw—that there are no hot hands—is wrong. Gamblers often speak of streaks of luck, or running hot, or being on a roll. Does this imply that they think some force other than chance is at work? Some may, although surely professional gamblers would not think of such a streak as anything other than a chance distribution of success. This hardly prevents them from reasonably commenting on a night's success as being a run of luck, or referring to themselves as having been hot. In other words, they *knowingly* assimilate streak shooting (of dice, say) to chance shooting. The latter is rather an explanation of, or an analysis of, what is understood by "streak."[13]

In sum, there are three prominent arguments that conclude there are no hot hands in sports. The first argument of the hot hands critics creates a tradition in the very act of destroying it. By making "success breeds success" a necessary condition of having hot hands, the critics have established a previously undefended and barely articulated account of hot hands only to demolish it. Instead I have argued that there are good reasons to reject "success breeds success" as a requirement for having hot hands. While it is true that many players believe that their future success is more likely when they are already hot, either this is no more than a belief that their current "hot" state has causal efficacy into the future, or inductive reasoning that their current high rate of success is evidence of future success. Yet neither possibility makes "success breeds success" part of the concept of having hot hands.

The second and third arguments offered by the hot hand critics are of a well-known skeptical pattern: set the standards for knowledge of X extremely high, and then show that no one meets those standards. The usual reply to this strategy, of which I availed myself, is to reject those standards in favor of more modest ones that charitably preserve our claims of knowledge. The skeptical insistence upon exceedingly rare streaks or statistically remote numbers of streaks as being the only legitimate instances of hot hands is arbitrary and severe. I have argued that "being hot" is a continuum, one that consists in simply shooting better than normal. And this obviously comes in degrees.

So what *is* proven by the hot hand studies? Some conclusions correctly drawn by the skeptics include (1) having a hot hand does not increase the chance of success for one's upcoming shot; (2) players who believe that their recent run of successful shots increases the chance of making their next shot are unjustified in this belief; (3) players perceived as streaky do not have more success runs than what is statistically expected; and (4) having a hot hand is not the result of a causal mechanism not describable by the laws of probability. Unfortunately, the skeptics erroneously infer that the previous results mean that there are no hot hands and that everyone is wrong in thinking otherwise. Instead I have argued that being hot does not have to do with the success rate, duration, or even frequency of streaks. It has to do with their existence. The conclusions to be drawn are (1) one has a hot hand when one is shooting better than average; (2) players often know when they are shooting better than average; and (3) observers can often tell when players are shooting better than average. This judgment of countless fans, coaches, and players is vindicated.

Notes

An earlier version of this chapter appeared in the *Journal of the Philosophy of Sport* 26 (1999): 79–87. Copyrighted by the International Association for the Philosophy of Sport. Used by permission.

1. Quoted in Amos Tversky and Thomas Gilovich, "The Cold Facts about the 'Hot Hand' in Basketball, *Chance* 2 (1991): 16.

2. Dean Smith, "Yes, Virginia, There Is a Hot Hand," http://www.rawbw.com/~deano/. December 21, 1997. Accessed July 1, 2005.

3. Stephen J. Gould, *Bully for Brontosaurus* (New York: W. W. Norton, 1991), 465.

4. Thomas Gilovich, Robert Vallone, and Amos Tversky, "The Hot Hand in Basketball: On the Misperception of Random Sequences," *Cognitive Psychology* 17 (1985): 302–3.

5. Robert M. Adams, "The 'Hot Hand' Revisited: Successful Basketball Shooting as a Function of Intershot Interval," *Perceptual and Motor Skills* 74 (1992): 934.

6. Gould, *Bully for Brontosaurus*, 468.

7. Gilovich, Vallone, and Tversky, "Hot Hand in Basketball," 310.

8. Gould, *Bully for Brontosaurus*, 467.

9. Gould, *Bully for Brontosaurus*, 467.

10. A standard deviation is a statistical measurement of how far a given data point is from the mean value of all the data points in a given data set. The larger the standard deviation, the further from the mean.

11. Gilovich, Vallone, and Tversky, "Hot Hand in Basketball," 296.

12. Gilovich, Vallone, and Tversky, "Hot Hand in Basketball," 311.

13. One possible objection here is that a distinction should be drawn between above-average success runs due in some identifiable sense to the player's skill and effort and those runs due to fortuitous deviant causal mechanisms. Only the former, goes the objection, are genuine examples of hot hands. Tossing five consecutive tails in a row with a fair coin is not an act of skill. Neither is birdying several holes in a row at golf through a series of bizarre shots and circumstances. Are these legitimate examples of hot hands? I feel the pull in both directions. My inclination is to say that hot hands are simply above-average success runs, however they are accomplished. I think this accords best with our everyday expressions of "running hot" or "being on a roll." Yet even if one insists on adding a clause requiring this success to be the result of some appropriate causal mechanism, my central point remains untouched. The core element of having hot hands is deviation above mean performance—not success breeds success, extreme statistical unlikelihood, or somehow outpacing chance, as the skeptics contend.

Tim Elcombe

PHILOSOPHERS CAN'T JUMP

Reflections on Living Time and Space in Basketball

MATHEMATICALLY, A SPACE that measures ten feet is the same distance anywhere in the world. The same can be said for time: ten seconds in Indianapolis is the same as ten seconds in Toronto, Buenos Aires, Munich, Sydney, or Beijing. But anyone who has ever played basketball knows that ten feet or ten seconds can be experienced in radically different ways in different situations. For a nine-year-old child, dreams of flying through the air to dunk a basketball are tempered by the seemingly insurmountable space between their outstretched hands and the bottom of the rim. A free throw to tie the game with no time left on the clock makes fifteen feet seem like a quarter mile. Two minutes on a clock ticks by at a constant rate of one second at a time. However, for a team holding on to a one-point lead in the championship game, two minutes can seem like an eternity. For aging hardwood warriors, including most basketball-playing philosophers, the length of the lunch hour usually (and thankfully) determines game time, and the court seems to grow longer with each passing year.

In this chapter, I explore how time and space are experienced pragmatically in the game of basketball. With the help of American philosopher John ("Dr. J.") Dewey (1859–1952), I explore basketball phenomenologically to deepen our understanding of how we actually live in time and space and to enhance our appreciation of the world's most "phenomenal" game.

Tape Measures and Ticking Clocks in Hoosierland

Nearly all basketball fans remember the scene in the film *Hoosiers* when the "pint-sized, hardly big enough for three syllables" Hickory Huskers first step onto the court in cavernous Butler Fieldhouse. The small-town Indiana high school team, in big-city Indianapolis to play an improbable state-final game against the mighty Bears of South Bend Central, is clearly overwhelmed by the enormity of the facility. To ease the tension, Hickory's wise and crafty coach, Norman Dale (played by Gene Hackman), first measures the distance from the hoop to the free throw line and then instructs Strap to place Ollie on his shoulders to determine the height of the rim. Measurements confirm that the basket is positioned fifteen feet from the free throw line and ten feet off the ground. "I think you'll find these are the exact measurements as our gym back in Hickory," says Coach Dale.

Coach Dale's simple strategy helps his awestruck players gain a sense of order and familiarity in the massive facility. His tactic also demonstrates a commonsense, analytical way of thinking about time and space. Although the Huskers are no longer in Hickory, the basic dimensions of the court are the same as in their home gym. Similarly, the seconds on the large electronic game clock will tick away at the same rate of speed as the smaller timer they use at home, in spite of the enormity of the event. Time and space on the basketball court, Coach Dale is implicitly saying, stand as unchanging constants—a commonality that binds huge facilities in big cities to tiny gyms in small communities.

Dewey helps us understand this phenomenon, noting that human experience is structured and continuous. Experience has form and recurrent patterns—a brute "isness" or durable quality.[1] But contrary to the theories of "experience" espoused by traditional claims of empiricists or idealists, this structured aspect of experience is "had" rather than simply "known." From a pragmatist perspective, we *live* ordered and habituated notions of time and space. Our experience is embodied and durable rather than disconnected or fixed.

Basketball nicely exemplifies the durable and uniform qualities of lived time and space. As Coach Dale points out to his players, basketball courts typically share equal dimensions—from basket heights to free throw and three-point line distances, and with some exceptions, court length and width. Time is also a fairly constant quality in basketball. Depending on the league, quarters or halves are the same length of time.[2] There are no rain-shortened contests or mercy rules. All Olympic basketball games, for example, last forty minutes of playing time.

The durable quality of lived time and space, particularly in a well-defined context such as a basketball game, gives continuity and meaning to the embodied experience. Basketball's form and structure create uniformity, a way to share experience and meaning with others. Without James Naismith getting the ball rolling (and eventually bouncing), basketball, as we "know" it, would never have existed metaphysically. And as Criswell Freeman reminds us, without the existence of some shared notion of a game we call basketball, "there would have been no epic battles between Chamberlain and Russell. And we would have missed that magic rivalry between Bird and Johnson. Pete Maravich would have been an anonymous lanky kid with droopy socks. And Hakeem Olajuwon would have been the world's tallest soccer goalie."[3]

Are the "Dimensions" Really the Same as in Hickory?

The durable qualities, however, are only one side of living time and space in basketball. Basketball also reveals what Dewey describes as the dynamic nature of our spatiotemporal experience and how we live *in* and *through* time and space. Such a "natural" transaction between humans and spatiotemporal dimensions, Dewey contends, is "an affair *of* affairs . . . a scene of incessant beginnings and endings."[4] Or as Los Angeles Lakers' übercoach Phil Jackson puts it: "Like life, basketball is messy and unpredictable. . . . [It] is a complex dance that requires shifting from one objective to another at lightning speed."[5]

To appreciate time and space, not as disconnected abstractions, but in an active, lived sense, it's helpful to consider the conclusion of the scene in *Hoosiers* mentioned earlier. After Coach Dale's tape-measure demonstration, the players walk off the court to change for practice. Although the tension has been broken, the still-awed looks on the Huskers' faces express the reality of the challenge they face. Despite Coach Dale's attempt to turn the dimension of space into a familiar constant, the players know that they will live *this* space quite differently than anything else they have ever experienced. Although the "dimensions" are the same, the basket and the court are very different from their tiny gym in the heartland of Indiana. Coach Dale knows they have entered a new "dimension" as well, quietly whispering, "It is big!" to his assistant coach as the team walks off the court to prepare for the climactic state championship game.

Depending on your age and current athletic ability, the height of the basket reveals different ways we live space. For young children, a ten-foot-high hoop is an unreachable peak. Just getting the ball to the rim as a young child is an accomplishment. In fact, to help young players live the thrill of experiencing the basket up close, adults lift them to dunk. And increasingly, the heights of hoops are brought down to the kids so they can experience the sensuous quality of overcoming the vertical challenges the game of basketball presents.

As embodied beings, we always bring to the court both the constraints and the possibilities of our physiology, history, psychology, culture, and so forth. For example, as we grow taller and expand our athletic abilities, ten feet becomes a more manageable height to deal with. Consequently, the various parts of the basket become something akin to a growth chart. First, we test our vertical possibilities by jumping and swatting at the hanging net. Next, we move to slapping the backboard, followed by touching and grabbing the rim. For a select few, dunking becomes the final phase. But regardless of how far we progress, a peak is reached where the rim is as close to us as it ever will be.

But alas, the circle of life (otherwise known as getting older) seems to raise the basket year by year after we reach our physical apex.[6] For this reason, as they age, seasoned hardwood warriors (including Michael Jordan when playing for the Washington Wizards) turn to "fundamental" basketball—a slower-paced, more horizontal version of the game that emphasizes passing, shooting, and screening. What little jumping is done is performed at great risk to the few Achilles tendons and anterior cruciate ligaments still intact.

On a temporal level, one great thing about basketball, something "vintage" athletes truly appreciate, is that one can "stop" time. Most games allow teams to call time-outs to rest, strategize, make substitutions, slow the other team's momentum, or stop precious seconds from ticking away. With the exception of FIBA—the governing body of international basketball—most basketball rules allow players a predetermined number of times (Chris Webber take note) to pause in the middle of the action when in possession of the ball and ask the referee to stop play. The same thing occurs every time the referee blows her whistle or the game-clock buzzer sounds as basketball time is suspended. The world does not stop turning, we continue to slowly age, clocks tracking "real" time keep ticking; but basketball time literally stops.[7]

Sometimes, in basketball, time only *feels* like it stops. For New York Knicks fans, the experienced time of Reggie Miller's majestic, high-arching, game-tying three-point shot in game 1 of the 1995 Knicks-Pacers play-off series far exceeded the mathematical time of its trajectory. Players "in the zone" often report a sense of time stopping or slowing down. Time in its scientific, objective sense never stops. But lived time in basketball stops both literally and experientially.

Werewolves Can Dunk? Must Be the Jump Shoes

The "always already" quality of time and space as both durable and dynamic opens space for rich, meaningful lived experience in basketball. This is clear when we see how humans are captivated by real or fictitious attempts to alter or manipulate time and space. Case in point: our cultural fascination with great leapers in basketball. Nothing captures our attention like the ability seemingly to defy gravity. I could complete a mathematical proof that would make John (not Steve) Nash green with envy, and only expect to receive polite applause. But if I can dunk, for a moment I become a king like LeBron "King" James. No matter how many camps I teach at, clinics I deliver, or teams I coach, the one constant question I get is: Can you (or could you) dunk? (For the record, I dunked twice. But give me a few more years and the number I remember will increase). Dunking a basketball provides instant "street cred" in our culture. The dunk is a celebration of youth, vitality, and power. For young athletes, it is a milestone to aspire to. For players in their prime, it is a symbol of their prowess. For aging athletes, it is a reminder of dwindling or never-realized physical powers.[8]

Marketers understand the social worth of having impressive leaping ability. Images of Michael Jordan soaring for a dunk earned him hundreds of millions of dollars in endorsements and made billions for Nike shoes. Many people will spend hundreds of dollars on vertical leap programs, ankle weights, jump-power machines, and of course, jump shoes.[9] We also see the cultural obsession with vertical leaping in the arts. Virtually every basketball movie includes a slow-motion scene featuring an improbable dunk. A werewolf in *Teen Wolf*, a kid in *Like Mike*, a dog in *Air Bud*, and, of course, Woody Harrelson in *White Men Can't Jump*. Even ESPN's middle-aged "PTPer," college basketball commentator Dick Vitale, got into the act, dunking "for the W" in a Pizza Hut commercial.

Why do we celebrate the dunk with such enthusiasm? The answer probably lies, in part, in our day-to-day relationship with gravity. For most of us, gravity keeps us firmly on the ground. As we get older, gravity seems to work even harder at keeping us grounded. Rarely do we summon our powers to try to lift our body vertically into the air. When we see athletes dunk, it seems as though gravity doesn't work on them as it does on us. And when we witness incredible leapers like Julius Erving, Dominique Wilkins, or Vince Carter soar high above the rim, they seem to defy gravity altogether, becoming, in "Pistol" Plato's famous phrase, a "moving image of eternity." We can't do that—few people fixed to the earth can—and so we find ourselves in awe of those capable of challenging a basic force that humans must deal with on a daily basis.

The same can be said for time. At one level, nothing is more familiar to us than time. In fact, as the great Enlightenment philosopher Immanuel Kant (1724–1804) pointed out, we can't even imagine having a thought or sensation that is not experienced as occurring in time. Yet most of us, if asked to define "time," would probably respond much as the philosopher Augustine (A.D. 354–430) did: "What then is time? If no one asks me, I know: if I wish to explain it to one that asketh, I know not."[10] Our rough-and-ready theoretical understanding of time is of something infinite and constantly moving forward. Our lived experience of time, however, begins and ends in radically different ways. Some games, including basketball, seem to create a separate realm of time. This notion of finite time moving toward a finite end creates a sense of drama. For that reason, plays that "cheat" the end of time resonate with us like no other basketball moment.

Children at camps where I teach, for example, are infatuated with a game called "buzzer beater." In this game the young players start at one end of the court while I count down a predetermined time period—somewhere in the vicinity of four to ten seconds. I always manipulate the rate at which the time is counted down, depending on the skill and age of the player. The players never notice that four seconds for Jenny is the same as ten seconds for Johnny, and quite different from four seconds for Jackie. It doesn't matter—living the final seconds of a countdown is what grabs them. The drama that the countdown creates captures the kids' attention, and if anyone makes an unlikely basket, heaving the ball from downtown, the atmosphere in the gym becomes electric. The same occurs at all levels of basketball. The sense of seeing the unexpected, the dramatic, as one watches a player hit a shot at the buzzer is akin to being there when someone wins a lottery.

Some might argue that the social significance placed upon seemingly overcoming the odds of time and space means that "heroes come cheap"—a sentiment expressed by a concerned schoolteacher in *Hoosiers*. And these criticisms may hold merit. Certainly the overemphasis placed upon the spectacular play in basketball is worthy of concern. As Phil Jackson notes, few players today come to the NBA dreaming of becoming good team players because they see that superstars with dramatic, eye-catching moves make the most money and garner the most media attention.[11] But the place of time and space in basketball goes far deeper than the dunk and the buzzer-beater. Part of the reason for basketball's worldwide popularity is that the game affords us the opportunity to live time and space in complex and nuanced ways.

5, 4, 3, 2 . . . I Was Fouled!

To understand the significance of lived time and space to basketball, it is helpful to look at the game in comparison with other sports. Basketball, I will argue, is the world's most "phenomenal" game because of its use of lived time and space. To defend this claim, I will first explain from a phenomenological perspective why time-regulated games are richer experientially than event-regulated games.

Scott Kretchmar, in an essay in *Baseball and Philosophy*, champions the moral and aesthetic superiority of baseball. His argument relies on the fact that baseball is an "event-regulated" game rather than a "time-regulated" one. Requiring players to play to the end of a game, to "honor the amount of mutual testing that was committed to at the start of the activity," as Kretchmar puts it, makes baseball a morally superior game to sports such as basketball, soccer, and football, in which stalling is a commonly used tactic. In addition, Kretchmar argues, time-regulated sports such as basketball and football are aesthetically displeasing because they "tend to unravel at the end."[12]

Kretchmar makes a forceful case for the moral and aesthetic superiority of baseball. Certainly there is a charming quality to event-regulated sports. Players cannot shorten the game by using stalling tactics. A degree of hope always remains despite the long odds a team may face in the ninth inning—it is not scientifically impossible to score a hundred or more runs even with two outs in the ninth. Consider as well the description of baseball by Michael Novak in his book *The Joy of Sports:* "Baseball players are watched one by one. Those who are not connoisseurs of every individual are bored by the (to them) tedious tempo of baseball. They want grand opera, not a string quartet. The game of baseball is civilized, mathematical, and operates upon the tiny watchlike springs of infinite detail—a step covertly taken to the left here, a batter choking up just an inch there, a pitcher shortening his step upon delivery by 2 or 3 inches. One must have a passion for detail to appreciate baseball."[13]

Undoubtedly many fans in the United States and elsewhere have a passion for baseball's detail, for the game's event-regulated subtleties. But we need to look more closely at the temporal descriptions of baseball offered by Kretchmar and Novak. Baseball moves forward discrete moment by discrete moment—like the *slow* ticking of a clock. The "infinite detail" and event-by-event quality of baseball at times renders the game "tedious" and "mathematical." One envisions an afternoon or evening at the ballpark as a sedate, relaxing experience interspersed with occasional moments of excitement and possibly a tense conclusion. This is why connoisseurship is required to truly love the game of baseball. If you don't revel in the analytical quality of baseball, you'll probably only find excitement in the "long ball"—something that traditionalists abhor.

Time-regulated sports, on the other hand, add a dimension that event-regulated sports, such as baseball, golf, tennis, and volleyball, lack, namely, the tension that arises from a ticking clock. Time takes on new meanings in the lived context of sport. Watching a clock tick down in the final minutes of a time-regulated game heightens the tension of a contest. In many ways, time is what makes sports such as basketball, hockey, football, and soccer most interesting. Teams that are behind must turn to riskier and more exciting strategies, including faster tempos and longer three-point shots in basketball, deep passes in football, pulling the goalie in hockey to add an extra attacker, and having all players push forward in soccer. The team in the lead must delicately balance the temptation to stall with the understanding that it could lose momentum should the game's outcome come into question. So while mathematically an event-regulated sporting event might appear more aesthetically pleasing, the lived tension and drama made possible by the ticking of a game clock points to the experiential superiority of time-regulated games.

To underscore this point, consider how time-regulated games could be changed to make them more like baseball. Basketball, for instance, could change the rules so that each team scores as many baskets as possible before the defense makes three stops (outs). Football, hockey, and soccer could make similar rule changes. No longer would it make sense to pull the goalie in hockey, to throw risky bombs in football, to push the tempo in basketball, or to send crowd-gathering crosses into the box in soccer. These sports instead choose to make use of time for the purpose of creating a sense of flow, to generate excitement by providing teams only a finite amount of time to gain an advantage over opponents. In this way, basketball, football, hockey, and soccer all use time to make their games more dramatic and engrossing.[14]

Most of us have at some point played an imaginary game of basketball. Nearly always these games come down to one last shot, with the score tied or our team trailing. As we move into position to score against a dominant imaginary defense, the countdown begins—four, three, two, one—and we launch the potential game-winning shot. If the ball goes in, for a moment we live like a champion. If we miss it, free throws with "no time left" to win the game await. Obviously we were fouled.

Good "Spacing"

The use of a clock in basketball puts it in a group of aesthetically superior sports including hockey and soccer. But its temporal quality is only one reason why basketball stands as the most "phenomenal" game ever invented. Once we consider the game's lived spatial quality, basketball clearly rises above all other sports from an experiential standpoint.

Basketball uses lived space better than any other sport. First, by hanging a basket ten feet off the ground, Naismith's invention makes it virtually impossible for opposing players to guard the goal. Goaltending rules further protect the basket from being defended by a defender as in soccer and hockey. Consequently, basketball becomes as much a vertical game as a horizontal game. Soccer and hockey, in contrast, are virtually horizontal. While the soccer ball and puck do leave the playing surface, the focus in both is on a single plane. Basketball, in contrast, builds a vertical dimension into the fabric of the game that enhances its experiential potential.

Even on the horizontal plane, however, basketball stands as the richest game from a phenomenological standpoint. For instance, the size of the basketball court in relation to the number of players enhances the artistry and excitement of the game. Five players for each team have enough room to spread out, yet all are potentially involved in the action at all times. Players cannot "hide" or "rest" on the far side of the court as they do in soccer, where the size of the pitch makes it impossible for all players to stay involved in the action. This is highlighted by the fact that in soccer a team can lose a player to a red card and still have a reasonable opportunity to win. Playing four against five (assuming the teams are fairly equal in ability) in basketball would undoubtedly result in a lopsided affair. Furthermore, with so much ground to cover, scoring opportunities in soccer are negated. Subsequently, the experiential quality made possible by the limits of time in soccer is reduced, as players cannot transition from one end to the other quickly enough to generate a consistent level of excitement.

Furthermore, basketball's comparative lack of reliance upon technology allows it to make better use of space than a game such as hockey. Hockey players—wielding fiberglass sticks, skating on a low-friction surface, and wearing extensive protective gear—move at a speed that reduces their freedom to explore. As a result, hockey players tend to race swiftly from end to end with relatively few scoring opportunities. Basketball, in contrast, makes little use of technology. Players run, jump, and shoot virtually without the aid of technological devices. Therefore the speed of the game is limited, not by technology, but by human possibility. Plays happen as quickly as humans move—not as fast as technology allows. This also explains why versions of basketball played on trampolines don't grab us, despite their heightened vertical appeal. We still love the horizontal, organic quality of basketball that is lost when the game is transformed into a technological sideshow that reduces the complexity of lived space.

The Phenomenal Game

Soccer rightfully holds the title the "beautiful game." But from an experiential perspective, basketball is the "phenomenal game." Basketball's optimal use of lived time and space, I have argued, makes it the richest sport for human experience. And as the original Dr. J says, "Nothing but the best, the richest and fullest experience possible, is good enough for man."[15]

Naismith's willingness to experiment by taking the best of other sports and melding them together to create basketball partially explains his gamewrighting genius. The result was a game that grabs us, a sport that reveals to us the potential to play *with* and *in* time and space. Although the conditions available determined basketball's original temporal and spatial dimensions, Naismith clearly possessed a brilliant intuitive grasp of how humans love to live time and space—something protected and enhanced for more than one hundred years by the gatekeepers of the game. Basketball, more so than any other popular game, has adopted Dewey's claim that "adjustment is no timeless state; it is a continuing process."[16] The game of basketball continues to evolve, to make the human experience in time and space more compelling. Officials constantly experiment with new temporal and spatial elements of the game, including scoring areas (such as the three-point line) and time features (for example, shot clocks). Spatial and temporal changes make possible new and richer experiences, allowing basketball to enhance the human dimension of time and space.

Basketball, more than any other sport, opens space for humans to meaningfully live space and time. In basketball, the interplay between humans, space, and time creates opportunities for magical moments unavailable to event-regulated, horizontal, or technology-reliant sports. Basketball touches people on a human level like no other game—hence its international popularity. The game continues to grow because it relies less on historical foundations and more on the experiential quality. Consequently, the game is no longer just an American sport, as evidenced by the fact that Spain and Argentina, at the time of this writing, hold the titles of world and Olympic champions respectively, while emerging NBA stars include international talents such as Steve Nash (Canada), Pau Gasol (Spain), Manu Ginobli (Argentina), Yao Ming (China), Tony Parker (France), and Dirk Nowitzki (Germany).

Coach Dale was right. The height of the basket in Indianapolis was the same as the height of the basket back home in Hickory. It is true that basketball has a sense of order and uniformity that includes the size of a court, the height of a basket, and the length of a game. But more important is the richness and complexity of experience that these durable dimensions make possible for basketball players and fans. Though effective, Coach Dale's psychological ploy had its limits: simply using a measuring tape and appealing to the mathematics of basketball couldn't supplant the unique and meaningful experience his players were about to encounter.

Basketball, in short, provides unique insights into how we live in and through space and time. Concurrently, appreciating time and space in a lived sense opens our eyes to the beauty and possibility of basketball. Leaving behind mathematical notions of time and space enables us to learn more about basketball. And what we learn about basketball allows us to achieve a deeper existential sense of the meaning of space and time.

Notes

Thanks to Greg "Skywalker" Bassham and Jerry "High Wire" Walls for their helpful comments on earlier drafts of this paper.

1. John Dewey, *Experience and Nature* (1938), in *The Collected Works of John Dewey: Later Works, 1925–1953,* ed. Jo Ann Boydston (Carbondale: Southern Illinois University, 1981), 1:75.

2. In the NBA, for instance, all games are played with four twelve-minute quarters. Elite international competitions, as well as college basketball in Canada and the United States, employ two twenty-minute halves. High school games in North America are played with eight-minute quarters.

3. Criswell Freeman, *The Book of Basketball Wisdom: Common Sense and Uncommon Genius from 101 Basketball Greats* (Nashville, TN: Walnut Grove Press, 1997), 13.

4. Dewey, *Experience and Nature,* 83.

5. Phil Jackson and Hugh Delehanty, *Sacred Hoops: Spiritual Lessons of a Hardwood Warrior* (New York: Hyperion, 1995), 7, 115.

6. I was recently amazed to stand under a ten-foot basket and look up. It seemed fifteen feet away.

7. Or, in rare cases, reverse itself, as in the 1972 Olympic final between the United States and the Soviet Union, when officials kept putting time back on the clock, allowing the Soviets three attempts to score the winning basket.

8. Who among us hasn't suffered the same moment of disgrace as George Costanza, the short, stocky, bald character in the television series *Seinfeld*? In one episode, George has to pick up Jerry at the airport because he loses a bet that he can touch the awning outside Jerry's apartment building. Similarly, golfer Phil Mickelson dealt with ridicule after awkwardly leaping into the air after making a putt to win the 2004 Masters. At some point, we've all tested our vertical leap, be it to touch an awning, to slap a backboard, or at least to swipe at the bottom of the net. If you spend any time at a gym with young teenagers, you're likely to see endless competitive attempts to touch the rim.

9. Who can forget another *Seinfeld* storyline when George, so impressed by Jimmy's ability to jump, orders a case of jump shoes to sell to sport retailers? Unfortunately for George, Jimmy slips on Kramer's drooled water and injures his leg. George must then demonstrate his jumping prowess and the impact of jump shoes for potential buyers—an unsuccessful career move to add to his failures as latex salesman, marine biologist, architect, and philanthropist.

10. *The Confessions of Saint Augustine,* trans. Edward B. Pusey (New York: Modern Library, 1949), 253.

11. Jackson, *Sacred Hoops,* 90.

12. R. Scott Kretchmar, "Walking Barry Bonds: The Ethics of the Intentional Walk," in *Baseball and Philosophy: Thinking Outside the Batter's Box,* ed. Eric Bronson (Chicago: Open Court, 2004), 270–71.

13. Michael Novak, *The Joy of Sports* (New York: Basic Books, 1976), 98.

14. Football, I would argue, must be removed from this list as a temporally superior game. The disjointed stops and starts of football make it more similar to an event-regulated game than to a dynamic time-regulated game like basketball, soccer, or hockey. Football can't compare with the fluidity of these other time-regulated games, with their quick transitions, the steady flow of the game, and the never-ending energy.

15. Dewey, *Experience and Nature,* 307.

16. Dewey, "The Need for a Recovery of Philosophy" (1917), in *The Collected Works of John Dewey: Middle Works, 1899–1924,* ed. Jo Ann Boydston (Carbondale: Southern Illinois University, 1976), 10:9.

Matthew H. Slater and Achille C. Varzi

PLAYING FOR THE SAME TEAM AGAIN

The following is a transcript of what might very well have been five telephone conversations between Michael Jordan and former Chicago Bulls coach Phil Jackson in early March 1995, just before MJ's comeback after more than a year pursuing a baseball career.

Day 1: The Conditional Comeback

Phil: Hello?

Mike: Hey, Phil, it's me. Is this a bad time?

Phil: It's never a bad time, as long as I'm not deep in meditation. I was just visualizing our next game. What's up?

Mike: Still thinking about my comeback.

Phil: Come on, Michael, give it a break. It'll be just like old times. Two words: Repeat Threepeat. Heck, why stop there? We'll stamp out championship trophies like a factory, trust me.

Mike: I just can't help wondering. With no Horace, B. J., Bill, Scott . . . is it *really* going to be the same team?[1] You know how important that is for me.

Phil: Getting philosophical in your old age, huh?

Mike: Time away from basketball got me thinking. If I'm going to be part of the team again, shouldn't I know what the team really is—whether it'll really be the same team as before?

Phil: Some might say that *you're* the team. But what do you suppose a team is?

Mike: I'd say that *we're* the team: all twelve of us, even JoJo.[2]

Phil: I'll pretend you said "all thirteen of us, including our beloved coach and spiritual leader."

Mike: That's what I meant.

Phil: Well, in that case, let me tell you: in a way your worry is warranted. If teams are just their players (and coaches), then it might seem that you can't ever play on the same team if the players aren't the same.

Mike: So I was right? We won't *really* be the same?

Phil: It depends on what you mean by "same."

Mike: Don't get all hair-splitty on me, now.

Phil: No really—think about it. "Being the same" is ambiguous. Things can be *qualitatively* the same or *numerically* the same. Our trophies are indistinguishable, except for their inscriptions: in other words, they're qualitatively the same. But they're not the same trophy: they are distinct. Numerically distinct trophies can be qualitatively identical. The question it seems you want answered is whether a thing can change yet be literally *one and the same thing*.

Mike: Right. How can it? If a team is just its players (and coach), how could it survive gaining or losing any of them? I'll tell Krause that I'll come back only if it's gonna be the same team, okay?[3] If we get *everyone* back together, I'll play.

Phil: So you think that having the same players is a sufficient condition for having the same team? That if you have the same players, you'd have the same team?

Mike: I guess that's what I'm saying. But now that I think about it, I figure it depends on you as much as Krause.

Phil: How so?

Mike: Well, you decide who plays what position. Even if we had all the same players, if you ran Cartwright at point guard and me at center, we'd have a problem. We'd lose (and you'd get fired)—and people might not recognize us as the same team. So perhaps merely having the same players back together isn't sufficient after all; we need them playing in the same positions.

Phil: I can guarantee that I'd never try Bill at point (I'll tell you about this nightmare I had sometime), but I can't guarantee that I won't make some minor adjustments. Remember when Doug Collins moved you to shooting guard and had B. J. Armstrong run point? Did that destroy the team or just make it better?

Mike: Ah, Doug . . . now *he* was a superstar's coach! "Give Michael the ball and stand back," he'd say. I hope that I get to play for him again someday. You know, I don't think I . . .

Phil: Ahem!

Mike: Sorry. Okay, I see the point: My "same players, same positions" criterion might be a bit strict, but it's hard to deny that it's a sufficient condition for team identity. If we have the very same players in the very same positions, that's definitely enough for it to be the same old team.

Phil: Granted. I guess now we also need to know what the *necessary* conditions are for your comeback. What minimum conditions must we meet for it to be the same team and to get you back?

Mike: It figures that you'd want both necessary and sufficient conditions.[4] I'll talk to my agent and get back to you.

Day 2: Teams Change

Mike: Hi, Phil.

Phil: Hi, Michael. Come to any conclusions?

Mike: My agent wasn't very helpful. He kept suggesting I ask the Jerrys to "show me the money."[5] But I think I'm going to stick to the strict criterion: it'll be the same team *if* and *only if* we have the same players playing the same positions.

Phil: Okay, but even if we managed it, the team wouldn't last for long.

Mike: Change is inevitable, I suppose.

Phil: Sounds like you wanna be like Heraclitus.

Mike: Who?

Phil: Heraclitus. An ancient Greek philosopher who thought that change was the only constant. He said that one could never step twice in the same river since the water would always be different.

Mike: Exactly!

Phil: Of course, even if the water stayed the same, *you* could never step twice in the same river since *you* are constantly changing too.

Mike: What do you mean?

Phil: How tall are you?

Mike: Six-six.

Phil: But you weren't born that tall. Remember that little boy in North Carolina cut from his high school team who was shorter than six feet?

Mike: I'm so tired of that story.

Phil: But it's a story about *you,* right?

Mike: I suppose you're gonna tell me it's not? That since I've changed—like the river water—I'm not really the same person?

Phil: I'm not telling you that. But if you think that rivers and teams can't survive any change of their parts, why think that people can survive such changes? You are qualitatively different from that little boy in North Carolina. Why think that you really *are* that boy?

Mike: Well, for one, my changes have all been gradual. I didn't go from five-eight to six-six overnight. When I left the NBA in '93, though, the team was radically and suddenly changed. It'd be as if someone replaced your brain—no one can survive that kind of drastic change.

Phil: I'm not sure I buy the analogy, but we're getting there. Surely teams too can survive *gradual* change, like other things. Perhaps what matters is not losing too many players all at once. Of course, if Krause went nuts and decided to replace all the players on the team before the season began, he'd have a different team on his hands, right? But players retire and new ones get drafted and traded all the time. None of those sorts of changes seem significant enough to affect the team's identity (present company excepted).

Mike: Thanks. Okay, maybe you're right. So while the "same players, same positions" condition is sufficient for team identity, it's not necessary. Some degree of change is unavoidable and acceptable, as long as it's gradual and continuous.

Phil: It seems to be the norm, in fact.

Mike: But what if the change becomes total? What if every player is gradually replaced until none of the original players are left?

Phil: For all we've said, it could still be the same team, so long as those changes were made slowly enough. Even you, Michael, constantly lose and replace cells all the time. As a result, your body probably has none of the same parts it had when you were a little boy.

Mike: So you think continuity, even when it results in a complete change in parts, is a necessary condition for team identity?

Phil: Perhaps. But I'm not so sure. It's not even clear that *all* abrupt changes in players should result in a team change. Suppose the whole team was lost in a tragic airplane crash. Most people would probably regard the team as going on in spite of this loss.

Mike: Let's not speculate about that.

Phil: It was just a thought. These matters are not easily settled. Perhaps if Krause fired everyone, the team might survive by virtue of the new players pursuing the same goal in the same way (running the triangle offense, playing tenacious D, bringing home the trophy, and so on).

Mike: What worries me now is that a lot seems to depend on Krause—on whether he wants to make the changes in the right way. I'm gonna call him and explain all this to him.

Day 3: Traveling

Mike: Phil?

Phil: Hi, Michael.

Mike: Answer me honestly: do I travel?

Phil: Michael, I think that life is a great journey and that everyone is traveling.

Mike: That's not what I meant, and you know it. Anyway, listen, about the team: maybe we're overthinking things. Say Krause fired us and replaced us with a bunch of rookies. They'd still play in Chicago, they'd still wear white and red at home, and all that. Don't you think it'd be the same team by virtue of playing in the same city and being called the same name?

Phil: Krause threatened to fire all of us, didn't he?

Mike: Oh yeah.

Phil: He wouldn't. But let's think about the suggestion that location is what matters for team identity, rather than sameness of players and positions or continuity of player change. Let me ask you: how many championships have the Lakers won?

Mike: Eleven, I think.[6] They were an awesome team, but we'll beat that record someday. Speaking of the Lakers, what's up with that name? There weren't any lakes in LA last I checked. Or what about the Utah "Jazz"—I've never heard of much of a scene there.

Phil: So I take it you've never heard of the *Minneapolis* Lakers or *New Orleans* Jazz, either? Teams travel too, Michael. In Minnesota—

"the Land of Ten Thousand Lakes"—"Lakers" is a perfect name. So what if it doesn't fit very well in Los Angeles? It was move or lose their best players to financial trouble. Likewise, we wouldn't bat an eye if the New Orleans Jazz became the *New York* Jazz.

Mike: You're right. Perhaps a team's city isn't as important as I thought.

Phil: Perhaps. On the other hand . . .

Mike: What now?

Phil: As before, we can look at the situation in two ways: either the move to LA destroyed the Minneapolis Lakers and a new team with the same name was created in LA, or one and the same team just moved—like you might one day move from Chicago to, say, Washington, D.C. In the first case, the Lakers have won six championships; in the second, they've won eleven: six in LA, five in Minneapolis.

Mike: I'm a little torn. I want to say that the Lakers just moved, but then again, I can't imagine our team moving to Cheyenne or Cheboygan. Even if everyone came with us (heck, even if Reinsdorf still owned it), it'd have a different feel, different home court, locker room, different fans—it'd be a different team.

Phil: Your loyalty is admirable, but maybe a little old-fashioned. Remember: in the early days of basketball, some teams were only loosely, accidentally associated with cities. Often, they were extensions of corporations. The Detroit Pistons began their existence as the Zollner Pistons of Fort Wayne, Indiana—they literally made pistons. Company owners like Fred Zollner would suit up factory workers for a few games a week. A few "barnstorming" teams traveled from city to city for a cut of the door. I heard of one owner who had reversible uniforms made so he could bring the same team through the same venue twice. People didn't realize they were paying to watch the same players again in different uniforms.[7]

Mike: I couldn't do that as a player: I'll always be number 23. Okay, so maybe things aren't so simple. We've got to think about this some more.

Day 4: The Team of Theseus

Mike: Hey, Phil. Listen, I've thought about it: I'm changing my number to 45.

Phil: So you're coming back?

Mike: Yeah. I still believe the strict "same players, same positions" criterion is sufficient for team identity, but I agree it's not necessary. Nor is it the *only* sufficient condition. I think you're right that the continuity criterion is fine, too.

Phil: The continuity criterion?

Mike: The thought that things can survive change so long as it's gradual enough. That works fine for teams, too. Perhaps it's not a necessary criterion, if you really believe that a team can survive the sudden loss of all its players. But continuity does seems sufficient for . . . what was it, arithmetical sameness?

Phil: Numerical. You were interested in knowing whether the team we're putting back together and the team we had before are one and the same team, as opposed to two different teams.

Mike: That's it. I promised myself that I would only ever play for one team.

Phil: I wonder, though . . .

Mike: What?

Phil: Well, we have two sufficient conditions for team identity, right?

Mike: Right, a strict criterion and a looser one, the continuity criterion. Teams can survive replacing a player or two every season even if it means eventually changing every player.

Phil: Okay. But now imagine the following happens. Krause trades Horace one season, Scottie the next, Bill after that, and so on until all of the present team has been traded away.[8]

Mike: I just said I've come to accept change. It would still be the same team, as long as the trades were sufficiently gradual. That's pretty much what happens to teams over time in the normal course of things, as with people who grow older and change their body cells.

Phil: But imagine that you were each gradually signed to an expansion team: call it the "Cheboygan Boars." So after a few years we would have two teams—the Bulls, which have proceeded continuously through the years (getting slightly worse each season) and then (suddenly) the Boars with a starting lineup of Michael, Scottie, Horace, B. J., and Bill—the familiar, championship-winning group.[9]

Mike: So?

Phil: So the question is, which team is really the Bulls? The team in Chicago that changes only gradually through the years, or the new team in Cheboygan that eventually comes to have all the same players as the Bulls do now? Each team meets one of the two sufficient conditions you've suggested.

Mike: Well, only one team would be named the Bulls. . . .

Phil: But of course names can be misleading: a team can survive a mere name and location change just as a different team can adopt an old team's name. To be clear, let's call the team in Chicago after all the gradual trades are completed the "Continuous Team." Then the question is: are the Bulls identical with the Boars or with the Continuous Team?

Mike: I see the problem.

Phil: Good. So the Boars are now indistinguishable from the original Bulls: the players are exactly the same—the coach too, let's suppose. They play like Bulls; they win like Bulls. The Continuous Team, on the other hand, may be struggling dead last with not one recognizable player. But ordinarily—if there were no expansion Boars—we'd regard the Continuous Team as the Bulls.

Mike: Well, it might be a nice reunion to play with the guys again on the Boars, but I don't think I'd be playing for the same team. Yeah, it'd be the same group playing the same positions and such, but there'd be a weird gap in the team's history. What would've happened to the Bulls in the meantime, before the Boars were assembled?

Phil: I suppose they wouldn't have existed. But I'm not sure. What happens to a watch when you take it apart and put it back together again? Does it cease to be for a while, or does it exist in a scattered, nonticking state?

Mike: Are you philosophers just interested in raising problems? You ever come up with any *answers?*

Phil: I've heard that before. But you must agree: not just any answer is a *good* answer.

Mike: I suppose there has to be a fact of the matter one way or another. But anyway, the continuity criterion doesn't force us to decide what it is. Let's just drop the strict criterion altogether. The Continuous Team would be the Bulls even if last year's players were playing in Cheboygan.

Phil: I still have my doubts. Consider this: the Bulls and the Pistons begin to trade players with each other and . . .

Mike: Are you crazy!?

Phil: It's just an example—hear me out. Imagine that the trades happen as before, one a year. This year they exchange a power forward, next year a shooting guard, the year after a center. Eventually all twelve players have been switched. Let the coaches switch too, if you like. The change is gradual, and your continuity criterion is satisfied. Would you say that the teams have stayed put? That the Pistons still play in Detroit and the Bulls in Chicago?

Mike: Argh! I don't know! I could never be a Piston, I know that.

Phil: Nor could any self-respecting Bulls fans cheer for the Pistons. But they'd certainly root for you, Scottie, Horace, Bill, and Dennis—even if you happened to play in Detroit. There'd be some years of confusion, to be sure (I can't quite picture you and Dumars together in the backcourt night after night).[10] But in the end, I know which team I'd think of as the Bulls, even if some cruel twist of fate had renamed them the Pistons. Think of it this way: If you and I gradually exchanged all our furniture, wouldn't you say that in the end your furniture just *moved* to my place, and mine to yours?

Mike: I suppose so.

Phil: So if we see the Bulls and Pistons as gradually switching names and cities, the continuity criterion can't be right.

Mike: Strike three . . .

Day 5: Fan Loyalty?

Mike: Phil?

Phil: Knew it was gonna be you.

Mike: Phil, do you really think that the fans would leave the Bulls for the Boars, or even for the Pistons? (If we all moved to Detroit, that is.)

Phil: Seems like a serious possibility. Especially if the Continuous Bulls play poorly.

Mike: So maybe we should take that into account. Is it the fans who decide who the Bulls really are?

Phil: That sounds a bit crude, but it's worth considering. Certainly what the fans think is not by itself enough to determine the identity of a team. If some mad scientist from Detroit brainwashed Bulls fans to suddenly root for the Pistons and speak of them as if they were the Bulls, that wouldn't make the Bulls the Pistons.

Mike: That's a little far-fetched.

Phil: True, but we have to be willing to consider even odd scenarios in testing our hypotheses. Anyway, you know how common it is for front-running fans to root for a team only if it's winning. Otherwise, if someday (David Stern forbid!) the Bulls became a mediocre team and fan support waned, we'd have to regard the team as being annihilated when it seems we should say that it just got worse and lost its fans.[11]

Mike: But in a sense it would be a different team.

Phil: In a sense, sure—but only a figurative sense. We're after the literal, metaphysical sense. The team would be *qualitatively* different. But I have trouble seeing fan opinion as either a necessary or sufficient condition for *numerical* team identity.

Mike: Maybe front-running fans are only *figurative fans.* Like false friends, they're not really friends. What if we say that a team is the same only if *loyal fans* continue to cheer for it?

Phil: "Only if"? I thought you weren't interested in necessary conditions.

Mike: Well, perhaps a bunch of necessary conditions will add up to a sufficient one. I haven't quite given up on continuity yet.

Phil: Okay, but your new condition looks like it might be circular. Aren't *loyal* fans precisely those fans that continue to cheer for the *same* team (even if it begins to lose)?

Mike: Say that again.

Phil: We have to understand what it is to be a loyal fan in order to understand what it is to be the same team, and vice versa. So we're no closer to solving the problem.

Mike: We *are* closer. We just need to find some other definition of fan loyalty. Anyway, that it's circular doesn't mean it's wrong.

Phil: True. Aristotle had a similar idea when it came to virtue: he thought that virtuous deeds were the ones virtuous people did.[12] But virtuous people are just those who do virtuous deeds.

Mike: Hmmm . . . virtuous fans? Let's just say the fans, for now.[13]

Phil: All of them?

Mike: A majority. And don't start playing with numbers now. You know what I mean: a good majority.

Phil: A good majority can gradually change. Initially they all stick to the Bulls. Then, gradually, one by one, the fans switch to cheering for the Boars—

Mike: Stop right there. I know everything changes, and that's why we have a problem in the first place. But let's say the fans *now.* Suppose we've got our two teams, the Continuous Team and the Boars, and those who used to cheer for the Bulls now cheer for the Boars. Those are the fans I mean. Do you think we should listen to them and identify the original team with the Boars?

Phil: Yes, I'd say so. But not just because of the fans. Remember, the Boars are supposed to have the same players and coach as the initial Bulls. So we have two elements supporting the view that the old Bulls are the new Boars: composition and the fans.

Mike: Hold on. Suppose the fans *didn't* follow the players but kept cheering for the team called the Bulls—the Continuous Team, located in Chicago. Then we would still have two elements: continuity and the fans. (Indeed, we would also have the location element, but never mind that.) So why are you saying that it's not just because of the fans? It seems to me that if we let the fans into the picture, they *would* make all the difference.

Phil: But then wouldn't everything be up for grabs? What a team is would be a matter of what the fans think.

Mike: Maybe. A bit like contemporary art: whether something is a piece of art would be a matter of whether we think it is.[14]

Phil: That might be right when we do aesthetics, especially these days. But here we are doing metaphysics, Michael. We are trying to nail down some good identity criteria for entities of a certain kind—teams. And you don't think metaphysics is a matter of opinion, do you? You don't think existence and identity are just a matter of what people think?

Mike: I surely *didn't.* I was looking for objective criteria for team identity, like composition, location, continuity. But then *you* suggested we take the fans into account. And that's right: the fans don't play on the team, but they sure seem to play a role in team identity; they somehow contribute from the outside. External factors may matter when it comes to determining which team we are part of, especially when the intrinsic factors don't seem to settle the issue.

Phil: Have you told the Jerrys about that?

Mike: I'm telling you. And I thought you'd be happy, since it was your idea.

Phil: I'm content. But I'm not a materialist—you know that.

Mike: Come on, I've seen your Montana ranch.

Phil: I meant in the philosophical sense; I don't believe everything boils down to physical bodies and processes. I'm happy to say that the team is not just you guys (and me); it's something *over and above* its actual members. And I'm happy to say that the extra bit comes from the fans, among other things. But that means that when the season starts, there will be two things after all: the *group* consisting of all of us, which exists and is what it is regardless of the fans, and the *team,* whose identity depends on the fans.

Mike: I don't like that. I'm definitely a materialist.

Phil: That's fine. You don't want two things in the same place at the same time. You want the team to be the group.

Mike: No, Phil, that would take us back to the initial deadlock between the composition criterion and the continuity criterion.

Phil: Then what?

Mike: That's where the fans come into the picture. None of the other criteria work because we are confusing two concepts: the group, with its composition, location, history, and so on; and the team, with its fans. You are saying these two concepts identify two entities, the group and the team. I'd say we've got two concepts and the problem is to see how they interact.

Phil: Holy Toledo Mud Hens: baseball did have an impact on you! Go ahead . . . keep swinging!

Mike: Wise guy. So we've got the group, that's for sure: a bunch of guys, with a coach—convention doesn't decide this. Now is this group a team? Yes, as long as they do certain things. *What* team it is, however— and whether it always counts as the *same* team—is up to the fans. It's not that we *are* the Bulls or the Boars. We *count* as the Bulls or as the Boars depending in part on what the fans think.[15]

Phil: Just like Clinton counts as the president so long as he plays a certain role and is properly acknowledged by certain laws?

Mike: That's the idea. Clinton definitely exists—he's part of this world, regardless of what people might think of him. That he's president, on the other hand, is a matter for some sort of social convention to decide.

Phil: So in our case you agree with me: we have a group *and* a team.

Mike: No. We have a group, period. And that group *counts as* a certain team only if the fans think so. A bit like art, if you like, but not because everything is up for grabs. Take a modern sculpture, say one of Henry Moore's *Large Forms:* there's a piece of bronze, shaped in a certain way, and the question is not whether there is *also* a sculpture, something over and above the bronze. The question is whether that piece of bronze counts as a sculpture—whether it has features that qualify it as an artwork. Maybe that's up for grabs, for different people may feel differently. But that is not a metaphysical question. It's sociology, you know. The only metaphysical question is whether the bronze is there, and that has a straight answer.[16]

Phil: I think I see. So tell me, Michael: how does this help you out?

Mike: Well, I guess I was after the wrong answer, because I was asking the wrong question.

Phil: You were asking whether the team we're putting together is the same old Bulls you used to play with.

Mike: Right. It turns out that I'm interested in two things: whether it'll be the same group, and whether that group will count as the same team. But it matters less whether the group is really the same, since different groups can count as the same team.

Phil: So have we been talking about group identity all this time? Are we not back at square one?

Mike: I'm not sure. Perhaps composition, continuity, and all that are criteria that the fans can use to decide where their allegiance lies. But perhaps group identity is a more subtle and fickle business than we had in mind. Perhaps there *are* no necessary and sufficient criteria informing their decision—the criteria may not even be *consistent.*

Phil: Okay, so where does this leave us?

Mike: I guess it depends on the fans. I'll come back only if they're happy. I'm sure it's gonna be a good group, whether or not it's strictly the same old group. I wanna be sure the fans think it makes a good team— their team.

Notes

1. Horace Grant, B. J. Armstrong, Bill Cartwright, and Scott Williams all left the Bulls during or after the 1994–1995 season.

2. JoJo English, an undrafted journeyman player not known for his offense.

3. Jerry Krause, general manager of the Bulls from 1985 to 2003.

4. In philosophical lingo, a "necessary condition" is something that *must be present* in order for something else to exist or take place. Being on the roster, for example, is a necessary condition of being a starter. A "sufficient condition," on the other hand, is something that *is all that is needed* for something else to exist or take place. Thus, in the NBA, having six personal fouls is a sufficient condition for getting expelled from a game; so is head-butting a referee.

5. Presumably Jerry Reinsdorf (the owner of the Bulls) and Jerry Krause (their general manager).

6. Of course, this number is higher now. Remember, these phone calls took place in 1995.

7. Mark Stewart, *Basketball: A History of Hoops* (New York: Franklin Watts, 1998), 48.

8. Evidently, Phil has read Plutarch's *Lives:* "The thirty-oared galley in which Theseus sailed with the youths [to Crete on a mission to kill the Minotaur] was preserved by the Athenians down to the time of Demetrius of Phalerum. At intervals they removed the old timbers and replaced them with sound ones, so that the ship became a classic illustration for the philosophers of the disputed question of growth and change, some of them arguing that it remained the same, and others that it became a different vessel." Plutarch, *The Rise and Fall of Athens,* trans. Ian Scott-Kilvert (Harmondsworth, UK: Penguin Books, 1960), 28–29.

9. So Phil has read Thomas Hobbes, too: "If the ship of Theseus were continually repaired by the replacing of all the old planks with new, then—according to the Athenian philosophers—the later ship would be numerically identical with the original. But if some man had kept the old planks as they were taken out and were to assemble a ship of them, then this ship would, also, without doubt be numerically identical with the original. And so there would be *two* ships, existing at the same time, both of which would be numerically identical with the original. But this latter verdict is absurd." Hobbes, *De Corpore,* pt. 2, chap. 11, para. 7.

10. Jackson is referring to Joe Dumars—a Detroit guard Jordan repeatedly played against in several testy and closely contested playoff series—as the best defender Jordan ever faced.

11. David Stern has been commissioner of the NBA from 1984 to the present.

12. Phil is referring here to Aristotle's *Nicomachean Ethics,* bk. 2.

13. Thomas Senor offers some interesting reflections on fandom in his "Should Cubs Fans Be Committed? What Bleacher Bums Have to Teach Us about the Nature

of Faith," in *Baseball and Philosophy,* ed. Eric Bronson (Chicago: Open Court, 2004), 37–55.

14. Sounds like Mike has read Nelson Goodman's "When Is Art?" in *The Arts and Cognition,* ed. D. Perkins and B. Leondar (Baltimore: Johns Hopkins University Press, 1977), 11–19.

15. Has Mike supplemented his reading of Goodman with John Searle's *The Construction of Social Reality* (New York: Free Press, 1995)? Unlikely, since the book came out at the time of this phone call. But the phrase "counts as" is really Searle's.

16. Mike must have read at least some of the papers that are now collected in Michael Rea's reader, *Material Constitution* (Lanham, MD: Rowman and Littlefield, 1997).

Daniel B. Gallagher

PLATO AND ARISTOTLE ON THE ROLE OF SOUL IN TAKING THE ROCK TO THE HOLE

WITH THE CLOCK stopped at twenty-six seconds, Patrick Sparks, the Kentucky Wildcats' best free throw shooter, steps to the line to shoot a one-and-one. His team is tied with Michigan State with a trip to the 2005 NCAA Final Four on the line. Although he's still a kid, he's been here countless times before. Shooting a free throw is as natural to him as breathing. But in this huge moment with the game on the line, the ball comes clanking off the rim into the opponents' hands. Dejected, Sparks slouches toward the bench, takes a seat, and feels the pathetic stare of every pair of eyes in the arena upon him.

Seconds later, after the Spartans sink a three-pointer, coach Tubby Smith puts Sparks back in the game with the score now 72–75. He gets the call and takes a jumper as the final seconds tick away. He misses. His teammate Kelenna Azubuike snags the rebound and breaks for the right corner to try another three. *He* misses. The ball ricochets off the front of the rim into the hands of—you guessed it—Patrick Sparks, who, after taking a hard bump from opponent Kelvin Torbert, launches a completely off-balance three-point desperation shot as the buzzer echoes through the arena. It bounces on the rim once . . . twice . . . three times . . . and yet a fourth, then miraculously eases into the net, sending the game into overtime. Sparks has changed from goat to hero in the space of twenty-six seconds.

Sparks's performance illustrates the dynamic relationship between two elements of the human soul that are essential to the game of basketball. Plato (427–348 B.C.), the father of Western philosophy, describes them as the spirited (*to thumoeides*) and the rational (*to logistikon*) parts of the soul. The spirited part of the soul is responsible for feeling and emotion, while the rational part is responsible for reasoning and understanding. The breakdown of Spark's rational soul as he consciously toed the free throw line was only overcome by the strength of his spirited soul as he unconsciously toed the three-point line. The history of Western philosophy, which Alfred North Whitehead (1861–1947) considered to be nothing more than a very long footnote to Plato, has had to grapple with how these two parts of the soul do and should relate to each other.

I'm a Soul Man

The modern game of basketball stands out as a perfect example of Plato's teaching on the soul. Both the spirited and the rational parts of the soul are absolutely essential to this great game. The spirited part of the soul was evident whenever Daryl Dawkins shattered a backboard with one of his thunder dunks, or Nancy Lieberman dove on the floor for a loose ball. The rational part was apparent whenever Bill Walton fired yet another perfect outlet pass, or John Stockton and Karl Malone ran one of their patented pick-and-rolls. Basketball exemplifies and reveals these two parts of the soul as few other sports can because of the delicate balance it requires between strength and touch, brains and brawn.

Basketball players use muscles, and muscles are primarily controlled by the spirited part of the soul. You have to exert bodily force on your opponent in direct proportion to the force he exerts on you. But you can't push or shove him. You can't tackle the player who has the ball. Unless you're playing ESPN's "streetball," you can't pull your opponent's jersey over his eyes and bounce the ball off his face. A player must remain "in control" yet play with great intensity and passion. This requires spirit under the direction of reason.

Coach Plato

So far, we've focused on two parts of the soul: spirit and reason. But Plato, in fact, distinguishes three parts: reason, spirit, and appetite. It is the appetitive power of the soul that is responsible for the basic bodily appetites, such as the desire for food, sex, sleep, and drink. The appetitive soul also clearly plays a role in basketball. Many a teenaged hoopster drools as much for the rock as he does for a double cheeseburger. But, according to Plato, it is the rational and spirited parts of the soul, and the ways they interact with each other, that separate humans from other animals. After all, my sister's golden retriever "Magi" drools more for a ball and a double cheeseburger than I do.

In the *Republic*, Plato offers a fascinating description of an ideally just and harmonious state as an extended allegory on the three-part structure of the human soul. For a society to operate smoothly, he says, three separate social classes are needed. Workers are needed to build houses, grow food, make clothes, and provide other basic necessities. Warriors are necessary to protect the state from the threat of attack and to maintain internal order. Rulers are needed to oversee and coordinate the various functions of the working and soldiering classes, as well as to provide overall leadership and direction. In Plato's analogy, each of these classes corresponds to some part of the soul. The workers in the *Republic* correspond to the power of desire (the appetitive soul), the warriors to the power of courage (the spirited soul), and the rulers to the power of reason (the rational soul). Each of these classes is essential to a safe, stable, and well-governed state. Just as the state won't operate smoothly if any one of them is absent, neither will the presence of any one of them alone be sufficient for a smoothly operating state. As Bill Bradley wisely reminds us, "a player is only one point in a five-point star."

A successful basketball team also mirrors the qualities found in the soul of a great individual player. Like the state, a good team needs workers, warriors, and rulers. Plato claims that citizens must be trained to have only the good of the state in mind. Political philosophers often point out how closely Plato's republic resembles a socialist state. For Plato as well as for Mao, dutiful citizens must give no thought to individual recognition or selfish gain but focus exclusively on promoting the common good.

Many championship teams would never have achieved such success had it not been for the unselfish play of "workers" on the team. Rather than scoring themselves, these players usually make it possible for others to score. Victory is impossible without them. Larry Bird urges us to "get the ball to the open man closest to the basket. That's your job on the offensive end. That's the only way you can win basketball games."[1] Although he could also shoot the three, most Blue Devil fans will remember

Bobby Hurley as an incredible playmaker who could slash across the court and feed the ball to his teammates again and again. Avery Johnson, currently head coach of the Dallas Mavericks, built his playing career on the reliable support he provided to his teammates by means of a steady stream of assists and outstanding ball protection on offense. Steve Nash won back-to-back NBA MVP awards in 2004–2005 and 2005–2006 because of his brilliant passing and unselfish play. Such players exemplify the indispensable value of "workers" in the Platonic republic of the basketball court.

The warriors of Plato's republic, in turn, must possess heroic courage in the face of danger. Their role in the state corresponds to the spirited part of the soul. They must be willing to take chances when the stakes are high. They are the ones who dive on loose balls and battle for the big rebound when the game is on the line. Patrick Ewing, Bill Laimbeer, Brian Cardinal, and Dennis Rodman stand out as examples of the warrior class of players in basketball. Often their style borders on the physically dangerous, as they play more effectively by relying on visceral rather than cerebral inspiration. In fact, in the *Timaeus*, Plato locates the rational part of the soul in the head, the spirited part in the chest, and the appetitive part in the gut.

Then there are Plato's rulers. Every successful team needs at least one player with the intelligence, poise, and leadership ability to carry his team to victory. Sam Jones, Willis Reed, John Stockton, Rebecca Lobo, Jason Kidd, Magic Johnson, and Isiah Thomas are just a few of the greats we might classify as "rulers." As Oscar Robertson once remarked, "The really great player takes the worst player on the team and makes him good." "Rulers" are able to elicit the best from their teammates but also to keep them in check when necessary.

Basketball is a game of fundamentals. Every player must possess the basic skills of dribbling, passing, rebounding, defending, and shooting. A kid must be taught and drilled in these fundamentals long before he or she can master the finer points of the game. After players learn these fundamental skills, they will discover how their individual strengths and weaknesses predispose them to a specific role on the team. Without leaving behind the general skills of shooting, passing, and dribbling, a player will go on to specialize. As former UCLA coach John Wooden likes to say, "Do not let what you cannot do interfere with what you can do."

Plato, too, finds individual citizens within the republic to be endowed with a variety of gifts that naturally predispose them toward fulfilling the particular functions of a worker, a warrior, or a ruler. Had Plato been a basketball coach, he would have strongly agreed with LA Lakers coach Phil Jackson that "good teams become great teams when the members trust each other enough to surrender the 'me' for the 'we.'"[2] A just and well-ordered society, while recognizing the value of individual dignity and personal freedom, must be based on a true sense of solidarity and the common good. Plato, in fact, went too far in subordinating individual freedom to social harmony, arguing, for example, for strict censorship of music and literature. Almost certainly there would be no *Shaq Diesel* in Plato's ideal state. On the other hand, if you've ever listened to NBA rappers Ron Artest, Kobe Bryant, and Chris Webber, you might think Plato had a point in excluding certain kinds of music from the republic.

Coach Aristotle

Like Plato, Aristotle loved to classify things into various categories. Ethically speaking, he says, there are four types of people: the virtuous, the self-controlled, the weak, and the vicious. Each of these types is determined by the way in which an agent's reason interacts with his or her inclination. In virtuous persons, reason and inclination are in harmony. For the self-controlled agent, reason masters inclination, but thought and desire are often opposed. Inclination usually wins out over reason in the weak agent, and in the vicious agent, both reason and inclination tend toward what is bad.

Let's say I want to improve my jump shot. I go to a shooting coach who notices that I have a bad habit of not squaring up my right elbow before my release. I'm already a pretty good shot, but I would improve my shooting considerably if I could correct this bad habit. I have, at least when it comes to shooting the basketball, a vicious character. Not only am I inclined to let my right elbow float away from my body when I jump, my reason actually urges me to do this because the rest of my habitually acquired bodily mechanics depend on the floating right elbow. In this way, both reason and inclination lead me to shoot in this skewed manner.

My coach first explains and demonstrates to me the correct positioning of my right elbow. Squaring my body more evenly with the basket, I am directed to visualize my forearm to make it perfectly perpendicular with the top of the square painted on the backboard. At first, this seems completely awkward and unnatural to me, and I miss almost every shot. My reason now tells me to shoot this way, but my inclination is to shoot the way I've always shot. I am now what Aristotle calls a weak agent. I know what is right, but my inclination leads me to do otherwise.

With practice, however, my body starts to respond to my brain, as Aristotle anticipated: "What we have to learn to do, we learn by doing." My elbow begins to assume the correct position more readily, and my set, jump, and release flow more fluidly. I still have to think about the movements, but usually my inclination follows my reason, and my shot percentage gradually climbs to where it was before. Patience and persistence have made me a self-controlled agent.

With still more practice, I notice that I have to think less and less about my shooting mechanics. My body adjusts automatically to the correct angle no matter where I am on the floor. Reason and inclination are now working together in harmony, and my shooting has improved significantly. My new shooting form now "feels right." Although I'm far from perfect, I have become a virtuous shooter.

Every good basketball coach, even if she's never read Aristotle, employs some version of Aristotle's theory of human excellence in teaching her players. First of all, one can't acquire a virtuous character merely by thinking about what's right. You can memorize every detail found in every book ever written on the mechanics of shooting, but you will only become a virtuous shooter by shooting.

Moreover, the only way to develop good shooting habits and become a virtuous shooter is by *repeated* shooting. As University of Louisville coach Rick Pitino says, it's not practice that makes perfect: it's *perfect* practice that makes perfect. If I make the first shot I take after repositioning my elbow according to my coach's instructions, it's probably a lucky accident. If I make the thousandth shot after repeated practice, and follow that up with the thousand-and-first, and the thousand-and-second, then my reason is in harmony with my inclination. "We are what we repeatedly do. Excellence . . . is not an act, but a habit," is an Aristotelian quote treasured by more than a few coaches.

Aristotle also teaches an important lesson about how we should theorize about ethics and excellence. Many contemporary moral philosophers, following the great German philosopher Immanuel Kant (1724–1804), believe that we can discover a lot about ethics just by sitting in our armchairs and spinning ideas out of our heads. By contrast, Aristotle believes that we must start theorizing about morality and excellence only after we have spent a great deal of time observing the real actions of real human beings.

Who's right, Aristotle or Kant? Well, ask yourself this: could anyone have figured out what a perfect jump shot looks like before the game of basketball was invented? Pretty clearly not. And it's instructive to think about *why* this would have been all but impossible.[3]

In the original rules of basketball, Dr. James Naismith's formulation of the objective was quite simple. "The object of the game is to put the ball into your opponent's goal. This may be done by throwing the ball from any part of the grounds, with one or two hands, under the following conditions and rules" (then followed his thirteen rules).

What Dr. Naismith's rules don't specify is the most effective way of putting the ball into your opponent's goal. They merely state that it may be done by throwing the ball with one or two hands. The first players of the game cared little *how* the ball got into the basket, as long as it got there legally.

How did players figure out the most effective way of tossing the ball into the opponents' basket? Through trial and error, of course. It didn't take long to figure out that you could prevent the opponent from blocking a shot if you kept the ball over your head. It also helped if you jumped into the air to elevate yourself over the reach of the defenders, or even jumped back in a fadeaway motion. Much later, Kareem Abdul-Jabbar went on to perfect his unstoppable sky hook. Players learned what worked through experience, not by armchair theorizing.

All of this illustrates another important teaching of Aristotle's, namely, that virtuous agents set the standard when it comes to human excellence. They disclose what is humanly possible by demonstrating *areté* (excellence or virtue). A good basketball shot is first achieved, and then it is formulated. We become good shooters largely by watching and imitating good shooters.

Basketball also provides a perfect example of Aristotle's famous teaching that virtue lies in a "golden mean" between too much and too little. In every area of human activity, Aristotle points out, there is the possibility of going wrong by excess or defect. Aristotle's classic example is the person facing grave danger. If a bold and decisive action is required and we react instead by running away, we are said to act cowardly. If we foolishly overreact to the threat, we act rashly. These are the two extremes. In the middle lies the virtue of courage. In a courageous person, reason and will act harmoniously so that he avoids both the excess of cowardice and the excess of rashness. Other human actions also have their distinctive extremes and means. When it comes to food and drink, to overindulge is gluttony; to refuse proper nourishment is abstemiousness; and to hit the right balance is temperance. Similarly, when it comes to spending money, the mean between stinginess and extravagance is liberality. Only when it comes to basketball, common sense, and philosophy, it seems, is it impossible to ever have too much!

The art of shot selection in basketball is a prime example of this doctrine of the golden mean. We have all known ball hogs who jack it up whenever the ball touches their fingers. Then there is the player who will look to pass even when he is alone in the lane with nothing more than a layup to complete the play. These are obvious extremes, but every player constantly has to decide: should I shoot or pass?

"Balance," as John Wooden says, "is the most important thing in basketball."[4] Yet as Aristotle notes, the precise mean is often very hard to determine. Virtuous persons can trust their instincts more than those who are merely self-controlled or weak-willed. Moral agents of these types are in greater need of direction and general rules to determine their course of action.

One of the things that made Michael Jordan such a phenomenal player was his uncanny ability to trust his instincts. He was well aware of his extraordinary abilities, but he was also aware of his limitations on an "off" day (as if he ever had one). He never hesitated to pass up a shot when he sensed that it had little chance of getting through the hoop. But he also never failed to take the shot when it really counted. "I never looked at the consequences of missing a big shot," he once said. "When you think about the consequences you always think of a negative result."[5]

Aristotle's doctrine of the golden mean is one of his most ingenious contributions to moral theory. It preserves ethical objectivity while recognizing the complexity and variability of the ethical life. In striving for the mean when it comes to shot selection, each player has to take into account his own personal abilities as well as the circumstances that surround a particular shot opportunity. Do I have the hot hand today, or does my teammate? Do we have enough of a lead to afford more selectivity in our shots, or do we need to close the gap quickly? How much time is left on the shot clock? Obviously, no player can afford to go through such a checklist every time he touches the rock, but that is precisely why he needs to be a virtuous player, so that the mean will be achieved through habit rather than through conscious choice.

Of course, there are times when you have no choice but to shoot. In such a situation, you have to rely on the spirited part of the soul trained and tempered by the rational part. At this point all preparation, all conscious thinking, is past. Now you must rely on the muscle memory of habit, flowing naturally from the virtuous character you have attained through persistent practice and repetition.

Patrick Sparks found himself in such a "no choice" situation when, through an amazing stroke of luck, the ball bounced off the rim and into his hands. And though it was amazing to watch the ball leave his hands as the buzzer sounded, the fact that it ended up in the basket was anything but luck.[6]

Notes

1. Larry Bird, *Bird on Basketball* (Reading, MA: Addison-Wesley, 1987), 26.

2. Phil Jackson with Hugh Delehanty, *Sacred Hoops: Spiritual Lessons of a Hardwood Warrior* (New York: Hyperion, 1995), 21.

3. See John Christgau's fascinating book *The Origins of the Jump Shot: Eight Great Men Who Shook the World of Basketball* (Lincoln: University of Nebraska Press, 1999).

4. John Wooden with Jack Tobin, *They Call Me Coach,* rev. ed. (New York: McGraw-Hill, 1988), 216.

5. Pat Williams, *Quotable Michael Jordan* (Hendersonville, TN: TowleHouse, 2004), 23.

6. Many thanks to John Kopson for counsel on examples.

Thomas P. Flint

THE BASKET THAT NEVER WAS

Prologue

THERE ARE EXACTLY 2.34 seconds remaining in the game to decide the conference championship, and it looks as though good old Yoreville U just might pull off an upset that will be world famous in Yoreville for a millennium. Yoreville trails Emeny by a single point, Yoreville has the ball, and Coach Quoats is using his last time-out to design a play. Actually, you and everyone else in the arena know what's coming: somehow or other, the ball is going to South Shore, Yoreville's famed shooting star. The players return to the court, the ref hands the ball to Yoreville's trusty guard Gard, and we're off. Gard inbounds the ball to his backcourt companion Dwibbles, who cuts toward the basket and passes, sure enough, to Shore. Shore hesitates for an eternal instant, then shoots. Shot, horn—which came first? You see the ball ascend, stop, descend, and . . . nothing but net. Yoreville roars, but then sees what you feared. The ref is waving off the points. The shot came too late, he says; the game clock had expired. There was no shot, and thus no points, and thus no victory, and thus no championship for Yoreville. Coach Quoats and half the crowd are livid, imploring the refs to check the monitors. They do, but the combination of poor camera angles and a technical gaffe render the available video evidence inconclusive. The call stands, and the crowd slowly leaves, angry and dejected. It's all over.

Or is it? The next morning at the office, your boss, Gervais, says he has something to show you. Gervais was at the game last night, in his usual front-row seat, and tells you he was recording parts of the contest with his new camcorder. "Take a look at this," he tells you as he starts the disc. And there it is, plain as day. From Gervais's perfect location, you can see the ball leave Shore's hand while the clock in the background shows .03 seconds remaining. "We was robbed!" you scream. "No doubt about it. Shore shot in time! Two points for us!" Gervais nods, and the two of you spend the next few minutes commiserating over the injustice of it all.

Act 1: Two Points or Not Two Points?
That Is the Question

As you return to your desk, though, confusing thoughts begin to assail you. The ball was shot before the horn: no doubt about *that* anymore. It went through the net—also indisputable. But does it follow that Shore hit a two-point basket? Well, you say, of course it does. Don't the rules say that a player "shall be awarded two points" or something along those lines?[1] So Shore really did hit a two-pointer—the refs just didn't call it. But if he hit a two-pointer, then Yoreville really earned more points than Emeny, whatever the official scorer said. And if Yoreville scored more points, then Yoreville really won the game, and hence the championship. So Yoreville is the real, true champion, no matter what the league says. Facts are facts, no matter what people (or refs, for that matter) say. Wasn't it Lincoln who once posed the question, "How many legs does a dog have if we call its tail a leg?" The correct answer, he said, was four, because it doesn't matter what we *call* a tail; the fact is, it just *isn't* a leg.

All this makes sense. But then you start to wonder. *Are* there really facts here no matter what the ref, the scorer, or the league says? Well, there's no doubt (in your mind, anyway) that there are physical facts in the neighborhood—facts about people, balls, nets, clocks, and so on— facts that are facts no matter what anybody says. Dwibbles passed the ball to Shore; the ball was shot before the horn sounded; the ball went through the net—all these are facts about the world, facts independent of anything we say or do about them.[2] But basketball's a game, and games don't just exist on their own, independent of what we say and do. They're governed by rules, and those rules create facts that wouldn't be facts without our consent. Take the three-point shot. Prior to 1980, there was no three-point shot in college basketball. Lots of players, of course, shot baskets from what we now refer to as three-point range. Did they *really* hit three-pointers, a fact that the refs perversely refused to recognize at the time? Of course not. Since the rules didn't allow three-point baskets back then, there simply *were* no three-point baskets then. Here, reality is created by convention. Maybe we should say the same thing about Shore—that since the ref didn't *call* it a basket, it *wasn't* a basket? Or is that to confuse what the *rules* say with what the *refs* say?

Act 2: Must Give Us Pause—To Know or Not to Know?

As you puzzle over these questions, it occurs to you that there's another reason to doubt that Shore really hit a two-pointer: it leads to truly goofy conclusions about what we know and don't know. Suppose we stick with the claim that Shore's shot was in reality good, and the refs just didn't recognize this fact about the world. It follows that you and Gervais know something that nobody else knows: that Shore's basket was good. You know that he *really* earned two points, that Yoreville *really* won the game, and that the *real* conference championship belongs to your beloved Yoricks.[3] Thousands of benighted fans—those who were at the game, or who read about it in the paper or heard the results on ESPN— *think* they know how many points each team got, which team won, and who the conference champion is, but they're all mistaken. They don't know; you do.

That sounds a bit strange. You like yourself (and sort of like Gervais), but can the two of you really know so much more about this sort of thing than anyone else does? Can everyone else be wrong about who won the game, and only the two of you be right? But wait a minute; *do* you really know? Emeny's center was twice called for goaltending. But you weren't sure at the time, and you're even more uncertain now. Was it *really* goaltending? Was the ball *really* on its way down when he swatted it away? Maybe, but maybe not. If it wasn't, then does it follow that Yoreville didn't *really* score those four points? If they didn't, then they still lost, even with Shore's buzzer-beater.

But wait another minute. Thinking back on it, there were lots of close calls in that game. How about those two shots Shore hit that you (and half the crowd) thought were three-pointers, but were called two-pointers? Maybe they really *were* three-pointers. How about that intentional technical foul call against Dwibbles at the end of the first half? You surely didn't think it was intentional. Maybe it really wasn't; maybe if we could look inside Dwibble's mind, we'd see that no intention to trip Emeny's guard was present.[4] On the other hand, remember those two out-of-bounds calls against Emeny at the start of the game? The Emeny bench surely didn't believe those two players were out of bounds; maybe they were right. And so on, and so on.

The more you think about it, the more it looks as if, once you start down the "Shore really *did* hit that basket" path, the less confident you become about what *really* happened in that game, or about what the *real* score was, or who *really* won. And not only for that game: surely the point, if valid at all, can be generalized. We'd have to say that nobody knows what really happened in just about any game.[5] You always thought you knew that UCLA's eighty-eight-game winning streak was ended by Notre Dame on January 19, 1974, but maybe it wasn't; maybe the Bruins actually won that game. (You smile at the thought, since you never cared much for Digger Phelps.) And what goes for games, of course, goes for seasons as well. How well you recall Michael Jordan's leading North Carolina to that championship back in 1982. Well, alas (you've always liked MJ), maybe *in reality* he didn't lead them to a championship; maybe they *really* lost in the first round of the NCAA tournament. Who knows? The same depressing conclusion seems to follow for individual players and their career statistics, too. *Officially,* Pete Maravich is the leading scorer in NCAA history, with 3,667 points. But, again, if you take the "Shore really scored" route, it looks as though the official statistics shouldn't cut much ice with you. "Officially, schmicially," you're apt to say. "Who cares what the record book says? How many points did Maravich *actually* have? Who *really* scored the most points? How many did he score?" And since there's no way for anyone to answer such questions, the upshot is that, for the most part, nobody knows nothin'.

That's such a goofy conclusion that you know you can't take it seriously. You have a clear and distinct memory of discussing skepticism in your Intro to Philosophy class, and you never could quite understand the amount of time and energy some philosophers seemed to spend trying to show that we do indeed know things. Whatever the philosophers might say, you're intent on saving Michael Jordan his championship, on securing for Pistol Pete his scoring record, and on maintaining for all of us our

knowledge of such accomplishments. And if that means denying that
Shore scored, so be it.

Act 3: Thus Conscience Doth Make Losers of Us All

There's another reason, it occurs to you, to question your "Of course
Shore scored" intuitions. Those intuitions have moral implications that
you wonder whether you should accept. You're actually quite a moralist
about basketball, as you are about all sports (except, of course, hockey).
You think that the rules of a game establish a code of conduct that the
participants have an ethical duty to follow. Coaches, especially at the
nonprofessional level, have an obligation to foster this reverence for the
rules in their players. Some coaches, you know, take a very different attitude toward the game; they actually encourage their players to get away
with whatever they can, to view the rules not as principles to be honored
but as obstacles to be overcome. Given the pressures to win in college
basketball, you can understand this attitude, but you still view it as a violation of a coach's responsibility toward his players. Teach them to do
their best, teach them to do all they can to win—but only if they can do
so fair and square.

Suppose we take the "Shore scored" line and insist that there are
facts of the game independent of what the refs say. Imagine, then, a game
in which the refs are noticeably lax about calling traveling. One step, two
steps, three steps—as long as you don't take four or five, it seems, they're
not calling a violation. Now, suppose you're the coach of one of the
teams. You know the rules regarding traveling, and it's perfectly evident
to you that honest-to-goodness cases of traveling are being ignored by the
officials. It's perfectly evident to the other coach, too, and he's responded
by telling his players, "Three steps are OK today, fellas; it looks like it's
not traveling until you get up to four." Now, what are you to do? There
are facts of the matter here, you remind yourself. There are rules in basketball; taking three steps is against the rules, whether the refs call it or
not; and it's wrong to encourage your players to violate the rules. So it
looks as though you should tell your players not to travel at all, in the
conventional sense of traveling. But is that really the right thing to do?
Won't you be putting your players at an unfair disadvantage if you tell

them to act in accord with rules that neither their opponents nor the game officials seem to be acknowledging?

Act 4: The Slings and Arrows of Outrageous Zebras

Well, that settles it. Shore didn't score. But just as you're about to leave thoughts of basketball behind and get down to work, you realize that something is still amiss. Shore didn't score. Why not? Because he wasn't in bounds? Shuffled his feet before he shot? Failed to put the ball through the net before the buzzer sounded? No, none of that. He didn't score simply because the ref said he didn't score; that was the only piece of the puzzle that was missing. If the ref had said he scored two points, then he would have scored two points. But what if he *had been* out of bounds when he shot, but the ref called it good? What if he *hadn't* put the ball through the basket in time, but the ref said he had? Lest you return to the goofy view you've already dismissed (you've decided to dub it "the Goofy View"), it seems that you have to say Shore would indeed have scored in these situations. But now a disturbing thought occurs to you. Basketball, like any good game, is supposed to be a game of rules. Yet it looks as though you're now being led to a position where the rules really don't matter very much. Shore gets his points if, but only if, the ref decides to give them to him. Basketball as rule-governed sport is morphing into basketball as tyranny of the zebras. And Tyranny of the Zebras (you're suddenly into giving things names) seems little if any better than the Goofy View.

The more you think about it, what makes Tyranny of the Zebras so odd a view is that it suggests that referees have a quality that Roman Catholics ascribe to the pope: the attribute of infallibility. The pope, say Catholics (or at least true-blue Catholics), can't be mistaken when speaking definitively on some issue of faith or morals. There's no guarantee that he'll speak grammatically or prudently or eloquently on such matters; and if he's speaking about, say, music or stamp collecting or baseball, there's no reason to pay much attention. But what he says about faith and morals cannot be wrong. And that's what the Tyranny of the Zebras suggests about the refs. They might be arrogant or ill-tempered or even confused about the rule book, and it's fine to tune them out if they start, well, pontificating about, for example, matters of faith and morals. But when it comes to making calls in the game, they can't be mistaken. Like the pope, within their sphere of authority, there's just no way they can get things wrong.[6] But you know that that just ain't so. Refs *do* make mistakes. Blown calls are as much a part of the game as blown shots. If a referee couldn't make a mistake, then why would knowledge of the rules be considered a requirement for becoming a ref? And why would referees ever examine videotape during a game and change a call on the basis of such evidence? Why change a call if there's no way the initial call could have been wrong? In this and so many other ways, don't referees signal that they *don't* think of themselves as infallible, that they *don't* view themselves as possessing unlimited or tyrannical power? If *they* don't buy into the Tyranny of the Zebras, surely we shouldn't.

Come to think of it, isn't the Tyranny of the Zebras in conflict with the very rules that establish the game? You think so, but you're not sure. Well, there's an easy way to find out. You look around to make sure that no one's watching you, then turn to your computer. You quickly find the rules online and, sure enough, uncover ample evidence of the restrictions placed upon, and the fallibility of, the officials. Rule 2, section 2, article 2 states, "No official has the authority to set aside any official rules or approved interpretations." That makes it as clear as clear can be; basketball is a game of laws, not of unfettered zebras. Nor are zebras infallible. For example, rule 2, section 5, article 2 says that "the officials *after making a call on the playing court* shall use replay equipment, videotape or television monitoring that is located on a designated courtside table . . . , when such equipment is available, to . . . (b) Ascertain whether a try for field goal that will determine the outcome of a game (win, lose, tie), and was attempted at or near the expiration of the game clock, was released before the reading of 0.00 on the game clock."[7] Note that the rule says the official *shall* (not *may*) check the monitor *even though he's already made the call.* This rule makes sense if the official can make a mistake in judging whether or not the shot was made in time; it would make no sense if officials can't get it wrong.[8] Similarly, rule 2, section 5, article 1i, states that officials can use a replay to determine "if a try for goal is a two- or three-point attempt"; again, why check the tape if your original verdict can't be mistaken? None of this language would be appropriate if the Tyranny of the Zebras were in harmony with the rule makers' vision of the game. One more reason, then, to oppose Tyranny.

Act 5: A Competition Devoutly to Be Judged

Where are you now, you wonder? You've rejected the Goofy View, the claim that there are mind-independent and (more importantly) ref-independent facts about points scored, games won, and so on. And you've also dismissed the Tyranny of the Zebras, which states that facts about points scored, games won, and so on are solely dependent upon the arbitrary edicts of referees or other officials, officials who can never be mistaken. The truth, you decide, must lie somewhere between these two extremes. But where? Should we say that Goofy is right about, say, buzzer-beating and points scored, but Tyranny is correct regarding traveling and games won? That sort of compromise has its attractions. But it also would lead us to say some amazing things—for example, that Yoreville really did score more points than Emeny, and there was no forfeit or subsequent disqualification of any sort, but Emeny really did win the game. Maybe that's the best we can do, but you hope not.

Perhaps the thing to do instead is to think more carefully about the role of the officials in a game. The Goofy View implies that referees operate more or less as historians, or at least as chroniclers. Their duty is to record what happened as accurately as possible. The rules of the game give them, in effect, a language for recording events: the player who impedes another's progress toward the basket is guilty of *blocking,* and he is recorded as having committed a *personal foul;* the player who puts the ball through the basket is said to have scored a *goal,* and two *points* are recorded in his name; and so on. But the events they are recording, according to the Goofy View, really have nothing to do with those who are doing the recording. Like Thucydides describing the events of the Peloponnesian War, the referee is endeavoring to record events whose occurrence doesn't depend upon their being recorded. And that independent existence of the relevant events also means that referees, like historians, can make mistakes; they can fail to notice what truly happened, or can judge that something happened when it really didn't.

You've already seen fit to reject the Goofy View, so you're not inclined to think of referees as historians anyway. It occurs to you, though, that there's another reason to question this way of seeing game officials. Historians need not have witnessed all of the events they record. Thucydides saw only a few of the occurrences he describes; other historians saw none. And such absence of firsthand observation hardly disqualifies one from serving, and serving well, as a historian. But witnessing seems crucial to being a referee.[9] Referees do not consult a number of witnesses, compare their stories, weigh their veracity, and eventually come up with a claim that, say, Gard traveled. They base their decisions on their own observations, not on those of others.[10] And that's a good reason, it occurs to you, not to think of referees as akin to judges or juries in a courtroom either, since the latter rely so obviously on testimony rather than on the direct evidence of their own senses.[11]

Still, maybe thinking of judges more generally is the right way to go. Maybe game officials are akin, not to judges in a court of law, but to judges who decide on awards in a contest, judges who are expected to make their awards on the basis of some publicly acknowledged rules. Lots of examples—some quite close to basketball, some not—come to mind here. The awarding of Nobel Prizes and the competitions for Oscars and Emmys are the kinds of contests you have in mind, though whatever rules there are here are often unwritten and rather vague. Dog shows or beauty pageants or competitive wine tastings may be better examples, but there's still a degree of looseness greater, it seems to you, than is present in contests such as basketball. Other sports—say, Olympic events such as diving or gymnastics—or other types of competitions (those amazing Coney Island hot-dog-eating contests, for example) seem to offer even closer parallels. And it seems to you that there are plenty of examples even where we would be somewhat less inclined to call something a contest. Remember when Gervais's wife was boring you at the office Christmas party last year talking about how the faculty in her department over at Yoreville went about selecting applicants to their graduate program? Everyone knew that there were, in effect, rules (loose and unwritten, but rules nonetheless) to follow in selecting the winning applicants. The quality of the university the candidate attended, her grade point average there, her scores on the GRE (or was it the GRRR?), the distinction of those who wrote letters on her behalf, and the quality of those letters—all of these were supposed to be weighed by those deciding to whom positions should be awarded.

And this notion of *awarding*, it seems to you, is what ties all these cases together and ties them all to sports officials such as basketball referees. The good judge, in basketball or any contest, is one who understands the rules of the contest and applies them correctly in making his award, whether he's awarding a Tony to an actor or three points to a Shore. Without his verdict, there simply is no award; with it, there is. To that extent, Tyranny is on track. But there still is a meaningful sense of a judge's being mistaken. For such an official has a duty to apply the rules properly. When he fails to do this—for instance, by giving Shore three points even though his foot was over the line—he has indeed made a mistake. But the mistake is not over whether Shore scored three points—*that* fact is indeed determined by his *saying* that Shore scored three points. The mistake is not so much one of failing to align one's *beliefs* with what *is;* rather, it is fundamentally one of failing to align one's *actions* with what *ought to be.*[12] Rules are akin to divine commands telling an official how he should act in different situations—"Thou shalt call a charge when the player with the ball runs into a defender who has established a stationary defensive position," or "Thou shalt not allow an offensive player to remain in the free throw lane for more than three consecutive seconds unless there is a shot," or the like. Judges in any contest have such rules to follow, to one degree or another, and (in the long run) the contest can flourish as a social activity only if those rules are honored. The good judge is the one who follows the rules correctly; the bad judge is the one who fails to do so.[13]

Epilogue

So South Shore didn't score. In an ideal world, he would have been awarded two points, Yoreville would have won the game, and the Yoricks would have been champions. In the actual world, they aren't champions, because they didn't win. Alas, poor Yoricks! And all because of the basket that should have been, but never was.

Notes

1. As you'll discover in a few minutes when you consult the official NCAA rules, the language actually reads: "A goal from the field other than from beyond the three-point line shall count two points." You'll find this wording in rule 5, section 1, article 1, which you'll locate online at http://www.ncaa.org/library/rules/2007/2007_m_w_basketball_rules.pdf.

2. Sure, sure, you've heard of Einstein, but you're confident that the theory of relativity doesn't really challenge any of the claims you're making about reality.

3. Campus legend has it that the team's distinctive nickname was bestowed upon it by Richard Tarlton, Yoreville's first president and reputedly a fellow of infinite jest.

4. You remember once reading that the official NCAA rules don't explicitly refer to a player's intentions when defining an intentional *personal* foul, but do when defining an intentional *technical* foul. As you'll discover in a few minutes, this is indeed the case. Rule 4, section 21, article 7 reads: "An intentional technical foul involves intentionally contacting an opponent in a non-flagrant manner when the ball is dead."

5. The "nobody" here and elsewhere is meant to cover only normal, merely human persons. God would presumably know the real score all the time. And it's at least conceivable that other nonhuman observers would suffer none of the epistemic uncertainty that flesh is heir to.

6. The popes of baseball (umpires) often seem attracted to this view. Think of Hall of Fame ump Bill Klem's famous remark, "It ain't anything 'til I call it." Come to think of it, not even a pope would say that. What he defines to be true can't be false, but it isn't made true by his speaking. If Mary was assumed into heaven (as Pius XII declared in 1950), she didn't have to wait around for his declaration before she could enter the pearly gates! But Shore doesn't score unless and until the ref says he does.

7. Italics have been added to note the section of the rule that seems to be especially pertinent.

8. One might think that, given this rule, Gervais's camcorder and the indisputable evidence it offers could have been used to reverse the official's call. Alas for Yoreville, such is not the case. See rule 2, section 5, article 1, A.R. 6.

9. The same goes, of course, for being an umpire in baseball, a point you recall having read in J. S. Russell's "Taking Umpiring Seriously: How Philosophy Can Help Umpires Make the Right Calls," in *Baseball and Philosophy,* ed. Eric Bronson (Chicago: Open Court, 2004), 87–103.

10. Obviously, an official can be blocked on a play and defer a ruling to one of the other referees. Still, he does this only if, and only because, he assumes that the other ref can appropriately make a ruling based solely on the testimony of his own senses.

11. It also seems to you, though you suspect others might disagree, that juries and judges, like historians, can be mistaken in a way that referees just can't. If the officials call Dwibbles for traveling, it follows that he traveled. But remember that French movie your girlfriend made you watch last year, *The Return of Martin Guerre*? There was a fact of the matter about whether the recent returnee to the village was identical with the Martin Guerre who had left years before, a fact that didn't depend on the decision of the court.

12. Obviously, beliefs have an impact upon action, and typically an official who makes a bad call does so because of a mistaken belief about some game-independent fact (such as whether or not someone's foot is on a certain line). Still, the official makes a bad call—makes an officiating mistake—if and only if the rules of the game

oblige him to act in a certain way (given the circumstances) and he doesn't act in that way. Whether his blown call is due to a mistaken belief about feet and lines, or to ignorance of the rules, or to malevolent intentions on his part is inessential to his action's being mistaken.

13. If you were a philosopher, you would probably feel obligated to point out to readers that the discussion here is in certain respects reminiscent of controversies concerning realism and antirealism in various areas of philosophy. And you would probably then go on to point out that an excellent general introduction to the disputes, along with suggestions for further reading, can be found in Edward Craig's article "Realism and Antirealism," in *The Routledge Encyclopedia of Philosophy*, ed. Edward Craig (London: Routledge, 1998), also available online at http://www.rep .routledge.com.

Michael L. Peterson

HOOSIERS AND THE
MEANING OF LIFE

HOOSIERS IS A feel-good movie about basketball that provides a rich glimpse into the human spirit. There are other great sports movies (such as *Rocky, Chariots of Fire,* and *The Natural*), but *Hoosiers* has it all. Based on the true story of the Milan Indians who beat Muncie Central to win the 1954 Indiana boys' high school basketball championship, this film holds you captive from beginning to end. If you're a sports fan, or a basketball fan, or even remotely interested in the meaning of life, then see the movie before reading this chapter.

Written by Angelo Pizzo and directed by David Anspaugh, *Hoosiers* (1986) was nominated for an Academy Award for Best Actor in a Supporting Role (Dennis Hopper) and Best Music, Original Score (Jerry Goldsmith). It handily topped the readers' poll in *USA Today* for best sports movie of all time. And both ESPN's Expert Panel and SportsNation Users polls ranked it the best sports movie. In 2001, the United States Library of Congress deemed *Hoosiers* "culturally significant" and selected it for preservation in the National Film Registry. Rereleased in 2005 in a two-disc DVD collector's edition, with a second disc that includes the Milan-Muncie 1954 game, this movie is a classic!

But why does watching *Hoosiers* affect us so powerfully? And how can *Hoosiers* lead us into reflection on the meaning of life itself? Before delving into these philosophical questions, let's nail down the flow of the movie.

Play by Play

The story line is compelling: a small school, shorthanded for players; a

controversial coach; turbulence surrounding the team; a romantic interest; a father-son relationship; a dark moment of despair, then victory
through perseverance, hope, and determination. This template, of course,
has been used in sports movies forever, but in *Hoosiers* the nostalgia for
Indiana in the 1950s, superb acting, and a thrilling musical score work
together to create a masterpiece.

Gene Hackman stars as Norman Dale, a formerly successful college
coach haunted by his past, who takes a coaching job at fictional Hickory
High School in the fall of 1951.[1] The opening scene pictures Dale sipping
coffee as he drives slowly through the Indiana countryside on his way to
Hickory. On the way, he stops briefly at a rural crossroads, where stands
a lone white clapboard church, before driving on. Upon arriving at Hickory High, Dale gets a less-than-affirming third degree from coteacher
Myra Fleener (Barbara Hershey). When he finds the principal, his long-
time friend Cletus Summers (Sheb Wooley), he's informed that this small,
rural school of 161 students has only six players on the basketball team.
To make matters worse, Hickory's star player, Jimmy Chitwood (Maris
Valainis), a troubled boy, has quit the team, causing great anxiety throughout the town.

Dale's early actions—failing Miss Fleener's interrogation, firing the
self-appointed assistant coach, and dismissing two players at the first
practice—don't win him any popularity contests. Players' dislike for
his fundamentals-oriented practice sessions, personality conflicts with
basketball-crazed townsfolk, and a string of early-season losses further
compound the coach's problems. Dale even hires the town drunk (Dennis Hopper as Shooter) as his new assistant, another not-so-savvy move
in the public eye or in the opinion of Shooter's son, Everett, who's on
the team.

In spite of losses on the court and conflicts off the court, Dale sees the
team "coming together" as they learn his system. At the lowest point in
the fortunes of the team, the town calls a meeting at a local church for the
purpose of dismissing Coach. Dribbling a ball all the way to the church
door, Jimmy makes an unexpected entrance. He strides to the front and
promises to return to the team—but only if Coach stays! With the coach
and the team getting a new lease on life, the winning begins, Myra starts
coming around, and Hickory hysteria is in full swing.

The team—Jimmy, Buddy, Rade, Merle, Everett, Strap, Whit, and the hapless Ollie—puts together a seven-game winning streak into the sectional finals, where it wins against Terhune.[2] The Hickory Huskers defeat Linton in the regional finals and end up in the dramatic state finals in Indianapolis against powerful South Bend Central. When these farm kids enter enormous Butler Fieldhouse before the big game, Coach brilliantly eases their apprehension by pointing out that the basket is ten feet high and the free throw line is fifteen feet from the basket—the exact same measurements as their gym back in Hickory. Billed as a massive underdog, the Huskers get way behind in the championship game and look like they'll soon be sent back to the cornfields and old tractors. Coach Dale calls a time-out to rally the team: "Maybe they were right about us. Maybe we don't belong up here." The team refocuses and goes on to pull off a thrilling last-second win.[3]

We can savor this movie at many levels. First, it's the perfect vehicle for a nostalgic history of Indiana basketball: peaceful farmlands, old gyms with gleaming wood floors and golden-toned wall tiles, cheerleaders with ponytails, the one-legged set shot, fanaticism for basketball, and every resident a walking encyclopedia of this great sport. Larry Bird, probably the most famous product of Indiana basketball, said of the movie, "Those guys got it right." Having grown up in Linton in the 1950s, I reply, "They sure did." (But, hey, Hollywood, it's the Linton Miners, not the Linton Wildcats!)

Second, in this wonderful setting, the movie's main plot is interlaced with engaging subplots: Coach Dale's respect for Jimmy's decision not to play earns Jimmy's and Myra's respect; Coach's dogmatic insistence on fundamentals, team play, and integrity brings out the best in his boys; friction with Myra blossoms into romance; Shooter gets an opportunity to rebuild his self-esteem and restore his relationship with his son.

Third, *Hoosiers* conveys so many great messages: the power of dreams fueled by drive, selflessness over individualism, the necessity of character, the need for courage in the face of great odds, the nobility of giving second chances, and the beauty of redemption. The grit and realism and sheer humanity of *Hoosiers* make it a microcosm of life itself. But if *Hoosiers* is such a microcosm, what important lessons does it teach us about life? Let's probe a little deeper.

Sports, Movies, and the Search for Happiness

We play and watch sports for fun and excitement—and for other reasons we won't explore here.[4] We watch movies for entertainment, perhaps to get our minds off ourselves for a while or to be transported to another place and time, whether fictional or not. But while fun and entertainment are part of life, they shouldn't divert us from thinking deeply about life. Consider those deep questions we ponder in our more serious moments: Why am I here? What does it mean to be a human being? How should I live? How can I be happy? These are attempts to solve the puzzle of the meaning of life. Existentialist thinker Albert Camus insists that "the meaning of life is the most urgent of questions." And nothing matters more than finding the answer.

A common stereotype of the search for the meaning of life is a person traveling to a far-off land (perhaps a mountain top in Tibet) and seeking wisdom from an oddly dressed, bearded, old sage. But what if the answer doesn't lie in what is extraordinary, esoteric, even mysterious? What if somehow the answer is much more related to ordinary life? In fact, what if the downright earthiness of *Hoosiers* is a tip-off (pardon the pun) to critical clues that help us make sense of life? One function of philosophy is to notice interesting features of the world so that its depth and wonder can be thoughtfully explored. Without having to go anywhere or do anything extraordinary, we simply need to see the clues around us everyday: personal decisions and attitudes, how we treat others, how we respond to adversity. In portraying some of these very common experiences, *Hoosiers* provides some amazing clues about the meaning of life.

At one level, *Hoosiers* is about a search. From the opening scene, Coach Dale is seeking to get his coaching career back on track. The town of Hickory is searching for basketball glory. Shooter is looking for self-esteem and connection with his son, Everett. All involved feel they need something to fall into place, something to make their lives work better, to make them happy. Aristotle (384–322 B.C.) says that all persons seek happiness. Everything that people do, whether consciously or unconsciously, is related to their search for happiness, for meaning and fulfillment.[5] But then what is it that will make us truly happy? What is the essence of happiness?

Aristotle discusses various things that people have taken as the "greatest good" *(summum bonum)* and thus the essence of human happiness. Some people think *pleasure* is the highest good. Pleasure comes in many forms—from the simple thrills of video games, to aesthetic appreciation, to sexual activity. *Fame* has also been proposed as life's great good, and we seek it in popularity, honors, awards, and even remembrance after death. *Power* has also been advocated as the chief good, whether political power or the power of self-expression. *Wealth and possessions* are often mentioned in the great debate over life's supreme good. We've all seen the bumper sticker: "Whoever dies with the most toys wins!" (I recently saw this crass message on a new yellow Porsche zipping in and out of traffic.) Since we're talking sports, we can't forget *physical health and appearance.* It is one thing to say that our physical condition supports the pursuit of higher goals. But with magazines such as *Shape, Cosmo, Allure,* and *Flex* at every checkout counter, preoccupation with image suggests that many take the physical to be the highest good in life.

What about you? What are you looking for? What do you think will make you really happy? Aristotle correctly says that many different goods are part of a happy life but that no single one of them can be made the essence of happiness. Aristotle taught that we can't understand real happiness until we first understand what a "human being" is, that is, what is unique about our humanity. For Aristotle, human beings are unique because of their capacities for rational thought and moral activity. These abilities set us apart from everything else on Earth—rocks, rutabagas, and even the great apes. Happiness, then, according to Aristotle, is the fulfillment of our distinctively human potentials. Since the human potential for intellectual contemplation is not the main focus of sports movies, let's explore the important theme of character in *Hoosiers* and see what it teaches us about happiness.

Winning according to Aristotle and Other Great Coaches

In sports, the point is to win—right? Obviously, in basketball, we want to win. Outscore the other team, beat the opponent. A rush of adrenaline, a moment of glory. But we can't always win, because circumstances are not under our complete control. In athletics we try to manage circumstances to our advantage: train hard, stay in condition, follow the game plan. Yet injuries, bad calls, unlucky bounces of the ball, and the talent of the opponent are variables beyond our control. Likewise, in life we try to manage circumstances, but things don't always go our way. This raises the question of what real "success" is and what it means to "win" in life. Viewed correctly, sports—and in this case basketball—provide situations in which we can learn attitudes and actions that apply to the larger arena of life.

Great basketball coaches teach that developing character is the most important form of winning. Tubby Smith, coach of the University of Kentucky Wildcats, tells his players, "Always strive to be the best person you can be. It will show on the court as well."[6] Although a demanding coach, Smith is known for taking a fatherly interest in his players' character development. He tries to teach them that the same qualities that make for a competitive basketball team make for real success in life: discipline, motivation, maximum effort, unselfishness, teamwork, loyalty, and commitment to the good of the whole. We can hear the echo of Coach Dale in the locker room before the Linton game: "If you put your effort and concentration into playing to your potential, to be the best that you can be, I don't care what the scoreboard says at the end of the game. In my book, we're going to be winners!" Dignity and self-worth are found in playing fairly and giving 110 percent, regardless of the outcome of the game. Sports is not all about the scoreboard. Work hard, follow the rules, do your best, help others, and you will be a winner in life.

Players with good character bring much more to the game of basketball than those without it. Obviously, some extremely talented players lack character. They may be poor students or magnets for trouble, and such liabilities injure their teams. And the behavior of some high-profile NBA players, both on and off the court, is clear evidence that talent is not always correlated with character. But even unparalleled individual talent is usually not enough to win consistently in team play. Acclaimed NBA coach Pat Riley (Los Angeles Lakers, Miami Heat) says that selfishness— what he calls "the disease of me"—destroys the teamwork necessary for consistent winning. Selfishness is the worst character flaw in team sports and clearly a major flaw in the big game of life. "Our significance," Riley explains, "arrives through our vital connections to other people."[7] We are all on many "teams"—family, job, sports—where we have to understand the dynamics of teamwork and not think "It's all about me." Remember Coach Dale telling the Hickory Huskers that the "five players on the floor function as one single unit. Team, team, team. No one more important than the other." Actress Ashley Judd, arguably the most famous Kentucky Wildcats basketball fan, says that "passing the ball . . . is the most spiritual element of the game. It's like a secret shared amongst kindred spirits."[8] Selfishness is put aside, and organic connectedness takes the team to a new level. The truth of interdependence and teamwork is so important that it is engraved on our coins: E pluribus unum, "Out of many, one."

In *Leading with the Heart,* Duke coach Mike Krzyzewski suggests that a key indicator of whether a person has his "self" in proper perspective is how much he cares.[9] Coach Dale models caring to his team and to the whole town: he cares about the boys on the team, the principal, his own integrity, and even the town drunk. In the locker room before the final game, after giving tactical instructions, Dale gets very personal with his team: "I want to thank you for the last few months. It's been very special for me." Then he asks the players why they want to win, what they care about. Merle answers with determination, "Let's win this'n for all the small schools that never had a chance to get here." "I want to win," states Everett, "for my dad." Buddy says, "Let's win for Coach, who got us here."

Caring makes real winners in the larger arena of life, and it's a kind of winning that doesn't require anyone else to lose. When asked at the end of a season whether it was a success, legendary coach Amos Alonzo Stagg was fond of saying, "Ask me in ten years and I'll tell you if it was a success." Time will tell if people care about the right things, and Stagg knew that.

Aristotle taught that character rests on habits that reflect moral principles: honesty, courage, self-control, and many more. The best coaches help student-athletes learn character lessons in basketball so that they can face life's full-court press. Dean Smith, former coach of the North Carolina Tar Heels, believes that character is essential. He reports telling players to "put academics first and basketball second" and to take their "citizenship role seriously."[10] Interestingly, this highly successful Carolina coach says that during recruiting visits he looked for signs of character in potential players: "If I witnessed a young man being disrespectful to his parents, I was concerned whether or not we should recruit him."[11]

Pat Summitt, legendary coach of the Tennessee Lady Vols, mentions accountability, among other traits, that make for success. "Accountability," she insists, "is essential to personal growth, as well as team growth. How can you improve if you're never wrong? If you don't admit a mistake and take responsibility for it, you're bound to make the same one again."[12] Summitt tells of once moving her players out of the plush, trophy-filled home locker room and into the visitors' bare locker room for a month to send the message that they weren't "paying the rent," weren't fulfilling their responsibilities. She reports that this tactic for motivating the team to strive for excellence made a bigger impression on her players than all the awards and hype surrounding the program.

Aristotle thought that morality is learned by doing. And basketball, like all sports, is best learned by doing. The other side of this is that teaching morality is a lot like coaching rather than, say, lecturing or simply verbalizing a list of rules. We learn basketball by practice based on good instruction in fundamentals, followed by drill, correction, and repetition. To teach a right-hand layup, the coach might say something like, "Okay, off the last dribble, shift your weight to your left foot, raise your right leg up, and release the ball with your right hand. Try it. No, that's not quite right. Back up and try that again with a little more rhythm. There, now you're getting it." Likewise, we learn moral virtues—such as loyalty, unselfishness, and initiative—by being "coached." A morally mature person, such as a parent or teacher, provides a moral example and guidance to those who are not as far along in their moral development. In sports, the coach has the opportunity to teach life skills and character right along with teaching the game. In *Hoosiers,* basketball becomes a wonderful venue for teaching and nurturing character.[13]

The most dramatic test of character for the Hickory Huskers comes in the title game against the mighty South Bend Central Bears. In this David-and-Goliath scenario, the Huskers are determined not to let the superior size and athleticism of the Bears intimidate them. Many basketball fans remember coach Jim Valvano (former coach of the North Carolina State Wolfpack, the improbable 1983 NCAA champions) speaking at the 1993 ESPY Awards, presented by ESPN, shortly before his death from cancer. Announcing the creation of the V Foundation for cancer research, he proclaimed that the foundation's motto would be, "Don't give up. Don't ever give up." The Hickory team simply refused to quit, refused to believe that they couldn't win. Courage, perseverance, drive, teamwork—all come together for the Huskers in that dramatic championship game because Coach Dale had created situations all season long in which they could develop those qualities. *Hoosiers* conveys an important message about the meaning of life: character is essential to our fulfillment as human beings. Character first, winning second.

Basketball and Redemption

While character is in principle under our control, we are not always consistent in acting on character. Sometimes we're weak, and we fail. But the dictum that character is essential does not tell us how to come back from a moral failure, particularly if the defect is serious and our comeback is dependent on the attitude of others. Here again *Hoosiers* contains a vital clue about the meaning of life.

Hoosiers wonderfully portrays the nobility of giving—as well as the liberation of receiving—second chances. Principal Summers graciously gives Norman Dale a second chance to overcome a dark deed in his past. Dale says, "I really appreciate what you're doing." Summers replies, "Let's not be repeatin' ourselves. Your slate's clean here. We've got a job to do." Knowing that one person shows faith in him and does not condemn him, Coach Dale throws himself wholeheartedly into working with the team. Criticism comes at him from virtually everyone in town, except for Myra's mother, Opal, and Shooter, who is not in a position to condemn anyone.

Throughout the movie, the theme of forgiveness is interwoven with the theme of character. Although character is a necessary condition for human fulfillment and finding meaning in life, it is not a sufficient condition. In light of moral frailty and failure, there has to be something more. The exercise of virtue today cannot erase the failure of yesterday. So, how do we think about moral weaknesses and blunders, particularly when they are the result of bad choices—either our own or someone else's? Even if those bad choices are in the past, they are still there, producing guilt, lowering self-esteem, spoiling one's reputation. We are in bondage to our less-than-stellar actions unless there is some way out.

Steve Smith, coach of the Oak Hill Academy Warriors, winners of six *USA Today* national boys' high school championships, says, "Players sometimes screw up, underachieve, or underperform—and the coach has an opportunity to get them back on track. We all have needed second chances in our lives." This three-time High School Coach of the Year explains, "There may have to be some consequences, but I try to structure situations for each individual player so that he can come back and fulfill his potential."[14] In *Hoosiers,* after Whit is dismissed from the team for being disrespectful, his father brings him back to practice. Whit is apologetic: "Sorry, coach, about walkin' out. I'd be obliged if I got myself another chance. It won't happen again. You're the boss." Coach accepts Whit back on the team and helps him get back on track.

Strictly speaking, character is attuned to moral right and wrong as well as the corresponding consequences. If we commit a wrong, morality may instruct us to make restitution, take appropriate consequences, or undergo punishment. But a morality of rights and wrongs per se doesn't teach us how to repair relationships. If a wrong has been committed by someone else, morality itself tells us to fit the consequences to the crime. It doesn't tell us how to make everything new again. That's exactly what we long for, something that will release us from condemnation and restore broken relationships. But that is up to the other person. Early in the movie, for example, Myra is moralistic and judgmental and refuses to give Coach a break. Her gradual change of heart becomes an interesting study of this point.

Hoosiers deals in a very earthy way with concepts of mercy, forgiveness, and the possibility of redemption. At the psychological level, forgiveness means overcoming negative feelings and judgment toward an offender, not by denying that we have the right to such feelings and judgment, but by endeavoring to view the offender with benevolence and compassion, while recognizing that he or she has abandoned the right to them.[15] Just think about it. Person X has done a huge wrong in the estimation of person Y, and Y has the right to her negative reaction. So, X has lost the "right" to Y's goodwill; but Y is able to show goodwill to X anyway. Myra's case is instructive along these lines. In many scenes, she cannot find it within herself to treat Coach Dale with respect. All along, she suspects that he's done something bad to put him in Hickory; later in the story she finds out the nature of his past offense. At the town meeting, however, she decides to show mercy by not publicly reporting his suspension from the college ranks for hitting a player. She's one more person who starts showing faith in Coach. Such actions demonstrate the human ability to transcend the strictly moral categories of justice, obligation, and retribution and move our thinking to a higher plane.

In psychology, most studies of attempts to act on this higher plane focus on the benefits of forgiveness for the forgiver. Forgiveness has been shown to rid the forgiver of negative, self-destructive feelings of hostility and resentment. But the benefits of forgiveness to the one being forgiven are enormous as well. Hannah Arendt, one of the foremost philosophers of the twentieth century, attributes the discovery of the role of forgiveness in the realm of human affairs to Jesus of Nazareth.[16] The Christian scriptures portray Jesus modeling to people a forgiving God and forgiveness having amazing effects on the people forgiven (e.g., Mary Magdalene and Zacchaeus the tax collector). The incredibly touching example in *Hoosiers* is Coach Dale's making Shooter an assistant coach and creating situations to build his self-esteem. Coach laid down some conditions, gave him some structure, and helped him start rebuilding his life, particularly his relationship with his son. Just think of the awful spot Shooter was in, being condemned by everyone. Even his son, Everett, protests to Coach: "He's a drunk. He'll do something stupid. He doesn't deserve a chance." But Shooter was given a tremendous gift: a new lease on life and the chance to set relationships on a new level.

Philosophers typically agree that we cannot change the past: the past is objectively what it is. Yet from a theological perspective it is fascinating to explore whether forgiveness is somehow the power to change the past. In a moral universe run by strict justice, the past cannot be canceled. But when mercy and forgiveness enter human affairs, although past actions are not changed, a new way of looking at them is provided. We are creatures who make meaning out of our lives according to the categories in which we think about ourselves and others. So, for the forgiver and the forgiven alike, forgiveness provides a way of reframing an experience that involves moral failings so that it is not as negative, not as destructive. Mercy and grace, both given and received, restore a sense of personal meaning and provide a positive, healing way of looking at the past. For-giveness is as close to changing the past as there can be. Forgiveness al-lows for a future that is not just a continuation of the past; it paves the way for breaking old patterns. The mobilization of so many human fac-ulties in the experience of forgiveness—compassion, intellect, will, imag-ination—gives birth to hope. Look at what it did in the life of Shooter. Forgiveness prevents an unerasable past from destroying the promise of the future.

If forgiveness in human affairs is not possible, then we are indeed the most miserable of all creatures. Jewish philosopher Martin Buber, speak-ing of human alienation, quotes the Fuegian saying, "They look at each other, each waiting for the other to offer to do that which both desire but neither wishes to do."[17] One of our deepest needs is forgiveness, although we often fail to give or receive it. Forgiveness, writes John Patton, is "not doing something but discovering something—that I am more like those who have hurt me than different from them. I am able to forgive when I discover that I am in no position to forgive."[18] Could this be part of Coach's motivation with Shooter? There is humility and surrender of false superiority involved in giving to others exactly what I myself need. When reminded of some wrong against her, Clara Barton, founder of the American Red Cross, is noted for replying, "I distinctly remember forget-ting that!"

Hoosiers and the Deep Structure of Reality

We admire the values of *Hoosiers*—the loyalty, courage, and drive that make for character as well as the all-too-rare quality of mercy, which so gracefully completes the film. It's definitely a heartwarming movie. And it makes us think, "Hey, this is the way things ought to be: a world where character breeds self-worth and achievement and where forgiveness makes possible amazing transformations." Yes, it is the way human be-ings ought to live, and it is essential to human flourishing. But, philo-sophically, we have to ask whether our identification with the values of *Hoosiers* is just wishful thinking or relates to something real. If such val-ues and our response to them are clues, where do these clues take our search for the meaning of life?

Put another way, in what kind of universe do the values of *Hoosiers* make best sense? If *Hoosiers* portrays something of "the way things ought to be," then this tells us something about the nature of reality itself. We are dealing here with the part of philosophy concerned with worldviews. A worldview is a general picture of everything: a theory of the nature of reality, the significance of humanity, whether there is a deity, the scope of knowledge, the place of morality, and the meaning of it all. Each worldview has its own beliefs about the "deep structure" of reality, or the way things really are at the most fundamental level. How would we envision the kind of reality—reality at its very core—that would give us an adequate answer to our question? Let's briefly survey some of the major worldviews and what they say about the values of *Hoosiers*. For a range of perspectives, let's look at a very diverse sample: naturalism, postmodernism, Hinduism, and theism.

Naturalism maintains that reality is physical or material. There is no nonmaterial reality, no God, no human soul, no absolute values. Naturalists typically see science, which is based on empirical method, as the paragon of human knowledge. For them, science reveals an impersonal universe with no morality or meaning or purpose. Bertrand Russell holds, for example, that our values are "the outcome of accidental collocations of atoms."[19] Another naturalist, Kurt Baier, says that individuals may find some "meaning *in* life" despite the fact that there is no overarching meaning *of* life.[20] So, within a naturalistic universe, we can subjectively approve of the values of *Hoosiers* and even embrace such values to give our lives some sense of fulfillment. But we can't claim that these values are the way things "ought" to be because there is no ought in a purely naturalistic universe, no objective moral ideals or norms. For naturalism, there is simply the brute fact of the natural physical universe. So, the values of *Hoosiers* really have no ultimate support in naturalism.

Postmodernism, in its extreme "deconstructivist" form, denies both that there is an objective reality and that human beings can know it. What we have are "linguistic descriptions" or "narratives" masquerading as reality. These narratives and the language they employ are used to keep one group in power at the expense of another (e.g., aristocratic, white, European males suppressing lower socioeconomic classes, women, non-Europeans). The dominant group or culture pretends that its narrative is superior, that the group possesses a "metanarrative" that judges all other narratives to be inferior or mistaken. Obviously, dramatic consequences follow for meaning and purpose, social and political affairs, and ethics and values. For postmodernists such as Jacques Derrida, no one narrative is superior to any other.[21] When properly deconstructed, the narrative of life implied in *Hoosiers*—which prizes traditional values— simply reflects the interpretation of a dominant social group and its attempt to maintain power by "normalizing" certain ideals. There really are no such values as fidelity, loyalty, dedication, courage, hope, and forgiveness. It is not just that postmodernism provides no support for the values of *Hoosiers;* it is downright hostile to them.

Disappointment with the secular viewpoints of naturalism and postmodernism may lead us to explore the great religious worldviews for more support. It is worth looking at *Hinduism,* one of the major religious systems of the East, for a different approach. Hinduism teaches that divine reality (Brahman) is the secret, hidden essence of everything. This means that our common belief that the world is made up of many individual persons and things is mistaken. The perception of reality as "many" is illusory. Hinduism teaches that distinctions we ordinarily make—between individual things, between good and evil, and even between personal and impersonal—do not apply to the Ultimate, or Brahman. Brahman is One. For this particular form of pantheism, then, the goal of life is to achieve consciousness, often through special forms of meditation, that we are one with Brahman. "Atman is Brahman," or the individual self is the Great Self.[22] At the most fundamental level of reality, there is no basis for our standards of good and evil, personhood as we know it, or even a concept of the divine as somehow personal. So, once again, the values and virtues so convincingly portrayed in *Hoosiers* have no place in this worldview.

Although we could survey more worldviews, it is starting to become clear what it's going to take for any worldview to be adequate. An adequate worldview must account for the incredible depth of personhood, including the values we cherish and virtues we admire. Inadequate worldviews miss this point in a number of different ways, either by reducing the personal to the impersonal (naturalism), by reducing the personal to the nonpersonal (neither personal nor impersonal; Hinduism), or by denying that we can know or say anything reliably about the nature of the personal (postmodernism). *Hoosiers* depicts something of the richness of what it means to be a person—the capacity for courage, conviction, achievement, compassion, and mercy—and compels us to revisit our earlier question: In what kind of universe do such attitudes and actions make best sense? In what kind of universe do they line up with the way things are? They obviously don't fit in a naturalist, postmodern, or Hindu universe, and they don't fit in an array of other universes envisioned by most other worldviews.

Having grown up in Indiana in the 1950s, I'm an instinctive realist. When I see people do good things and resonate with those actions, and when I admire certain values, I think that these things are something real, that they reflect something of the way things are. I think this about the wonderful human qualities in *Hoosiers*. Back in rural Indiana, we also had a saying: "Water cannot rise higher than its source." It is preposterous, then, to think that the personal reality we know—indeed, the personal reality that we *are*—is supported by a universe that is less than personal itself at its very core. Naturalism, postmodernism, and Hinduism just begin the long list of worldviews that, in effect, assert that water rises higher than its source. But the Hoosier in me says no way.

The worldview of *theism* holds that ultimate reality is intensely personal and that this personal reality is God. God brought everything else into being: finite personality as well as the physical world. The prospects for finding valid clues in our search for the meaning of life are much brighter when the most important aspects of personhood as we know it can be anchored all the way down to the deep structure of reality. Finite personal reality argues for an infinite personal source.

Among theistic religions that recognize ultimate reality as personal, *Christianity* specifically maintains that the being of God is interpersonal, social, and relational. And this infinite personal life is perfectly morally good. Such goodness, then, is the kind of goodness that aims at the best for created persons (honesty, courage, fidelity, and so forth) and enhances relationships. Although we never achieve perfect moral character, the theme of character in *Hoosiers* leads us to recognize a theistic universe as its only adequate support. To develop character in this universe is actually to reflect in our own lives something of the way things really are, and thus to find something of the meaning of life. It is not that nontheists or non-Christians can't have moral character or approve of some moral values, but the reality of character and values in personal life receive no ontological support from other worldviews, whereas they do from theism.

Christianity also has much to say about mercy and forgiveness under the general concept of grace. Grace tells us that the God who is morally perfect also has unlimited love for persons—that in spite of our moral failings God offers forgiveness and redemption. Some of the religious accoutrements of *Hoosiers*—meetings in church to discuss basketball, preachers traveling with the team, and frequent prayers for basketball games—serve as "window dressing" suggesting a religious zeal for Indiana basketball. But the Christian symbols also suggest the kind of universe in which the drama takes place: a universe in which moral character is important and in which forgiveness is possible. No wonder we identify with the character dramatized in *Hoosiers* and long for the forgiveness it depicts to be operative in the way human beings relate to one another. The beauty and nobility of forgiveness, as we now see, are rooted all the way down to the very heart of reality.

The nature of this deeply personal universe—deriving from an infinite personal source—is such that character is necessary for our own personal fulfillment and that forgiveness is necessary for repairing relationships and giving new hope. This is surely the way things ought to be. Christian theism says that this is indeed the way things are. Thomas Aquinas (1225–1274) explains that God's nature itself is love. Creatures may possess properties that are distinct from their natures (as a person might or might not have love), but in God love is identical with God's nature. This means that the very heart of reality is personal-relational love. And this love "wills the good of others, and loves everything that exists."[23]

Morality and mercy in human affairs, then, reflect perfect love at the core of reality and teach us that love is the key to life. The closing scene of *Hoosiers* features a little boy shooting hoops in the old Hickory gym, dark, empty, quiet, filled with wonderful memories. As the camera closes in on the 1952 championship team picture mounted on the wall, we hear Coach's voice saying, "I love you guys."

Notes

1. Scriptwriter Angelo Pizzo reveals in the trailer that the character of Coach Dale was initially inspired by Woody Hayes, who had to leave Ohio State after punching a Clemson player during a bowl game on national television. Pizzo, who attended Indiana University and was a huge IU basketball fan, also based the coach on Bobby

Knight, with his emphasis on "fundamentals" and "four passes before a shot" phi-losophy. Both of these real coaches, like Coach Dale, have aggressive personalities and short fuses. In the film, Dale, a former coach of the national champion Ithaca Warriors, was banned from college coaching for hitting a player. By contrast, the ac-tual Milan coach, Marvin Wood, was a young, happily married, soft-spoken man who was well liked by both the townsfolk and the players.

2. When Coach Dale visits Shooter to keep him on track, he says, "We got ten games to play, right? We're going to be a tough team to beat. Now you come along for the ride." Ray Craft, associate commissioner of the Indiana High School Athletic Association, who was high scorer in the actual Milan-Muncie game and appeared in the film as the person who meets the team bus at Butler Fieldhouse, interprets Dale to mean that there are ten games to win all the way through the championship (Ray Craft, interview by author, May 12, 2006). But the alert viewer knows that after that conversation with Shooter, the movie shows only games against Decatur and Dugger before the sectional finals. On Craft's interpretation, there would be five games not shown. Also, sectionals and regionals in Indiana—all single-elimination—usually in-volve two games at each level before semistate and state playoffs. The movie simply does not get bogged down in this level of detail.

3. Jimmy Chitwood of *Hoosiers,* who makes the last-second shot to win the game at 42–40, is based on the character of Bobby Plump, the shy Milan sharp-shooter who sank the final shot against Muncie in 1954 to win 32–30. Milan was behind in the fourth quarter, pulled even, and then Coach Wood told Plump to hold the ball and take the last shot.

4. See Michael Mandelbaum, *The Meaning of Sports: Why Americans Watch Baseball, Football, and Basketball, and What They See When They Do* (New York: Public Affairs, 2004). Also see the *Journal of the Philosophy of Sport* for occasional discussions of this topic.

5. Aristotle, *Nicomachean Ethics,* trans. Richard McKeon (New York: Ran-dom House, 1947), bk. 1.

6. Tubby Smith, interview by author, December 18, 2005.

7. Pat Riley, *The Winner Within: A Life Plan for Team Players* (New York: Putnam's Sons, 1993), 16.

8. Ashley Judd, "More UK Games, More Chances to Savor the Pass," *Lexing-ton Herald-Leader,* March 25, 2005, C5.

9. Mike Krzyzewski, *Leading with the Heart: Coach K'S Successful Strategies for Basketball, Business, and Life* (New York: Warner Business Books, 2000), 78–79.

10. Dean Smith and Gerald Bell, *The Carolina Way: Leadership Lessons from a Life in Coaching* (New York: Penguin Press, 2004), 101.

11. Smith, *The Carolina Way,* 100.

12. Pat Summitt, *Reach for the Summit: The Definite Dozen System for Succeed-ing in Whatever You Do* (New York: Broadway Books, 1998), 39.

13. See the discussion of character building in basketball by Gregory Bassham and Mark Hamilton in this volume.

14. Steve Smith, interview by author, May 10, 2006.

15. See Luke Witte's moving and insightful discussion of this theme in this volume.

16. Hannah Arendt, *The Human Condition* (Chicago: University of Chicago Press, 1958), 242–43.

17. Martin Buber, *I and Thou,* trans. Walter Kaufmann (New York: Charles Scribner's Sons, 1970), 70.

18. John Patton, *Is Human Forgiveness Possible? A Pastoral Care Perspective* (Nashville: Abingdon Press, 1985), 25.

19. Bertrand Russell, "A Free Man's Worship," in *Why I Am Not a Christian* (London: Allen and Unwin, 1957), 107.

20. Kurt Baier, "The Meaning of Life," in *Philosophy: Contemporary Perspectives on Perennial Issues,* ed. E. D. Klemke, A. David Kline, and Robert Hollinger (New York: St. Martin's, 1994), 378–88.

21. Jacques Derrida, *Of Grammatology,* trans. Gayatri Chakrovorty Spivak (Baltimore: Johns Hopkins University Press, 1976).

22. *Upanishads,* Kaivalya Meditation, bk. 11.

23. Thomas Aquinas, *Summa Theologica,* pt. 1, Q 20, A 1 and 2, in *Aquinas: A Summary of Philosophy,* ed. Richard Regan (Indianapolis: Hackett Press, 2003). Also see the biblical statement "God is love" (1 John 4:8).

THE LINEUP

FRITZ ALLHOFF is assistant professor of philosophy at Western Michigan University, where he specializes in ethical theory, applied ethics, and philosophy of biology. He has published scholarly articles in *American Journal of Bioethics, Cambridge Quarterly of Healthcare Ethics, History and Philosophy of the Life Sciences, International Journal of Applied Ethics, Journal of Business Ethics,* and *Kennedy Institute of Ethics Journal.* He has also edited or coedited a number of anthologies, including *Beer and Philosophy* (forthcoming).

GREGORY BASSHAM is chair of the philosophy department at King's College (Pennsylvania). He coedited *The Lord of the Rings and Philosophy* (2003) and *The Chronicles of Narnia and Philosophy* (2005) and is the coauthor of *Critical Thinking: A Student's Introduction* (3rd ed., forthcoming).

MYLES BRAND is president of the National Collegiate Athletic Association (NCAA). He formerly served as president of the University of Oregon and Indiana University. He also was professor of philosophy at several universities, and he has published extensively on topics in the philosophy of mind, action theory, and analytic metaphysics.

PEG BRAND is an artist and associate professor of philosophy and women's studies at Indiana University–Purdue University Indianapolis. She has edited *Beauty Matters* (2000) and coedited *Feminism and Tradition* *in Aesthetics* (1995). She is currently working on a book manuscript with accompanying original illustrations entitled *Beauty below the Surface: Feminist Visual Parodies.*

SCOTT A. DAVISON is professor of philosophy at Morehead State University in Morehead, Kentucky. He is the author of a number of scholarly articles and philosophical essays written for a general audience, including a chapter in *The Lord of the Rings and Philosophy* (2003).

DIRK DUNBAR is the director of the joint interdisciplinary humanities program at Okaloosa-Walton College and the University of West Florida, where he teaches courses in philosophy, religion, and environmental humanities. He is author of *The Balance of Nature's Polarities in New-Paradigm Theory* (1994) and numerous articles on ecocentric thought in music, literature, religion, philosophy, psychology, and popular culture.

TIM ELCOMBE is an assistant professor of physical education and kinesiology at Brock University in St. Catherines, Ontario, and a recent PhD graduate of Pennsylvania State University in sport philosophy. His research projects and published works consider sport and physical culture from an experiential and sociopolitical perspective. He is also a former national-level basketball coach in Canada.

THOMAS P. FLINT is professor of philosophy and director of the Center for Philosophy of Religion at the University of Notre Dame. Flint publishes and/or teaches in philosophical theology, philosophy of religion, metaphysics, the history of political theory, and classical Greek drama. He wrote *Divine Providence: The Molinist Account* (1998), edited *Christian Philosophy* (1990), and coedited (with Eleonore Stump) *Hermes and Athena: Biblical Exegesis and Philosophical Theology* (1993). Along with his colleague Michael Rea, he is editing *The Oxford Handbook of Philosophical Theology* (forthcoming).

DANIEL B. GALLAGHER is assistant professor of theology at Sacred Heart Major Seminary in Detroit, where he specializes in medieval aesthetics and metaphysics. His more recent articles have appeared in *Topics* on *General and Formal Ontology* (2006), *Etudes Maritainiennes,* the *Latin Americanist,* and the *New Oxford Review.* He affectionately dedicates his essay to Paul Berg—coach, philosopher, priest.

STEVEN D. HALES is professor of philosophy at Bloomsburg University. He has a PhD from Brown University and has published six books, including *Relativism and the Foundations of Philosophy* (2006) and *Beer and Philosophy* (forthcoming). He has also published numerous articles in epistemology and metaphysics and has lectured widely. In 2006 he was named Bloomsburg's Outstanding Teacher of the Year.

MARK HAMILTON is a professor of philosophy and NCAA faculty representative in charge of compliance for athletes at Ashland University. He specializes in sports ethics and has published a number of essays in the Popular Culture and Philosophy series.

BERNARD JACKSON JR. has held appointments at the State University of New York at Cortland, Ithaca College, and the Hobart and William Smith Colleges. He specializes in the philosophy of law, applied ethics, and modern philosophy and has strong interests in the philosophy of sport and African American philosophy.

THOMAS D. KENNEDY is professor and chair of the Department of Philosophy at Valparaiso University in Indiana. He works on eighteenth-century Scottish philosophy, philosophy of art, and bioethics as well as moral theory.

KEVIN KINGHORN is philosophy tutor for undergraduates at Wycliffe Hall, University of Oxford, and is also assistant professor at Asbury Theological Seminary in Wilmore, Kentucky. He has written philosophical articles on such popular culture topics as the superheroes, *The Chronicles of Narnia,* and the films of Alfred Hitchcock. He is also the author of *The Decision of Faith: Can Christian Beliefs Be Freely Chosen?* (2005).

R. SCOTT KRETCHMAR is professor of exercise and sport science at Penn State University. He is a founding member of the International Association for the Philosophy of Sport and served as its president. He has been editor of the *Journal of the Philosophy of Sport*, is a fellow in the American Academy of Kinesiology and Physical Education, and has authored a popular text in the philosophy of sport.

DAVID K. O'CONNOR has been a member of the faculty of the philosophy department at the University of Notre Dame since 1985. He works in ancient philosophy, ethics and political philosophy, and philosophy and literature. He is the director of the undergraduate program in philosophy and literature.

MICHAEL L. PETERSON is professor and chair of the philosophy department at Asbury College in Wilmore, Kentucky. He is author of *With All Your Mind* (2001) and *God and Evil* (1998) and is the lead author of *Reason and Religious Belief* (3rd ed., 2002). He is editor of *The Problem of Evil: Selected Readings* (1992) and lead editor of *Philosophy of Religion: Selected Readings* (2006). He is general editor for the Blackwell Exploring the Philosophy of Religion series of books and managing editor of the journal *Faith and Philosophy*. In addition to teaching and writing, he is director of the Transformations Project at Asbury College, funded by Lilly Endowment Inc.

REGAN LANCE REITSMA is assistant professor of philosophy at King's College (Pennsylvania), where he specializes in ethics and action theory.

MATTHEW H. SLATER obtained his PhD in 2006 from Columbia University and is currently an assistant professor of philosophy at the University of Idaho. Working on issues in metaphysics and the philosophy of science, he has published articles in *Philosophy of Science, Philosophical Studies,* and the *Monist.*

ANAND J. VAIDYA is assistant professor of philosophy at San Jose State University. He does research in epistemology and the philosophy of mind and has coedited an anthology on business ethics.

ACHILLE C. VARZI is professor of philosophy at Columbia University. He is the author or coauthor of several books in logic and metaphysics, including *Insurmountable Simplicities* (2006), *An Essay in Universal Se-*

mantics (1999), *Parts and Places* (1999), *Theory and Problems of Logic* (1998), and *Holes and Other Superficialities* (1994). Currently he is an editor of the *Journal of Philosophy* and an advisory editor of the *Monist, Studia Logica,* and *Dialectica.*

DEBORAH A. WALLACE is the director of the elementary gifted program in the Lake-Lehman School District, in Lehman, Pennsylvania. She has published on critical thinking in the elementary grades and on multicultural education. A lifelong basketball player, she played in the Division III national championship game in 1985.

JAMES M. WALLACE, a professor of English at King's College (Pennsylvania), has contributed twice to the Popular Culture and Philosophy series and is a coauthor of *Critical Thinking: A Student's Introduction* (3rd ed., forthcoming).

JERRY L. WALLS is professor of philosophy of religion at Asbury Theological Seminary in Wilmore, Kentucky. Among his many books are *Heaven: The Logic of Eternal Joy* (2002) and *The Chronicles of Narnia and Philosophy* (2005; coedited with Gregory Bassham).

STEPHEN H. WEBB is professor of religion and philosophy at Wabash College. He has published eight books, including *Good Eating, Taking Religion to School, American Providence,* and *The Divine Voice.* He has also contributed to *The Chronicles of Narnia and Philosophy.* His most recent book is on the political theology of Bob Dylan.

LUKE WITTE played college basketball at Ohio State University and spent four seasons with the Cleveland Cavaliers. After graduating from Asbury Theological Seminary in 1993, he served for many years as family ministry team leader at Forest Hill Evangelical Presbyterian Church in Charlotte, North Carolina.

INDEX